ADMINISTRATORS
AND READING

Administrators and Reading

edited by THORSTEN R. CARLSON

A PROJECT OF
THE INTERNATIONAL READING ASSOCIATION

HARCOURT BRACE JOVANOVICH, INC.
New York Chicago San Francisco Atlanta

ISBN: 0-15-500780-7

Library of Congress Catalog Card Number: 70-190464

Printed in the United States of America

Preface

In 1966, the International Reading Association made a commitment to publish three volumes on key areas affecting reading instruction. Committees were appointed to draft outlines and select outstanding contributors for these volumes.

The IRA committee and the authorial group proceeded on the assumption that many administrators are uninformed about reading instruction and reading problems. They believed that all means should be used to reach administrators with the latest research and thinking in reading. This volume, then, dealing with administrators and reading, is a distillation of hours of planning by the total committee, subcommittees, and the authorial group.

The book discusses the issues that have arisen in the controversy over reading. Part I explores the administrative roles and responsibilities essential to effective reading instruction. Such issues as the definition and structure of the reading program, leadership roles of administrative personnel, organization of the staff for instructional service, acquisition and effective use of local, state, and federal resources, and home and community involvement in school programs are examined. Part II deals with strategies for improving instruction that emphasize measurement, the use of varied media, and staff development. The needs of disabled readers and those of deprived children are considered in the concluding chapters of this section. Part III is a discussion of innovative practices in reading instruction at the elementary and secondary school levels. Part IV stresses the importance of a knowledge of developments in educational research and a willingness to bridge the gap between innovation and practice.

This is not just another book on the teaching of reading. It is written by administrators and reading specialists for administrators. Their experience represents all levels of administrative responsibility. The contributors, though having had complete freedom in writing, have been encouraged to be relevant and to illustrate from their experience and research. The book has been designed to suit a readership of administrators who serve in various capacities and in small, intermediate, and large districts. We believe it will have a unique and compelling appeal for them.

Many issues and problems are not covered. No single book can exhaust the subject. The articles will undoubtedly, however, stimulate thinking along new directions, provide new information for some, and encourage all to pursue the curriculum area of reading at greater depth. More expertise in reading curriculum will eventuate in more effective leadership and in turn will improve instruction. No effort is too great when the reading competence of our youth is at stake.

Mildred Dawson, 1966–1967 IRA President, read the entire manuscript and did extensive editing. Ralph Staiger, Executive Secretary-Treasurer of the IRA, has followed the progress of the project with concern and interest. His continuing support has been invaluable. The committee on *Administrators and Reading* played a major role in developing content and format, and reviewed each chapter manuscript. The committee consisted of Paul J. Avery, Rexel Brown, Levin B. Hanigan, Theodore Harris, William Kendrick, Lawrence O. Lobdell, James Loughridge, Russell Meyers, Gertrude Whipple, Earle E. Wiltse, and Ellsworth Woestehoff.

I would also wish to express my appreciation to Mrs. Dorothy Lassen, Sonoma State College, who gave uncounted hours of assistance in correspondence and preparation of the manuscript. My thanks also to George McCabe and John Lawrence, Chairmen of the Division of Education and Psychology, who gave continued encouragement and support.

THORSTEN R. CARLSON

Contributors

Paul J. Avery
Superintendent of Schools
Mercer Island Public Schools

Morton Botel
Professor of Education
University of Pennsylvania

George B. Brain
Dean of the College of Education
Washington State University

Thorsten R. Carlson
Professor of Education
Sonoma State College

Margaret Chisholm
Dean of the School of Library
    and Information Services
University of Maryland

Muriel Crosby
Formerly Associate Superintendent
Wilmington Public Schools

Bjorn Karlsen
Professor of Education
Sonoma State College

William Kottmeyer
Formerly Superintendent of Schools
Saint Louis Public Schools

Walter McHugh
Professor of Education
California State College at Hayward

Richard Madden
Professor Emeritus
San Diego State College

Kenneth E. Oberholtzer
Formerly Superintendent of Schools
Denver Public Schools

H. Alan Robinson
Professor of Education
Hofstra University

Gertrude Whipple
Formerly Assistant Director of
    Language Education
Detroit Public Schools

Ellsworth S. Woestehoff
Chairman of the Department of
    Curriculum, Teaching and Super-
    vision
The University of Rochester

Elaine V. Wolfe
Assistant Professor of Elementary
    Education
University of Northern Colorado

Contents

III. Innovative Practices   209

IV. Research—The Key to the Future   265

ADMINISTRATORS
AND READING

Introduction

Thorsten R. Carlson

Instructional excellence is dependent upon administrative leadership and expertise in curriculum and teaching. In smaller administrative units, the administrator should, ideally, be expert in all curriculum areas. This expectation may be impossible for most administrators and it may be necessary to select certain crucial areas for emphasis. For several reasons, knowledge in the area of reading instruction would seem to merit a high priority.

First, no area of educational responsibility seems to be more potentially explosive; reading instruction has become a political issue at the national level. A concerned public has forced administrators to take a first-hand interest in the reading program.

Second, the advent of massive federal funding and special support in many states has lent importance to the reading program. Testing programs have also focused attention on reading. Professional controversies over reading methods and procedures have received publicity in widely circulated newspapers and magazines causing the public to turn to teachers and principals for advice and information.

Third, providing reading materials (authorship, publication, promotion, and sales) is big business. The cost of materials to implement a reading program has become a sizable factor in the educational budget. It has been estimated that at least 50 percent of all money provided for instructional materials in the elementary school is allocated to the field of reading. High standards of ethics generally prevail, but with the entrance of many firms into the field, unprofessional promotion of materials and systems seems almost inevitable. So the administrator must be knowledgeable.

The administrator of larger educational units will find it difficult to maintain expertise in all curriculum areas. He will need to make provision and provide support for assistance by specialists. Administrative and specialist leaders in reading will need to exhibit depth of understanding and practical expertise in

1

such areas as the complexity and nature of the reading process, learning theory, varied methods of teaching reading, needs and problems at different educational levels, the science of language or linguistics, assessment of reading competence, reading disability, diagnosis and remediation, materials for instruction, learning theory, and research.

The Domain of the Administrator

IN-SERVICE EDUCATION

In-service education is of crucial importance to effective teaching. This has always been true. However, the need for more effective in-service programs is more vital today than in any earlier period for several reasons.

First, pre-service training is probably no more effective and possibly less effective than ever in the past. Undergraduate students typically have too little contact with children. Professional course work is often minimal, superficial, spotty in coverage, poorly integrated with teaching experience, and therefore incomplete and often nonrelevant.

In addition, certain built-in motivational advantages of in-service training make it particularly viable and important for the schools of today. Since in-service training is close to the tasks and responsibilities at hand, it is usually more relevant than pre-service training. The competencies achieved in this training, as well as the understandings and insights gained, can immediately be put into practice in the classroom.

Administrators are finding that traditional practices in in-service education are not productive. In the late afternoon, the jaded teacher derives little from the typical "rehash" provided by a consultant from the school district, a publishing house, or a college or university. The administrator needs to know and use newer techniques such as workshops, demonstrations, video tapes, and films. Closed-circuit TV as a means of instructional improvement is also in the offing. A teacher will be able to view her teaching and, with the help of the principal, seek ways of improvement.

The teaching staff and the administration should play the key roles in the development of in-service programs for their schools. Under such conditions there can be some assurance of programs that have relevance to the needs of the school. Also, with a personal investment in a program, the teacher is more likely to display an interest and a sense of responsibility for the effectiveness of the programs.

CURRICULUM DEVELOPMENT

The administrator must be dedicated to the idea of involving the staff in curriculum development. Such a challenging task requires the best thinking of all.

Also, through the process, each participant becomes more knowledgeable and increases his personal investment in the total effort.

As the staff and administration develop a program, they must recognize the importance of experimentation and innovation. The new and novel seem to be related to the effectiveness of reading programs. Some innovation leavens the entire program—even the instruction that conforms to the already established program of the school. The freedom to innovate and experiment is in itself an important teaching right. An administrator must be catholic enough to be able to live comfortably with and respond creatively to such practices, and more— to provide leadership for those who wish to experiment and innovate.

SUPERVISION

The administrator must similarly be concerned with innovations in supervision. The old patterns of supervision are no longer tolerable. The administrator needs to be familiar with the newer patterns such as teacher-administrator joint evaluations of reading instruction. With this procedure, the teacher and administrator can set mutual goals for the improvement of instruction.

HUMAN RELATIONS

The administrator needs to keep foremost in mind that he works with pupils, the public, and teachers. Effective human relations can be his greatest asset. This seems obvious, but it is surprising how easily people become statistics— the administration of things and processes becomes paramount—and the administrator, in his minimal contacts with pupils and staff, becomes at best humanitarian, but not truly human.

When the administrator really works with people, he realizes the complexity of the task and the many and varied problems involved. This realization fosters humility—an important asset to any administrator. A full realization of the complexity of the teaching-learning process discourages authoritarian solutions and suggests instead the use of problem-solving approaches in the improvement of the total learning environment.

The administrator needs to be a good listener, but not passive and inscrutable. He should have and is entitled to have opinions, but his thinking should be subject to change in response to evidence, reflection, and dialogue.

He must be committed to the team approach. As such, he must be willing and eager to give credit to those on the team—pupils, teachers, the public, and others in the administration. Paternalistic attitudes reflected in expressions such as "my teacher," "my staff," do not encourage sincere team efforts.

The administrator should understand the mechanisms of behavior and recognize them in his own actions and in the actions of his staff. Sometimes frontal responses and natural reactions are not the most effective. The administrator needs to know the causes of particular behavior and then should handle that behavior in ways that help individuals without causing them to lose face or their sense of personal worth and competence.

Barriers to Leadership

Undoubtedly, mediocre teaching can be attributed, at least in part, to administrators' lack of background in the teaching of reading. Inadequate background often stems from too little emphasis on curriculum and instruction in the training of administrators. It also results from lack of classroom experience, especially at the primary-grade levels. Both the Harvard Study by Austin and others[1] and the Conant report[2] bear out this contention.

Administrators of all levels of school organization must, in the current milieu, be informed on the teaching of reading. This is important even when the details of the administration and supervision of the programs are delegated to specialists.

Administrators are beset by many demands that are only tangentially, if at all, related to instruction. Forms, reports, schedules, inventories, records, and budgets conspire to chain them to their desks. In addition, there are the demands for their time from the administration of the nonteaching staff and from the parents and the community.

Summary

With the controversy over reading instruction now in full view, it is essential that school administrators be aware of the problems involved in establishing an effective reading program and equally aware of the current attempts to arrive at solutions to these problems. Unfortunately, a variety of factors conspire to keep the administrator from becoming an informed leader in reading.

Only a few procedures for implementing effective reading instruction have been mentioned in this introduction. It is the purpose of the remaining chapters to examine the issues and suggest possible alternative approaches to increase the reading competence of students.

[1] Mary C. Austin and Coleman Morrison, *The First R: The Harvard Report on Reading in the Elementary Schools* (New York: Macmillan, 1963).

[2] James B. Conant, *Learning to Read* (Princeton, N.J.: Education Test Service, 1962).

I

Administrative Roles and Responsibilities

1

The Obligations of School Administrators to the Reading Program

Paul J. Avery

Introduction

The 1970's will be a stormy decade for American schools and the men and women who represent them; for they have been catapulted out of cozy backwaters and thrust into the rough and tumble world of social ferment.

School personnel have ridden and subdued the tiger of educational reform movements periodically, but the educational reformers of this decade are trained revolutionaries and represent three converging revolutions—the cultural, the scientific, and the humanistic. Each revolution is predicated on the proposition that the key to man's survival on this planet is the development of a new kind of educational system to sustain and enrich all of the people. Schools everywhere have become storm centers of conflicting ideologies; educators are being compelled to re-examine their priorities and their justification for existence. Scholars and school administrators no longer tred those cloistered halls where there was "time yet for a hundred indecisions, and for a hundred visions and revisions, before the taking of toast and tea."[1]

Reading As a National Priority

The knowledge explosion and the liberation of the common man from absolute dependence upon his environment and the mercy of his Lord took a giant step five centuries ago when the first Gutenberg Bible rolled off the press.

[1] T. S. Eliot, "The Love Song of J. Alfred Prufrock," from *Collected Poems 1909–1962*, copyright 1936 by Harcourt Brace Jovanovich, Inc., copyright © 1963, 1964, by T. S. Eliot. Reprinted by permission of Harcourt Brace Jovanovich, Inc., and Faber and Faber Ltd.

With mass production of the written word, the ability to read was no longer a mysterious status symbol to be learned solely as an exercise in erudition. Men of perception and ambition quickly realized that the art of reading was a lever to free themselves from the bonds of ignorance and gain stature in the society of man.

In time, it was accepted as common sense that reading was a basic skill which ought to be mastered by all free men as the key to sustained economic self-sufficiency and effective citizenship. In colonial America, the establishment of schools to teach reading and other useful arts became a matter of pride in each new frontier settlement. With surprising docility, Americans initiated the practice of taxing themselves in order that all children should have the opportunity to learn to read.

Today, with nearly two centuries of practice in the teaching of reading behind us, it is shocking to be told that the number of Americans who cannot read or write runs into the millions, that there are many more millions whose deficiencies in reading prevent them from achieving full productivity, and that our network of public schools still produces a disproportionate number of non-readers, problem readers, retarded readers, marginal readers and indifferent readers.

A Survival Literacy Study, conducted by the National Reading Council, has reported that 4.3 million Americans must be considered functionally illiterate in modern society, and that as many as 34 percent of Americans are limited—by inadequate reading skills—in their ability to achieve their full potential in modern society.

So critical is this problem that on September 23, 1969, the U.S. Commissioner of Education, James E. Allen, Jr., felt duty-bound to proclaim that the right to read was "as fundamental as the right to life, liberty, and the pursuit of happiness."[2]

Commissioner Allen warned educators not to get bogged down in debate over "methods of teaching reading, but to organize all possible resources toward eliminating reading deficiencies which exist among more than a quarter of our population. He equated failure to acquire basic reading skills and a "desire" to read as being a "barrier to success that for many young adults produces the misery of a life marked by poverty, unemployment, alienation, and in many cases, crime."

Commissioner Allen's declaration of man's fundamental right to read was widely heralded by the American press and a public which has historically supported public education to the extent that it has confidence that children are being taught to read. Where this confidence level is high, the public has tended to be generous in its support of schools. Where the confidence level has deteriorated, public support of schools has become critical and grudging.

Suburban Birmingham, Michigan, is an ideal example of parental support

---

[2] James E. Allen, Jr., address before the National Association of State School Boards (September 1969).

of a vigorous reading program. There, when school Superintendent John Blackhall Smith proclaimed his belief that "the most important skill taught and the skill most needed by every individual remains reading. No school system can deny this responsibility; it must have the top priority at the instructional level"—97 percent of the parents of Birmingham elementary school children responding to a survey expressed full agreement with the Superintendent and 78 percent expressed satisfaction with the level of reading attained by their children.[3]

Reading in the Sixties

During the momentous years between the launching of Russia's Sputnik and the landing of the first Americans on the moon, more schools were built, more children educated, more teachers trained, more money was invested, and more innovations were attempted than in all of the previous decades of American education put together. The sixties appeared to be rich and productive years in education with exciting advances made in teaching of mathematics, the physical sciences, and foreign languages in particular. The emphasis shifted from the teaching and memorization of facts to the teaching of concepts, inquiry and research methods. Subject matter content was shifted downward in the grades as it became apparent that younger children could comprehend concepts beyond previous expectations. An unprecedented burden was placed upon young pupils to read advanced subject matter content critically and purposefully, which in turn placed increasing pressure upon teachers of young children to engage in intensive instruction.

In the wake of this pressure, the reading market became inundated with new and improved packaged methods of instruction, each accompanied by testimonials from teachers who reported that by simply following the directions on the package, they were turning out better readers faster than ever before. The claims and counter-claims became so confusing that at the 1966 annual convention of IRA a "buyer be wary" policy was adopted. It was further asserted that "distributors of reading devices or materials have an ethical obligation to submit their products to fair scientific trials before marketing and to make data of these evaluations available to all prospective purchasers."

During the years from 1960 to 1969, new sources of funds were injected into public education via the National Defense Education Act and other congressional appropriations. These funds made it possible for school districts to readily purchase all kinds of instructional materials, equipment, supplies, programs, and personal services. Simultaneously, districts were offered impressive financial incentives to engage in bold experimental programs and projects.

Certainly, the sixties will be remembered for the emphasis placed on the application of modern technology to the teaching of reading. Through the use

[3] The Birmingham Public Schools, *Reading Survey 1965–1968*, p. 101.

of programmed readers, automated devices, and a plethora of learning systems, individual pupils can work to develop proficiency in reading skills, while teachers can concentrate on helping children to expand and develop their creativity, curiosity, insight, and enthusiasm for learning.

We might predict that the great advancement in the seventies will be achieving full recognition of the all-importance of the teacher-learner relationship in learning to read, incorporated with direct involvement of the learner in shaping his reading program.

The Responsibility Gap in the Sixties

In the board room, the classroom, and the faculty lounge, educators engaged in profound argument over status quo methods and procedures in the teaching of reading versus bold new approaches to the entire reading process. Experimentation placed new stresses on working relationships which were expressed in symptoms of tension, defensiveness, and divergence from the main task. Administrators, many of whom were still smarting from the humiliating battle of the fifties over "why Johnnie can't read" tended to shy away from direct contact with the reading program. More and more reading consultants working in school districts observed a breakdown in communications between administration and staff, which worked to the detriment of the reading program.

The charge that, by and large, administrators were insensitive to and nonsupportive of the reading program came to the attention of the Board of Directors of the International Reading Association and, in 1966, President-elect H. Alan Robinson called for the formation of a special committee at the national level to close the gap between the school administrator and the reading specialist. Dr. Robinson was convinced, from his own studies in several midwestern and eastern school districts, that a vital factor in the improvement of reading instruction was the degree to which the building principal involved himself with and gave support to the reading program. Dr. Robinson also concluded that "a chief function of the top school administrator is to be sure that the status quo is being challenged and changed when necessary."[4]

The twelve-man committee on administration and reading met for the first time at the 1967 IRA convention in Seattle and drew up initial plans which matured into a three-year program of regional and national seminars, dialogues, workshops, and institutes involving reading teachers, reading consultants, curriculum personnel, and school administrators.

During these three years of dialogues, it became apparent that very real animosities existed between administrators and reading specialists. The follow-

[4] See H. Alan Robinson, "New Patterns in Secondary Education," Chapter 13 in this volume.

ing complaints which may strike a familiar note with the reader were extracted from impromptu discussions.

Administrator: Seventy percent of the kids in our district are reading below grade level, yet all of the reading personnel are tied up in a clinical program that works with less than 20 kids a year.

Reading Specialist: We worked every night for three months preparing a budget request for a developmental reading program at the junior high school level. The entire program was red-penciled in the Superintendent's office without a word of explanation.

Administrator: Each of our elementary schools now has a full-time librarian and a well-stocked library. They seem to stand empty most of each day.

Reading Specialist: Before approving the working drawings for our new elementary school, the Board of Education cut out all seminar rooms, the curriculum library, and the resource center. Our principal didn't raise one objection.

Administrator: We had a very promising district-wide reading project under way. The director resigned in order to write a book and teach at the university and the project fell apart at the seams.

Reading Specialist: The Superintendent returned from a national convention and proudly announced that he had purchased a new comprehensive phonics reading program for all elementary grades. He was completely unaware that our local reading committee had studied the program the previous year and had rejected it.

Once the differences were recognized and discussed, those in attendance at these group sessions were willing to close ranks and address themselves to the identification of facets of the reading program where administrative intervention and planning were necessary and desirable. Viewed in this perspective, teachers began to describe situations where the lack of administrative involvement had inhibited effective reading instruction. As one specialist stated, "I used to feel that I had to work around the administration in order to upgrade the reading program. I have since found that without informed administrative leadership I don't get anywhere."

As might be expected, teachers view the involvement of administrators in accordance with their own experience. If the teacher works within an administrative environment that is supportive and creative, he is able to give specific examples of tasks performed by his administrator which were invaluable to the success of the reading program. Conversely, if the experience has been with vacuous or repressive leadership, this fact is given as a reason for the failure or dissolution of the program.

Obligations of the Administrator

The conclusion drawn from these dialogues is that most teachers feel insecure to a substantial degree about the teaching of reading. They want guidance, encouragement, in-service training, time for planning, and relief from some of the obstacles which inhibit effective reading instruction. They feel that their principal or their superintendent has the power to help them with the reading program, and that their administrators have an obligation to exercise their power to perform the following functions:

1. To try to improve the quality of reading instruction in the classroom.
2. To establish an attitude and an atmosphere which enhances the reading program.
3. To provide optimum conditions to assist each child to learn to read.
4. To budget sufficient funds to implement an effective reading program.

IMPROVING THE QUALITY OF READING

Ninety percent of all reading instruction begins and ends in the classroom and approximately 60% of the formal reading instruction received by the typical child during his school career takes place in the primary grades.

During the era of the one-room schoolhouse, the wise teacher utilized older children to assist younger children in learning how to read. The upper-grade student was provided with a practical reason for continuing to review and improve his own reading skills in order to carry out the responsibility which was assigned to him.

When schools became larger and the grade level system went into effect, the responsibility for reading instruction gravitated to the first-grade teacher. Our country's folklore is full of reminiscences relating to the indomitable spinster ladies who hammered the sounds of the alphabets into the heads of an endless procession of first-grade children, with such a no-nonsense manner that it would seem few children dared to become reading failures.

Although reading instruction still is centered around the primary grades, a profile of the reading teacher is that of a young woman who will teach, at the most, a dozen years and only two to three consecutive years in one teaching situation. Her career is interrupted, often in midyear, by marriage, pregnancy, transfer of her husband, or an inexplicable urge to move to far-off places. She is unsure of her adequacy to teach reading and it is probable that she was enrolled in less than three courses in the teaching of reading or language arts at her college of education. She is resentful that she receives little help from consultants, principals, or department heads and must rely on the good nature of other teachers in the building for advice and assistance. She feels that the district has not provided her with a sufficient amount or variety of basic and supplementary reading materials to engage in the kind of individualized instruction in reading that she has been told about. She is intensely frustrated and disturbed that she has no time during the day for lesson planning, learning how to work with the materials and equipment available, or simply to sit down and compose her nerves.

One young teacher stated, "I was instructed to report to the district for an orientation workshop one day before school opened. At the workshop they told me that I would be teaching beginning reading by the ITA method. I didn't even know what they were talking about."

Another teacher confessed, "When I walked into that classroom and saw thirty pairs of eyes looking at me and begging me to teach them how to read, my knees almost gave way. At first I was afraid the principal would barge in and find how terrible I was doing but no one came into my room the entire year."

Writing in the January 1969 *Phi Delta Kappan,* S. Alan Cohen reports "Every study of the level of instruction in American classrooms concludes that, in general, the instruction in reading is at best mediocre and often poor."[5] Cohen substantiates his conclusion by citing a number of studies which show that teachers are ignorant of basic principles of phonetics, phonemics, and phonics, and have little or no knowledge of what is involved in conducting a good reading program. Cohen blames the administrator who knows that intensive instruction brings about positive results but who does not implement such instruction either because he does not really know how, or because he does not want to.

Dr. Walter McHugh, professor of education at California State College, Hayward, California, believes that the most important factor in improving the reading program in the classroom is to train principals to be instructional leaders in reading. "Someone," said Dr. McHugh, "must assume the role of instructional leader, change agent and evaluator. This challenge falls squarely on the school principal. No other person can assume this role."[6] In his studies of a number of California school districts, McHugh found that after principals had been trained to assume instructional leadership (and were accepted by teachers in this role) there was a marked improvement in reading achievement.

---

[5] S. Alan Cohen, "Local Control and the Cultural Deprivation Fallacy," *Phi Delta Kappan* (January 1969), p. 257.

[6] Walter J. McHugh, *Current Administrative Problems in Reading,* IRA Highlights of the 1967 Pre-Convention Institutes, p. 25.

ESTABLISHING THE PROPER ATMOSPHERE

By their words and actions, school administrators at all levels provide clues to staff members which determine the real status of the reading program in the school hierarchy. Jean P., a reading consultant in a suburban school system, recalls, "We were trying to generate enthusiasm for a reading workshop which was to be conducted in the district. A luncheon was planned and we invited the superintendent to be present and introduce the speaker. His secretary told us that he couldn't make it because our luncheon had been scheduled on his Rotary day. This has happened so many times we have stopped asking." Jean and her staff have concluded that their superintendent has little interest in reading instruction.

By contrast, when P. S. 192 in Harlem exceeded national averages for reading on standardized achievement test scores, a statistic which set it apart from other New York City schools in disadvantaged areas, the Council for Basic Education sent George Weber to the school to determine how this reading success had been achieved. Weber commented on several unusual characteristics of the school. Prominent among these characteristics was the "personality" of the principal, "certainly the drive, the courage, the imagination, warmth, intelligence and knowledge of the man must be maintained. Could a lesser man have presided over such an effort?" Weber was equally impressed with the atmosphere of the school: "There is also the expectation of success and a businesslike quality on the part of the teachers and staff . . . everyone at the school, including the children, contributes to an atmosphere of success and excitement, and joy in success rather than failure."

The entire field of interpersonal relationships and the interaction between administrator and teacher has been minimized in the preparation and selection of school administrators. Consequently, some administrators take a long time to learn that they must be both alert and responsive to the basic needs of their faculty members. Few educational researchers have been able to measure the effect of the principal's attitude on reading instruction as accurately as the first-grade teacher who stated matter-of-factly, "Every time my principal walks into the classroom the temperature drops thirty degrees."

PROVIDING OPTIMUM CONDITIONS

It is still hard to find a school district or a school that is willing to give every child an even break in learning how to read. Each school has its own customs by which it determines the instructor to whom each child is assigned, the amount of time allocated for reading instruction, the precise age at which all children may commence reading instruction, the materials all must master, and the method by which all will be instructed. If any child fails to make sense out of the process the first time around, he and his parents are presented with the unpalatable prospect of "taking a second dose of the same medicine" under the identical conditions which resulted in failure the first time.

Most of the several thousand school districts in the United States operate programs on the expectation that all pupils will remain with the district from kindergarten through graduation. There is little or no accommodation for the pupil who transfers into a program in midstream.

Such a pupil usually enters a school system unaccompanied by relevant data from his former school district to assist in his placement, and when data is forthcoming it is frequently disregarded. The child might be fortunate to find that his new school is using procedures for learning with which he is familiar; however, it may be the child's bad luck to be shuffled from midpoint in an ITA program to midpoint in a language-experience program, or from an individualized program to a traditional program, or from a remediation program to an accelerated program, without any orientation or acclimatization.

He may find himself a year or more advanced, or a year or more retarded, in terms of the level of performance now expected of him. The only advice he or his parents may be extended during the transition is the prescription "Don't be unduly alarmed—most students who come from your part of the country are at least a year behind our program—let's keep him where he is for another month. If things don't work out, we can always put him back a grade."

Children can experience the same kind of problem moving from one school to another within the same school district, and occasionally the transfer from one room to another within the same school will be as disorienting to a child as a transfer between geographic regions. My scrutinizing of case studies of problem readers has always revealed children whose deficiency resulted from having received bits and pieces from highly divergent approaches to reading instruction.

Few school districts have developed (and few administrators have urged the adoption of) systematized procedures to inventory each individual child's basic strengths and weaknesses, and to use that inventory to recommend placement with a teacher and a reading program which offers him the best possible chance of experiencing success in learning. Nor do schools employ reliable screening devices designed to sound the alarm before an individual child experiences the damaging effects of frustration and failure.

Until schools are organized and funded to periodically assess the progress of individual pupils and to utilize the results to prescribe instructional methods which are particularly appropriate to the pupil, there will continue to be a noticeable proportion of children completing the primary grades with little interest in reading and with insufficient grounding in word-attack skills to mature as independent readers. For these children, the intermediate grades and the junior high school years become a nightmare. Each subject area has its own textbooks, special vocabularies, symbols, and concepts which must be deciphered and mastered for passing grades. Those children who continue to lag in classroom performance begin to exhibit deviate behavior of inattention, truancy, hostility, and rebellion.

Generalizing upon his studies in Bucks County, Pennsylvania, Morton Botel has estimated that as many as ten to fifteen million pupils in the United

States may be suffering from over-placement in reading material. By this he means that junior high, secondary, and college students have such heavy assignments in reading materials in each of their subject areas that their limitations in the act of reading itself have immeasurable effect upon general performance. He feels that the frustration accompanying over-placement in reading material can produce symptoms which are commonly associated with dyslexia.[7] Although Botel's studies have been widely disseminated, administrative practices and policies in school districts seldom contain provisions to reduce the incidents and frustration of over-placement as described by Botel.

Individualized instruction in reading, in its fullest sense, has been an unattainable goal in most school systems. This condition does not result from lack of interest or skill on the part of the instructional staff, but it arises from the sheer number and diversity of pupils, the transiency of personnel, and the inadequacies of materials to sustain and supplement an individualized program.

Performance Contracting. At this writing, several school districts are experimenting with the concept of "performance contracts" with private companies. The first of these performance contracts was awarded by the Texarkana, Arkansas, School District to the Dorsett Educational System of Norman, Oklahoma. The Dorsett Company contracted to raise the reading and mathematics level of students by one full grade level in 80 hours of instruction, or to forfeit some payment from the school district for each student who made no progress during the instructional period.

Encouraged by the availability of federal money from the U. S. Office of Education and the Office of Economic Opportunity, similar performance contracts with private industry have been announced by the Dallas Public Schools, the Portland, Oregon, Public Schools, Seattle Public Schools, and at least 16 other school districts in fifteen states. A number of companies, namely Singer-Graflex, Westinghouse Learning, Alpha Learning Systems, and Learning Foundations, Inc., are anxious to engage in performance contracting services for school districts on the basis that if they fail to produce measurable results within a stipulated period of time they will not be paid.

Performance contracting by private industry is appealing to some educators and appalling to others. With no forewarning, a challenging and competitive alternative to existing instructional practices has been thrust upon the school establishment. Administrators have an obligation to become intelligently critical of the application of performance contracting in the classroom. Once we begin to pay instructors in direct ratio to the measured achievement gains of the learner, it becomes necessary to institute rigorous safeguards to protect against fraud and deceit. Just as the alchemist appeared to be able to produce gold where none existed, so could a cunning instructor appear to produce

[7] Morton Botel, *Dyslexia, Diagnosis, and Treatment of Reading Disorders* (C. V. Mosby Co., St. Louis, 1968), Chapter 12, p. 121.

measurable achievement gains where none existed. It will also be necessary to protect the learner against harmful pressure designed to force him to achieve. Every experienced administrator has had some occasion to deal with cases of over-anxious teachers who will go to incredible lengths to appear to be doing a better job of teaching than their associates. An increased incidence of fraudulent teaching could be a hazard emerging from performance contracting in the schools.

In modern technology, there exists the capability to develop comprehensive, definitive, and stimulating systems of individualized instruction, keyed to in-class instruction or independent study, and modifiable to accommodate children of differing backgrounds, perceptions, and interests. Administrators in the coming decade must become fluent in the language of technology and craftsmen in the utilization of technology to achieve desired educational goals.

BUDGETING THE READING PROGRAM

Most school personnel are abysmally ignorant of the realities of school finance, collection of revenue, and budget preparation. Allocations of funds and accountability for expenditures has become a highly technical and complex specialization in a school operation. Having remained at arm's length from the budgeting process, instructional personnel collectively maintain that inadequate financial support has been the root cause of any and all deficiencies in the instructional program. Teachers have uniformly demanded more equipment, more supplies, more planning time, more in-service programs, more audiovisual materials, more supplementary materials, smaller classes, and more paraprofessional help. They have argued interminably that so long as these standards are not met, they should not be held accountable for mediocrity of performance.

Despite the fact that almost one-sixth of the annual federal operating budget, 30 to 50 percent of many state budgets, and 40 to 70 percent of local tax collections are expended on public education, educators continue to clamor for increased funds. However, as competition among public agencies for dollars grows keener and the signs of a taxpayers revolt becomes more evident, administrative personnel are commencing to talk about *the establishment of educational program priorities; the distribution of funds in accordance with priority needs; the development and maintenance of standards of accountability to assure that the expenditure of funds is matched by corresponding anticipated results.*

Traditional Budgeting Practices. Program budgeting is being widely studied as a new approach to the establishment of accountability in school finance. Heretofore, budgeting has been divided into broad and ill-defined categories which have made it virtually impossible to hold anyone accountable for the expenditure of funds in relation to a specific educational objective. Beyond that, it has been virtually impossible to determine the actual amount of funds which are being allocated to any specific educational function.

Although budget categories differ from state to state, the following sample would serve as recognizable categories in most school districts:

Budget Categories	Percent of Total Budget
Administration	4%
Instruction	72%
Pupil Services	2%
Food Services	6%
Pupil Transportation	2%
Operation of Plant	9%
Maintenance of Plant	3%
Community Services & Misc.	2%

Within each of the above broad categories, a series of subcategories is established, usually in accordance with an accounting manual issued by the state government. Under the major budget category of *Instruction,* for example, the following subcategories may exist:

1. Administration of Instruction
2. In-service Education
3. Textbooks
4. Library Books
5. Teacher Salaries
6. Principals' Salaries
7. Counselor Salaries
8. Extra-Curricular Salaries
9. Paraprofessional Salaries
10. Audiovisual Supplies

Assume that a school district decides to initiate a prereading program in kindergarten in order to identify children with potential reading problems. The specifics of the program call for the assignment of one full-time teacher and one full-time teacher aide, along with the part-time services of a school psychologist, two reading specialists, the school librarian, and school nurse. A substitute teacher will be required for ten consecutive afternoons while the regular teacher holds individual conferences with parents of the children. Supplies which will be ordered for the program include a special selection of library books, a variety of preselected program reading materials, a series of diagnostic test batteries, a set of phonograph records, and a set of pre-programmed tape cassettes. The equipment which will be required includes a custom-built library cart, a four-drawer filing cabinet, two filmstrip projectors, a movie projector, and twelve portable tape recorders. A consultant from the nearby university has been hired to visit the classroom two days a month and evaluate the results of the program which are scheduled to be published in a district publication. A twelve-passenger school bus will be used daily to transport kindergarten students to and from the district reading center.

The total budget of this program has been established at $125,000 for the school year. Utilizing the type of budgeting practices described above, the cost of this program would be spread out among four major budget categories and further subdivided into eight subcategories of the budget. The program would have such anonymity that the most exhaustive examination of the district budget would fail to reveal its existence, let alone the amount of funds which were appropriated to operate the program. Financial accountability for the program would be distributed among a number of department heads, several of whom would be uninformed of the existence or purpose of this particular program.

Program Budgeting. Under a system of program budgeting, once a program has been identified, it bears a code number and all costs associated with the program will be so designated. One individual will have the primary responsibility for managing all funds and approving all expenditures carrying that code number. Each subsequent year, when the budget is prepared, the program will come under automatic review and reassessment. If after a thorough evaluation the program is determined to be ineffective, all funds previously carrying the designated code will be released for other priority projects.

Program budgeting relates the educational activities and services of a school district to the cost in specific dollar amounts. It provides data which will enable educators to exercise their professional judgment in designating priority goals of the school district. It provides the teacher, the parent, and the taxpayer with the opportunity to find out for himself where school dollars are really going and to help participate in setting and evaluating the school district's priority allocations.

With the assistance of such techniques as program budgeting, administrators will train themselves and their staff to distinguish the less effective instructional practices. They will learn how to get promising programs started, expanded, or stopped on the basis of objective data. They will have the fortitude to deal with unreasonable resistance to change and, most important, to place educational planning above the trivia of day-to-day administration.

Conclusion

How do school administrators perceive their role in handling the forces which will shape education in the 1970's? Will the administrators serve as a catalyst for change or as a caretaker of tradition? The administrator will become increasingly burdened with demands for reforms both from within his faculty and outside his faculty. He will face complex decision-making tasks which are beyond the ken of his present training and experience. Surely, the school administrator who perceives his role as a choice among ignoring the forces of change, resisting them blindly, or embracing them indiscriminately will not survive the decade of the 1970's.

The new directions prescribed for education in the seventies beg for the kind of administrative leadership which dares to risk failure in order to discover better ways of teaching children. We need the kind of administrator who will involve himself in planning and implementing the reading program and who will keep abreast of the growing research and literature on reading instruction, and apply his knowledge toward the eradication of reading failure.

BIBLIOGRAPHY

Borton, Terry, *Reach, Touch and Teach* (New York: McGraw-Hill, 1970).

Brameld, Theodore, *The Climactic Decades: Mandate to Education* (New York: Praeger, 1970).

Goodlad, John, M. Francis Klein et al., *Behind the Classroom Door* (Worthington, Ohio: Charles A. Jones, 1970).

Gross, Ronald and Beatrice Gross, *Radical School Reform* (New York: Simon & Schuster, 1970).

Raths, Louis E., *Teaching for Learning* (Columbus, Ohio: Charles E. Merrill, 1969).

Rosenthal, Robert and Lenore Jacobson, *Pygmalion in the Classroom* (New York: Holt, Rinehart & Winston, 1968).

2

A Modern Reading Program
for This Season

Gertrude Whipple[1]

To be a good program, a reading program must serve the contemporary society. A good reading program can be described as Robert Bolt has described a good man. "A man for all seasons is a good man . . . good in the sense that a good car is good, or a good plow, or a good knife. Good for what it's *for*. A good knife is a sharp knife because a knife is for cutting."[2] But what is a reading program *for*? What kind of a program is a good one? Before we can answer these questions, we need to define *reading*.

In a limited sense, reading may be defined as the ability to comprehend the written word. In the larger sense—since man is a social creature living in a complex society—reading is the ability to translate what is comprehended from the printed page into action. The action may be for or against the ideas presented; it may occur immediately or at some later time. Often ideas drawn from the printed page are stored in the conscious or subconscious mind and become a part of the information, attitude, and idea bank that will influence or determine later behavior.

Now we can say what reading is *for*. It is to help children become socially informed and adaptive adults. To be a well-informed and socially effective person, a child must learn how to make full use of printed factual data as the basis for his emotional and intellectual reactions. The reading program must lead him through the evolutionary changes that will contribute to his personal and social development.

A reading program for this season has another urgent purpose, it must act as a social lever. The effective reading program lifts one's aspirations, nourishes appreciation of the beautiful and artistic, encourages integrity, and

[1] The following persons served as advisers in the preparation of this chapter: Patricia Eastland, Teacher, Detroit Public Schools; and W. Dean Edmundson, Region Superintendent, Detroit Public Schools.

[2] Robert Bolt, "A Modern Man for All Seasons," *Esquire*, vol. 58, no. 6 (December 1962), p. 149.

develops concern for persons different from one's self. In our divisive society, we cannot afford to neglect this use of reading.

Today we are in desperate straits as we attempt to defend our record in teaching children to read. We must measure the benefits of our present program, evaluate its effectiveness, and set hard priorities. Only by assessing the present program will we be able to sensibly plan an increasingly effective reading program for the future.

Ten Standards for an Effective Reading Program

The effectiveness and needs of a reading program can be reasonably judged by using the evaluation form in Figure 2.1. (See page 22.)

Obviously, none of the standards in Figure 2.1 is sufficient by itself. All are needed in the achievement of an effective reading program. One good feature practiced to excess works miracles, but the reduced attention to some other feature puts the program out of balance. Take the sixth and ninth questions above; number six is concerned with the basic program; number nine, with compensatory and remedial measures. Too much concentration on the latter results in too little on the former, and too little attention to the ninth handicaps the attainment of the sixth. Both deserve proper emphasis in the total program to ensure proper balance.

This chapter explains more fully what is involved in each of the ten standards and indicates how to direct a district or a school reading program toward the achievement of these standards.

DEFINES ATTAINABLE GOALS
CONGRUENT WITH LONG-RANGE PURPOSES
FOR ALL PUPILS

One reason why children do very poorly in reading is that many teachers give reading lessons day after day without knowing what they are trying to accomplish. Specific goals that promote the long-range purposes are needed in planning the classroom reading program, in choosing suitable reading materials, in devising learning activities, and in selecting and preparing tests or other instruments to appraise the instructional results.

However, the teacher cannot determine his part in the total reading program independently for he is a member of a team. Only the principal or the supervisory reading specialist is in a position to perceive all facets of the reading program in proper perspective. Therefore, it is the principal or specialist who must act as team leader, guiding the faculty toward sound decisions regarding specific goals for day-by-day teaching.

A successful definition of goals depends upon a good organizational climate

FIGURE 2.1

Under the column marked "Effectiveness," use one of these three symbols: 2—superior or strong; 1—average or adequate; 0—inferior or weak. Endeavor to make your judgment broadly applicable to different schools and school levels in the district.

Effectiveness   *Need*

Does the district reading program

.... 1. define attainable goals congruent with long-range purposes at each school level for all pupils?   ....

.... 2. relate reading to listening, speaking, and writing activities?   ....

.... 3. reach all pupils, however different?   ....

.... 4. extend from preschool through high school (and college)?   ....

.... 5. provide reading instruction and extended practice in all school subjects in which children read?   ....

.... 6. provide for the appropriate introduction, integration, and maintenance of reading skills and abilities?   ....

.... 7. make reading materials and equipment available to pupils under conditions suitable for reading growth?   ....

.... 8. establish valid standards and procedures in the selection of superior reading materials and equipment?   ....

.... 9. make special provisions in reading for divergent learners and disabled readers?   ....

.... 10. utilize appropriate tools and procedures for continuing appraisal and improvement of reading instructions?   ....

Under the column marked "Need" above, rank in order from 1 (highest) to 10 (lowest) the priority you would assign to each of the above characteristics to improve the district reading program.

On another sheet indicate specific steps which might be taken to improve each.

within the school. The relationships of the principal, teachers, pupils, reading specialist, and parents must be based on the conviction that their interests are inseparable. The effective principal shows concern for the teachers and builds an environment in which each individual has an opportunity for achievement and personal reward. In this atmosphere of openness and trust, the principal can then help the team develop a degree of consensus on specific goals and the means by which they can be achieved. The following is an example of how one principal initiated work on the problem of consensus.

First, the principal observed reading instruction in the various classrooms over a period of time. As he observed, he used a checklist to record what was being taught; he also noted the extent of adaptive instruction to meet pupils' needs.

Second, he started in-service education with this principle of leadership in mind: the staff should participate in every phase of a survey analysis—interpretation and evaluation of the findings, decision making, planning, and re-evaluation. At a faculty meeting, he presented a summary of his checklist findings, commented on several strong points to arouse interest, then invited comments and reactions. Among other things, the teachers pointed out that enrichment of experience was stressed in only one grade, that far greater emphasis was given to answering fact questions than to getting main ideas, and that certain important aims were almost completely neglected.

Third, the principal raised probing questions such as: What are the specific goals of teaching reading in any school? Which goals deserve emphasis in our school? How do these goals differ from grade to grade? Are they the same for all pupils?

Finally, using professional books as guides and thinking in terms of their own pupils, the staff gave some time to a study of these questions. Through further discussion, the teachers began to define and understand appropriate goals at each level as they kept in mind the pupils' backgrounds and capabilities.

A program "for all pupils" is one that "defines attainable goals" and thereby empowers each child to do his best. Each child wants assurance that his skills are equal to the reading tasks he is asked to carry out. No parent would demand that his child become the world's greatest mountain climber or nuclear scientist. Likewise a parent should not demand arbitrarily that his child attain a certain reading ability at a given time.

Thus, a modern program provides whatever means are necessary for each individual to learn to read up to his capabilities. This is exactly the opposite of laying down one set of specific goals and reading experiences for all children.

READING RELATED TO LISTENING, SPEAKING, AND WRITING ACTIVITIES

Our society depends upon verbal communication to such an extent that it is hard to imagine existence without some kind of spoken and written language. Indeed, it has been suggested[2] that much of our civilization would disappear if we could not communicate with one another.

The communication process depends upon the unique contribution of each

[2] F. K. Berrien and Wendell H. Bash, *Human Relations: Comments and Cases* (New York: Harper and Row, 1957), p. 21.

language art. None is sufficient by itself. For effective communication, the language arts must be used together and, therefore, taught in proper relationship.

School systems throughout the country have issued thousands of curriculum guides that stress the interrelationships of the language arts. The practical significance of these relationships has often been indicated by the stress placed on the importance of studying pupils' needs in the various areas of communication. In addition, emphasis has been repeatedly given to the need for reserving a large part of the school day for developing all phases of communication.

However, after surveying the reading practices in more than 1000 school systems, Austin and Morrison reported that most teachers did not use these guides.[3] One supervisor who was interviewed said that either teachers did not know the curriculum guide existed; or if they knew it existed, they did not have a copy; or if they had a copy, they could not find it.

The teachers' failure to use the curriculum guides may partly account for the poor practices frequently observed by the Harvard survey team. For example, oral reading was not taught as a means of communicating ideas to others. Most frequently seen was the obsolete "barbershop" ("Next, next") or "taking turns" style of oral reading.[4]

> Around the circle
> Or up the row
> You read orally
> Till I say whoa![5]

Consequently, the oral reading was routinish, purposeless, and unplanned. No wonder it was characterized by mispronunciation, inadequate phrasing, word-by-word reading, and finger pointing.

On the basis of field study observations, Austin and Morrison give this report of the development of reading comprehension skills:

> A few teachers are doing an excellent job of developing these important skills, but far too many fail to set purposes for reading, to relate story content to pupil experiences, to provide discussion opportunities to clarify misconceptions, to identify pupil strengths and weaknesses, and to adapt instruction to individual needs.[6]

Why is oral discussion ruled out when reading is taught? Why is reading seldom taught as a vital means of communication? Why are the language arts not taught in an integrated program? Several reasons are suggested by Austin and Morrison:[7] (1) the curriculum guides outlining policies of integration

---

[3] Mary C. Austin and Coleman Morrison, *The First R: The Harvard Report on Reading in Elementary Schools* (New York: Macmillan, 1963), p. 59.

[4] Ibid., pp. 44–46.

[5] Mary C. Austin and Coleman Morrison, *The First R: The Harvard Report on Writing in Elementary Schools,* copyright 1963 by the Macmillan Company and reprinted with permission.

[6] Ibid., p. 68.

[7] Ibid., pp. 59, 239–40.

have been allowed to become "dust collectors"; (2) none of the school systems surveyed had recently appraised their reading programs, so the school administrators were unaware of the weaknesses in their programs; (3) many staff members responsible for defining program policies did not observe classroom instruction.

Obviously, most of the participating administrators had decided to install an integrated language arts program. Did they arrive at the decision independently or by working with those who must carry out the policy? *How* we do whatever we have decided to do is every bit as important as *what* is to be done. If teachers, principals, and central staff members, working together in a good social climate, consider the relative values of separate subject teaching versus integrated language arts instruction, the benefits of the integrated language arts program will become readily apparent to all. And as a result, the integrated language arts program will most probably appear in practice as well as in theory.

REACHES ALL PUPILS, HOWEVER DIFFERENT

As Greene has so aptly said, "We cannot disregard the basic law of human nature that each child is a 'custom-made job.' "[8] No two children in a class are alike. Each has his particular strengths and weaknesses. Each responds differently to the teacher. It follows that each child requires the kind of reading program that will benefit him as a distinct individual.

To what extent are differentiated programs offered in schools at present? In the vast majority of elementary classrooms, the chief concession made to the individuality of children is that of sorting them into two or three reading groups, usually on the basis of scores on a reading test. Since such scores represent only one aspect of ability, the children in a group still differ in numerous other important characteristics. However, most teachers equate the reduction in range of ability with homogeneity and make their instruction in each group uniform. All the pupils in a group must carry out the same reading activities using the same reading materials at the same time. School principals need to convince teachers that even after pupils have been sorted on some one basis, many important individual differences still exist within every group, and instruction should be adapted to meet the needs of each child.

More often than not, the teacher does not become acquainted with each child as an individual, does not make detailed observations of each, does not give diagnostic tests to discover the child's particular capabilities, and does not keep adequate records of individual progress. Thus the teacher is unable to adjust reading experiences to individual needs and modify these experiences as needs change.

[8] John D. Greene, quoted by Harry W. Sartain, "Organizational Patterns of Schools and Classrooms for Reading Instruction," Chap. 6 in *Innovation and Change in Reading Instruction,* Sixty-Seventh Yearbook of the National Society for the Study of Education, Part II (Chicago: University of Chicago Press, 1968), p. 209.

In view of the present-day clamor for better reading instruction, it is imperative that we develop and use effective ways to individualize reading instruction. First, schools need to be staffed with teachers and principals who not only exhibit educational knowledge and teaching skills but also human understanding. The teacher-pupil relationship can be a motivating force that makes the difference between failure and success in reading. A good tone for learning is set by the teacher who believes that all children in his class are teachable and who respects, trusts, and encourages each child.

Second, the teacher's ability to differentiate instruction ought to be aided by the best possible school organization. In the elementary school, the one-teacher-per-class pattern would seem to be superior to any form of departmentalizing the academic subjects. This pattern allows for a more flexible time schedule. The teacher has fewer children and can, therefore, become better acquainted with each. In the departmentalized plan, the teacher must follow a rigid time schedule because of the movement of pupils from room to room. Also, since the teacher must meet more than one class a day, the load of individualization is so great that most teachers are overwhelmed before they have taken a single step.

Third, the stage will need to be set for adaptive instruction by the proper distribution of schoolbooks to classrooms. In a very real sense, a book supply tells the teacher the kind of instruction the principal has in mind. For instance, what is a principal saying to his staff about pupil guidance when he supplies each teacher with enough copies of a basic reader for all pupils and furnishes few or no other reading materials?

On the other hand, what is he saying when he makes evaluations of a teacher's book supply in light of information about the particular pupils? When he provides the teacher with various sample books to try out in the classroom? When he supplies basic readers on various levels of difficulty and a variety of other reading materials? More clearly than any words can say, he is encouraging the teacher to reach all pupils.

Fourth, principals and supervisors need to show teachers alternative methods of grouping so that they will realize that children's current reading needs should dictate the basis for organizing instruction. Small, flexible groups can be organized on bases such as reading attainments, need for instruction in some special reading skill, and preferences for various independent-reading activities. Thus a child may work in different groups, and regrouping can take place often during the school year. Also, while a teacher works with a small group, the tasks at which the other pupils work independently may be more or less individualized.

Finally, the administrator who wants to reach all pupils will see what can be done in his district to reduce class size. He will also encourage classroom experimentation to evaluate various organizational schemes now being advocated —team teaching, pupil-team reading, nongraded classes, and the promising aspects of individualized reading, particularly self-selection of reading materials and pupil-teacher conferences.

EXTENDS FROM PRESCHOOL THROUGH COLLEGE

A good program for this season extends from the three-to-four age level to at least two years beyond high school.

When to Begin Reading Instruction. Because of the differences in the way children develop physically and mentally, it is difficult to say at what age children should be introduced to reading. It is customary to start systematic reading instruction at the age of six. For late-developing six year olds, however, most schools postpone reading for a few months, a semester, or a year. Slow-starting children have been identified mainly by mental age and scores on reading readiness tests. However, research has shown that many of the reading readiness tests have little predictive value, that correlations of mental age with reading age are low at the end of the first year, and that the best time to introduce reading depends not only upon the nature of the child himself, but also upon the nature of the reading program. Some materials and methods can be used successfully by a pupil at the mental age of five, whereas others would be too hard for him at the mental age of six.

We also understand that preparation for reading begins in the home long before the child enters school. The early years are especially important in determining the child's oral language development, a key factor in reading readiness. As a result of this new emphasis on language development, preschool classes are being established to help three and four-year-old deprived children increase their language ability. There is a prediction that schooling for three and four year olds will become even more common in the relatively near future. Usually the preschool curriculum stresses oral language growth and concept development through a multisensory approach. Hopefully, one or two years in preschool and another in kindergarten will properly equip most deprived children to begin reading soon after entering the first grade, and may well facilitate learning to read for more privileged children.

Quite different innovations are now being made for able children. In fact, the findings of certain recent studies cast new light on the whole concept of reading readiness. Durkin's studies of children who learned to read early showed that some five year olds could recognize a minimum of eighteen words in their preschool years.[9] In other studies some type of informal reading has been offered to experimental classes in the kindergarten and the effects noted.

For example, Brzeinski carried out a kindergarten study over a five-year period that involved 61 experimental classes with the same number of control classes.[10] The reading activities for the experimental groups lasted 20 minutes a day. The activities included practice in auditory discrimination of letter sounds, in visual discrimination of letter forms, and in the use of con-

[9] Dolores Durkin, "Early Readers—Reflections After Six Years of Research," *The Reading Teacher,* vol. 18, no. 1 (October 1946), pp. 3–7 (see p. 5).

[10] Joseph E. Brzeinski, "Beginning Reading in Denver," *The Reading Teacher,* vol. 18, no. 1 (October 1964), pp. 16–21.

text clues and initial consonants in identifying words. The results in reading readiness favored the experimental classes. Later Brzeinski and others reported that only the experimental pupils whose reading programs were adjusted thereafter through grade five continued to progress.[11]

Such studies have led to the acceleration of reading instruction for capable five year olds. These are children who have lived in a verbal environment. They have acquired a large vocabulary of words and meanings, skills in handling oral language, and a love of books and stories. They have taken trips to a variety of places with someone along to answer their questions. This mental stimulation has prepared these children for some kind of reading instruction in the kindergarten.

Unfortunately, the kindergarten curriculum is seldom adapted to developing the varied interests and abilities of the individual child. All children are given the same traditional experiences in games, singing, skipping, coloring, and storytelling with little or no thought given to adapting these experiences to challenge and develop the individual child. Thus, essential to a good kindergarten program is an ever-increasing emphasis on individualizing and updating the curriculum.

Much can be done to bring about the necessary improvements if the administrator keeps these five imperatives in mind.

1. Provide a kindergarten in every school.
2. Reduce the size of kindergarten classes so that teachers can give more attention to the individual child.
3. See that a greater variety of learning experiences is included in the kindergarten program, and that there are more small-group and individual activities.
4. Do not allow any child to be pushed into reading, but give informal reading experiences to children who are ready to read or have begun reading.
5. Encourage first-grade teachers to realize that some children start learning to read at home, others start in the kindergarten, and still others at varying times in first grade; and, therefore, good first-grade reading instruction is adjusted to the attainments of the particular child. Not every child should start first grade with a reading-readiness book or a first preprimer.

When to Bring Reading Instruction to an End. Just as we must vary the time of initiating reading instruction, so we must vary the time of terminating it. Reading instruction, as nearly as possible, should end for a young person when he has approached the distant goals of the reading program (see page 21).

---

[11] Joseph E. Brzeinski, M. Lucille Harrison, and Paul McKee, "Should Johnny Read in Kindergarten?" *National Education Association Journal*, vol. 56, no. 3 (March 1967), pp. 23–25.

These include the social goal of ability to participate in the development of a good society.

In preparation for such a society—one in which the members think, learn, and act without prejudice—students must be taught to observe, listen, and read critically. They must have practice in utilizing reading to help solve controversial problems. Such practice entails guidance of the student in assembling pertinent information through the use of reference tools and study skills. Students must also learn to debate and discuss crucial problems objectively in light of their reading and to seek new sources of information as needed. Furthermore, they must develop a taste for reading to learn which will carry over into adult life.

Instruction in these advanced skills is the obligation of the secondary school and college. Unfortunately, the typical secondary school of today does not assume this responsibility. In a large number of secondary schools and colleges, the staff provides no reading guidance at all. In other schools, reading instruction is offered, but it does not cover all the essential aspects of reading. In still other schools, the responsibility for reading instruction is assumed by trained teachers, but the other teachers, feeling inadequate to the task, take no responsibility for teaching reading. Relatively few schools and colleges base their programs upon demonstrated needs or make periodic evaluations to see whether students are achieving the learnings sought.

Secondary school and college administrators are in key positions to improve the current practices. They alone can sensitize the staff to the need for assessing the extent of the reading problems in their schools, for developing an adequate program to satisfy these needs, and for securing the reading materials, facilities and equipment to carry out such a program.

Many practical questions usually arise in campaigns undertaken to improve reading. To aid school officials, Mildred Dawson has compiled an excellent book on high school reading programs.[12] This publication can be used to answer the questions of staff members who have had little or no preparation in this field.

Also teachers and school officials can find much concrete help in H. Alan Robinson's chapter in this volume, Chapter 13, "New Patterns in the Secondary School."

PROVIDES READING INSTRUCTION AND EXTENDED PRACTICE IN ALL SCHOOL SUBJECTS IN WHICH CHILDREN READ

Because it is radically different from basic reading, reading in various curriculum areas requires definite guidance. In a content subject, reading serves chiefly as a tool to help children acquire the basic concepts of the subject, to use these concepts in reaching sound generalizations, and to follow the type of

---

[12] Mildred A. Dawson, Comp. *Developing High School Reading Programs* (Newark, Del.: International Reading Association, 1967).

thinking typical of that subject. For example, the vocabulary and thinking patterns in mathematics are almost totally different from those in history. Indeed, the reading instruction is of value only as it contributes to the goals of the given subject.

This fifth standard can best be promoted by the principal of the school. He can appraise the present teaching practices in his school, identify weaknesses, and secure the cooperation of teachers in improving instruction. Six questions must be answered as a school official observes curricular reading in classrooms and then shapes the program along better lines.

1. Does the teacher use reading only when it is the most effective medium for the teaching purpose? For example, a book should rarely be used as an initial approach to a unit of study in a curriculum area. To teach some of the processes in electing a president, for instance, seeing a voting machine and taking part in a mock election is much better than starting with a verbal description.

This is true because most students, even those at the secondary level, are too immature in reading to acquire the broad, abstract understandings of the content subjects through reading alone. They often need to have a background for thoughtful reading built in advance through the use of visual and auditory aids, explanation by the teacher, discussion, recall of related experiences, and the like. Then the books may be consulted to verify, enrich, and extend the ideas. By such means, the student can gain new concepts and insights with a depth and range of meaning.

2. Is the reading idea-centered rather than fact-centered? The good teacher emphasizes the basic understandings in the subject as opposed to the memorization of the facts. The questions he asks the pupils are broad-based and significant, certainly not concerned with too much detail. The teacher often uses the problem-solving technique. He leads the children to define a problem, recall related experiences, collect and interpret necessary data, draw tentative conclusions, and test conclusions by further reading.

3. Is the semitechnical vocabulary of the subject definitely taught? This vocabulary includes both familiar words used with new and unfamiliar meanings and also words that are new in form as well as meaning. We know that pupils have many misconceptions of familiar word forms used in a semitechnical sense in a content field. One study has shown, for instance, that such simple concepts as *river* and *desert* are misinterpreted by many third-grade pupils. They thought that a river was a body of water that flowed from bank to bank, and a desert, a stretch of land on which one would see camels and Arabs.

4. Do the reading activities utilize the various ways of reading that are useful in the given content subject? For instance, in social studies several types of silent reading are needed, including skimming, cursory reading to gain a general idea, reading for literal meaning, and critical reading. Oral reading is seldom useful. Under the slow oral method, the listeners gain bits of detailed

information rather than the broad meanings which the author has tried to convey.

5. Are the books used in the classroom suitable in reading difficulty, up to date in content, and of sufficient variety? Do they include not only textbooks, but supplementary, reference, and trade books? Morton Botel has said that we are using the wrong book for 25 to 30 percent of the students.[13] They either read the book with very limited comprehension or take excessive time to cover the material.

With the many changes occurring in the world today, many of our earlier doctrines have become obsolete. Yet many schools continue to use outdated reading materials such as geographies that teach temperate, torrid, and frigid zones, or present the idea that the wind systems of the world are the result of heating at the equator and cooling at the poles.

6. Does the teacher provide library books to individualize reading and to encourage extensive reading that enriches the child's ideas and makes the subject "come alive"?

PROVIDES FOR THE APPROPRIATE INTRODUCTION, INTEGRATION, AND MAINTENANCE OF READING SKILLS AND ABILITIES

As Helen Huus has said, "the basic skills are the central focus of a sound reading program."[14] Extensive attention has been given to identifying and listing basic skills. Professional articles, curriculum guides, and teacher's manuals for basic readers all list reading skills, sometimes by the hundreds.

During the past fifteen years, schools have been criticized for their neglect of one of these areas—phonics. Parents, taxpayers, and other lay critics have claimed that the public schools have no strong program of organized phonics. The critics charge that the only method used is the look-and-say method, or memorization of words by sight. The whole blame for poor reading results is laid on lack of instruction in the decoding of the sounds the letters represent. According to the critics, this lack is the chief explanation of why so many disadvantaged children are retarded in reading. This lack is also presented as the reason for high illiteracy rates among young adults and why employers find that many job applicants are unable to read well enough to fill out simple application forms.

While these charges seem greatly oversimplified, unfair, and unrealistic, it is safe to say that all those directly concerned with the reading program believe that the public schools can teach reading much better than they now do.

[13] Morton Botel, duplicated outline prepared for the Metropolitan Detroit Reading Conference, 1964.

[14] Helen Huus, *Innovation and Change in Reading Instruction,* Sixty-Seventh Yearbook of the National Society for the Study of Education, Part II (Chicago: University of Chicago Press, 1968), pp. 129–30.

Therefore, we must subject our word recognition techniques to careful evaluation.

Actually, most teachers and school officials realize that decoding is a basic tool for all children if they are to become self-reliant readers. However, the use of meaning clues, word form clues, structural analysis, and the dictionary is also basic to word recognition. These skills must be taught if the child is to become a truly independent reader. No one can ensure the identification of all new words by equipping children with any one aid, such as phonics. Often a word can be perceived and recognized only through the combined use of several aids.

The critics advocate the early introduction of phonics. They indicate that learning to read consists of mastering a code involving the correspondence of sounds and their visual symbols, and that children should learn at once to translate letter forms first into sounds and then into words. According to these critics, emphasis on meaning can come later.

Let us take a look at the children who come to school. Some children know the alphabet when they come to school and can distinguish sounds in words or even read words. On the other hand, there are many children who, at this stage, are unable to distinguish sounds in the words they hear and say or to even make correct speech sounds. These children are often unable to name a single letter. Consequently, there is a great need for differentiation in instruction in phonics and for wide variation in the rate at which the instruction is provided.

The child needs a background of experience (1) in perceiving speech sounds through various listening and speaking activities; (2) in distinguishing likenesses and differences in speech sounds, (3) in hearing and using the letter names as speech sounds are discussed. For some children, such a background is developed at home in the preschool years with or without direct instruction; for others, the background must be developed at school. Only when the child has had such a rich background of listening and speaking experiences is he ready to study sounds as they are related to reading. Without it, practice in sound-symbol relationships is a waste of the child's time.

Even when the child is fully prepared for the phonics program, it must be remembered that isolated practice on phonics apart from context, while necessary, is inadequate. Each time a new phonetic learning is developed, children need opportunities to apply it to unfamiliar words in context. As Constance McCullough has said, "no letter, no word, no sentence, no paragraph is an island . . . the interpretation of sound and meaning is relative, because context determines what sound a letter shall be given and what meaning a word or phrase or sentence or paragraph shall have."[15]

Just as meaningful instruction in the phonics program must take place within the reading context, so the various reading skills must be presented within an

---

[15] Constance M. McCullough, "Balanced Reading Development," Chap. 9 in *Innovation and Change in Reading Instruction*, Sixty-Seventh Yearbook of the National Society for the Study of Education Part II (Chicago: University of Chicago Press, 1968), p. 324.

integrated reading program. Certain skills, as Heilman has indicated,[16] complement one another and should be learned *concomitantly*. Examples are "learning sight words," "associating printed letters with speech sounds," and "profiting from context clues." Overemphasis on any one of these to the exclusion of the others might predispose the child to rely on it and therefore hinder his growth on a long-term basis. On the other hand, the skills of dictionary usage require a sequential approach over a period of years.

The integrated nature of an effective program of reading skills is well illustrated by the analysis prepared by Helen M. Robinson.[17] This analysis consists of sample questions to consider in appraising the scope and adequacy of skill instruction. Robinson's analysis, quoted below, can be used not only to identify the essential reading skills, but also as a basis for evaluating current skill instruction.

1. Does instruction promote the various aids to readiness for reading and word perception and provide for their development?

Auditory discrimination	Visual discrimination	Meaning clues	Word form clues	Details of form	Phonetic analysis	Structural analysis	Use of dictionary

2. Does instruction stimulate growth in various attitudes and habits involved in a clear grasp of the meaning of what is read (comprehension)?

An inquiring attitude	Attention to meaning (literal and non-literal)	Attach right meaning to words	Fuse meanings into sequence of ideas	Grasp author's thought pattern	Interpret in light of broader context	Answer specific questions

3. Does instruction stimulate growth in a variety of comprehension abilities?

Details	Main ideas	Cause and effect relationships	Sequence of ideas (time, place, logic)	Comparison	Mood	Sensory imagery

[16] Arthur W. Heilman, "Sequence of Skills in Reading," *Current Issues in Reading*, pp. 123–24 in Vol. 13, Part 2, Proceedings of the Thirteenth Annual Convention (Newark, Del.: International Reading Association, 1969).

[17] Helen M. Robinson, "Sample Questions to Consider in Appraising the Scope and Adequacy of Reading Programs" (mimeographed form prepared for NDEA Institute, 1967), pp. 4–5. Quoted with permission of the author.

4. Does instruction stimulate growth in the types of interpretation that are integral parts of appreciative and critical reading?

Determine relevance	Recognize relationships	Evaluate against a standard	Test validity of inferences and conclusions	Use problem-solving techniques	Formulate own valid conclusions	Apply to new situations

5. Does instruction promote assimilation of ideas and information?

Alertness to new ideas	Recall of related experience	Effective association	Resulting changes in attitudes and understandings	Use in future reading and thinking

6. Does instruction cultivate the attitudes and skills involved in effective oral interpretation?

Clear grasp of author's meaning	Sensing the message to be conveyed	Using devices such as intonation, pause and emphasis to convey meaning	Adjusting to audience	Effective use of voice, expression and gesture

7. Does instruction promote flexible rates of reading?

Achieves a variety of rates	Adapts to purpose	Adapts to types of materials	Adapts to difficulty of materials	Adapts to experiential background

What makes Robinson's analysis especially relevant to our purpose is that it can be used to help teachers see the interrelationships of reading skills and to provide for integrated teaching. According to Robinson,[18] there are five major skill aspects: (1) word perception, including recognition of words and their meanings; (2) comprehension of both literal and implied meanings; (3) reaction, both intellectual and emotional; (4) assimilation by exercising critical judgment, creative thinking, and combining ideas from reading and

[18] Helen M. Robinson, "The Major Aspects of Reading," Chap 3 in Reading: *Seventy-Five Years of Progress,* Supplementary Educational Monographs, no. 96 (Chicago: University of Chicago Press, 1966), pp. 28–29.

previous experiences; and (5) rate of reading. The first four of these major aspects are covered in sample questions 1 through 6 above. As Robinson says, all four aspects may function concurrently in a reading situation. The last major aspect, rate of reading, is covered in question 7. This aspect "develops from considerable competence in each of the four other aspects."

In addition to the interrelationships of the major skill aspects, the subskills, stated in a row below each question, are also integrated. Consider the clues to word recognition below question 1. Each clue supplements the others. All the clues should be taught with simple content as soon as possible and then used together in identifying new words.

The subskills taken together show the scope of an adequate program of skill instruction. When a principal observes reading instruction in a particular classroom, he may keep a record of what was taught by making a mark in the little box above each observed skill listed. If such tabulations are made for all the reading classrooms (a separate sheet for each classroom) over a sufficient period of time, a principal can get a good idea of his school's actual reading-skill program. Sharing the results of his survey with the teachers can lead to questions and discussion about the introduction, integration, application, and maintenance of reading skills. Such discussion has inestimable value in effecting teaching reforms.

MAKES READING MATERIALS AND EQUIPMENT AVAILABLE TO CHILDREN UNDER CONDITIONS SUITABLE FOR READING GROWTH

Successful teaching of reading skills and abilities requires not only good instruction but also enough appropriate reading materials. The quantity of these depends on the financial support of the reading program. The superintendent, besides supplying the staff and scheduling classes, supports the program with teaching tools. He gives every teacher as large a supply of suitable reading material and equipment as the budget permits. If the budget is not adequate, he exhausts every means to secure the necessary funds. Then the teacher does not have to "beg, borrow, or steal" to obtain what he considers essential to teaching reading; nor does he have to supplement the normal allotment for materials out of his own pocket, as many teachers do today.[19]

Among the items needed in classrooms are: basic readers and several texts for each content subject adapted to the various levels of reading ability; supplementary books related to single themes; easy books with high interest appeal; anthologies; reference books including dictionaries, encyclopedias, and atlases; appropriate newspapers and magazines. Varied types of visual and auditory aids should also be available with the necessary machinery for their use, e.g., programmed materials, tapes and worksheets, and films and filmstrips.

Each elementary school needs a well-stocked school library with a trained

---

[19] Austin and Morrison, *The First R,* op. cit., p. 69.

school librarian in charge. Classrooms also need libraries with a sufficient number of trade books of varied content representing different reading levels.

The principal of the school seeks parental cooperation in making appropriate children's books available in the home. He indicates to the parents the need for providing a quiet time and a study space for students during their out-of-school hours.

Another step in attaining the aforementioned standard is that of helping teachers make the classroom a learning laboratory. Such a laboratory creates the conditions under which reading growth is most likely to take place. The classroom is neither barren nor "interior-decorated." Rather, the environment is functional; pictures, exhibits, and the like reflect the units of study under way and are changed from time to time to fit new teaching purposes. The assorted reading materials arouse the children's curiosity and start them on a search for new understandings. Committee rooms off the main classroom are used by individuals or small groups of pupils for discussion and the solution of problems. The teacher and the pupils are cooperative and sensitive to the rights of others.

Admittedly, the foregoing pattern for teaching is ideal. But with some such ideal in mind, a principal has an ultimate goal—a standard toward which to work and against which to appraise present attainments.

ESTABLISHES VALID STANDARDS AND PROCEDURES IN THE SELECTION OF SUPERIOR READING MATERIALS AND EQUIPMENT

The need for careful selection of reading materials is obvious in view of the great increases in the number, variety, and cost of such materials. But, under pressure of time and with limited personnel to make an evaluation, far too often the only basis for the choices is hasty inspection or haphazard testing of the materials in classrooms under subjective conditions. Small wonder that administrators aware of this situation are concerned that selection of materials be improved.

Since books represent the largest and most widely used category of reading materials, let us consider some of the difficulties of book selection. Among the problems that need to be solved are the following: (1) organizing the work of book evaluation so as to distribute it throughout the school year; (2) obtaining expert advice in special subject-matter areas; (3) selecting with children's needs and curriculum objectives in mind; (4) ensuring that enough objective information is assembled to show the relative merits of the books being considered; and (5) coordinating the work of those participating in the selection.

In order to establish valid standards and procedures for selection of the best books, an administrator needs to guide the book committee through two basic steps. One step is that of establishing valid standards for evaluation. To minimize the work but ensure good selection, some book committees choose several criteria of major significance in satisfying the particular students' needs; then, with the time and effort available, the committee makes a careful, objective appraisal using these important criteria. If the list of standards is too long, too much attention may be devoted to appraising very minor items. Also, too much weight is likely to be given the trivial items in summing up the ratings. The second step involves making impartial evaluation of the books in light of each major standard. The clearer the definition of the standard, the easier it is to use it in the selection process.

Much of what has been said about problems of careful book selection also applies to the evaluation of the many types of new materials and equipment available for teaching reading.

MAKES SPECIAL PROVISIONS IN READING FOR DIVERGENT LEARNERS AND DISABLED READERS

There are several kinds of problem children who require special services if they are to attain their reading potentials. First, and perhaps of greatest concern to teachers, is the constitutionally *slow learner*. As described by Sterl Artley,[20] he is a child who "has a low potential for growth resulting from low native capacity," i.e., IQs of 70 to 90. Slow learners "lag behind about a year in mental growth when they enter school. They lag one year in intellectual growth for each six years of chronological growth. . . . There is one such learner in every four of five pupils in the typical classroom."

Artley indicates that the slow learner shows definite limitations in defining, reasoning, generalizing, and seeing relationships. However, the difference from the average child is not of kind but of degree, "a case of less than." The chief problem with the slow learner is that of lowering teachers' sights to what the child's intellectual powers will permit, seeing that adapted instruction is provided, and encouraging teachers to appraise his growth in terms of his potential. He must be helped to succeed at his level.

Another kind of problem child is the *underachiever*—the child who does not perform up to his potential. There are slow underachievers, average underachievers and bright underachievers. The problem in the case of all three groups is easiest to solve when there is early identification of the child's deficiency. At an early age, he is more likely to respond well to program adjustment.

Unlike the underachiever, the *reluctant reader* possesses the requisite reading skills. Reluctant students are those who are not motivated to read and apparently get little satisfaction from reading. During a library period, they shun reading and inspect the illustrations of the book or look through one book after another. The major problem is to identify and overcome the causes of the reluctance, which are often deep-seated.

Still another group are the *children without,* from low socio-economic areas. According to J. W. Getzels, "their capacity to be interested has been im-

---

[20] A. Sterl Artley, "Reading Instruction for Slow Learners," a paper given at the Sixteenth Annual Meeting of the Metropolitan Detroit Reading Conference, 1959, p. 1.

paired," they are "in an inferior position physically, intellectually, and emotionally," "their educational and occupational aspirations tend to be depressed," and "their time orientation is shorter."[21] These disadvantaged children need compensatory learning opportunities.

Impaired interest in learning to read can be corrected by a variety of steps. The teacher may demonstrate the pleasure of books by skillfully reading aloud stories that the children can appreciate and enjoy. Popular stories are usually those that include an appropriate kind of humor, are action-centered, do not involve an undue amount of description, have well-developed characters, and will excite the child's imagination. The teacher may get good books into the child's home by introducing the class to public library services, both within the library building and through the neighborhood bookmobile. Or, as was done in Detroit, administrators can purchase large numbers of suitable paperbacks and sell them at cost to parents and children.

In addition, there are partially sighted, blind, emotionally disturbed, and otherwise seriously handicapped children who require highly specialized services.

In the past, most of these disabled children were not identified until the middle grades. They were allowed to fail repeatedly in the regular classroom, thus multiplying their reading difficulties. When corrective instruction was undertaken, it was given by regular classroom teachers who had no educational background or experience in the specialized techniques required. Often the only reading materials used were basic readers and skill workbooks.

In contrast, a modern reading program identifies divergent and disabled pupils upon entering school or as early as possible thereafter. The program is responsive to these children. The persons assigned to work with disabled readers are well prepared to make diagnoses of reading disabilities and to provide the specialized help needed. The specialist has access to a reading center well supplied with diagnostic materials and equipment, a variety of instructional reading materials, library books, and mechanical teaching devices such as pacers and programmed learning machines. Ample time is allowed the specialist for individual and small-group work.

In a modern program, slow learners who are left in regular classrooms are assigned to teachers who understand relative growth rates. The teachers realize that these children will show growth but that it will not be as rapid as that of the average pupils. The teachers are careful to see that slow learners do not compete against better students but only against their own records. The teacher considers growth the important thing and appraises it in terms of each slow learner's reading potential.

In modernizing programs for divergent and disabled readers, several administrative procedures are necessary: (1) building staff competence in

---

[21] J. W. Getzels, "The Problem of Interests: A Reconsideration" in *Reading: Seventy-Five Years of Progress,* Supplementary Educational Monograph No. 96 (Chicago: University of Chicago Press, 1966), pp. 104–105.

identifying such pupils early; (2) providing in-service training for teachers who must meet the unique needs of these pupils; and (3) providing an adequate budget for the services planned.

UTILIZES TOOLS AND PROCEDURES FOR CONTINUING APPRAISAL AND IMPROVEMENT OF READING INSTRUCTION

Let us assume that the reading program of a school district has been rated on standards 1 through 9 of the evaluation form shown on page 22. This accomplished, the district superintendent has a composite profile of the different features of his reading program. Usually he will note at once that there are both strengths and weaknesses.

What can be done to improve the reading program in light of the findings of the appraisal? The findings will need to be studied and the priorities considered and acted upon by all concerned—administrators, supervisors, teachers, and parents.

Action cannot be taken overnight. Before the staff members make a move, they will require time to "shift gears." Then they will need to decide on their specific goals in strengthening the program. They will also have to decide how each of these goals can be achieved. Then they are ready to proceed step by step in accord with the priorities.

An example of effective action is that taken in the Banneker District of St. Louis by Dr. Samuel Shepard and his staff.[22] (The schools in this district were attended by disadvantaged children.) First, Shepard induced the principals and teachers in his district to face the cruel fact that the academic achievement of the pupils was disgracefully low. He presented the results of objective measures of skill achievement in graphic form. He explained that group intelligence tests are inaccurate because of their environmental loading and that a child's limitations in learning are largely determined by his drive and determination. Thus he endeavored to convince the teachers that disadvantaged children can learn, given the proper climate, materials, and instruction. Second, he worked with the parents to develop an understanding of the relationship between formal education and the number of dollars one brings home in his pay envelope. He sought to motivate the parents' interest in the progress of their children and to encourage higher aspirations.

Such attention to reading is almost certain to lead to concrete improvements in the school's programs. It is no wonder that today's reading program in the Banneker District is inspiring the students to make the most of themselves. They are given a chance to achieve their full potential in the years ahead!

[22] Kay Ware, "Ways to Develop Reading Skills and Interests of Culturally Different Youth in Large Cities" in *Improving English Skills of Culturally Different Youth*, Bulletin 1964, no. 5, of the U.S. Department of Health Education and Welfare, Office of Education (Washington, D.C.: U.S. Government Printing Office, 1964), pp. 150–51.

Conclusion

It surely would seem that we do not want, and cannot afford to have, an out-dated reading program. We need a modern reading program that challenges each student while providing him with definite ends that he can work toward with self-confidence. This is a complex program, language-centered, subject-wide, skill-promoting, adaptable, never rigid. A reading program for this season is not just one straight-line program but a program with many varia-tions, one that is "custom made" for the individual child. It must provide the means by which all children can become concerned adults able to participate effectively in our society.

BIBLIOGRAPHY

Austin, Mary C., and Coleman Morrison, *The First R: The Harvard Report on Reading in Elementary Schools* (New York: Macmillan, 1963).

Dawson, Mildred A., comp., *Teaching Word Recognition Skills* (Newark, Del.: International Reading Association, 1971).

Harris, Albert J., ed., *Casebook on Reading Disability* (New York: David McKay, 1970).

Harris, Albert J., *How to Increase Reading Ability*, 5th ed. rev. (New York: David McKay, 1970).

Ornstein, Allan C., and Philip D. Vairo, *How to Teach Disadvantaged Youth* (New York: David McKay, 1969).

Passow, A. Harry, Miriam Goldberg, and Abraham J. Tannenbaum, eds., *Education of the Disadvantaged* (New York: Holt, Rinehart & Winston, 1967).

Robinson, H. Alan, comp. and ed., *Meeting Individual Differences in Reading*, Supplementary Educational Monographs, No. 94 (Chicago: University of Chicago Press, 1964).

Robinson, H. Alan, comp. and ed., *Recent Developments in Reading*, Supplementary Educational Monographs, No. 95 (Chicago: University of Chicago Press, 1965).

Robinson, Helen M., ed., *Innovation and Change in Reading Instruction*, Sixty-Seventh Yearbook of the National Society for the Study of Education, Part II (Chicago: University of Chicago Press, 1968).

The Journal of Reading, a periodical published October through May; secondary reading (Newark, Del.: International Reading Association).

The Reading Teacher, a periodical published October through May; elementary reading (Newark, Del.: International Reading Association).

3

A Proposed Staff Organization
for Reading–Language Arts

Morton Botel

Few school systems have sufficient assistance from specialists in reading;[1] most probably will never have enough specialized help. Consequently, the superintendent needs to be resourceful in devising ways of effectively using the talents of whatever reading specialists are available. In his efforts he must consider the philosophy or emphasis of the reading program. He must determine whether the specialist should work primarily with teachers, with pupils, or with some combination of the two.

If the reading–language arts program is regarded as a developmental program concerned with the reading, language, study skills, and attitudes of all pupils—kindergarten through grade 12—in all subjects, the reading specialist must direct his efforts toward the professional development of teachers. If, on the other hand, the reading program is regarded as a remedial program, the reading specialist will focus directly on those children who are underachievers in reading.

The author's experience as reading specialist in Bucks County, Pennsylvania, indicates that reading problems exist largely because teachers ordinarily do not adjust their instructional programs to the uniqueness of each pupil, taking into account his levels of ability and current achievement, his rate and best ways of learning, as well as his interests. Therefore, the major effort of the reading–language arts specialist should be directed toward the professional development of teachers.

As a rule, remedial programs should be initiated only when the total pro-

---

[1] The use of the term reading specialist and reading program in the chapter should properly be extended in actual practice to reading–language arts specialist and reading–language arts program.

gram of the school has been updated to provide for the range of differences in each classroom. Most reading specialists will assert that when a reading program is geared primarily to problem cases, many teachers are disinclined to work with pupils whose reading does not come up to grade level. They feel that the inability of pupils to read and comprehend their textbooks represents retardation in reading and requires remedial help. On the other hand, if the focus of the reading program is developmental, each teacher will be encouraged to provide in many ways for the wide range of reading levels. The latter policy is more positive and generally more effective.

Schoolwide Reading Problems

What are the practices which foster the development of inefficient reading skills and attitudes? In 1952 and 1953, the author made a survey of the status of reading instruction in 52 Bucks County districts in an attempt to answer this question. A number of significant and pervasive practices and problems in typical classrooms were evident.

1. More than 25 percent of the pupils were assigned reading books and content area textbooks that were too difficult. This resulted in disinterest, discouragement, discipline problems, and poor understanding.
2. Many teachers seemed inclined to ask dull and trivial questions rather than stimulating and crucial ones that would guide pupils to understanding the content of these books.
3. Oral reading was often conducted on a turn-by-turn, sight approach leading to hesitation, poor intonation, and general dullness.
4. Few library books were readily available to pupils, particularly to the poor readers.
5. Word-attack skills were frequently neglected or taught in a haphazard way. There was little effort to relate such instruction to pupils' current needs.
6. Pupils who had difficulty associating oral language with its written counterpart were rarely given reinforcing tactile and kinesthetic experience with written forms to enhance their perception, attentiveness, and memory.
7. Pupils were infrequently taught how to study independently, or how to vary their reading rate to suit different purposes, or the level of difficulty of material.
8. Reading, spelling, and handwriting, as well as grammar and word usage, tended to be taught as discrete subjects rather than as interrelated language arts. Written expression seemed to be an ignored art.

A Schoolwide Strategy Is Needed

When the foregoing instructional practices exist, a schoolwide strategy for reading improvement is needed. The reading program should seek to eliminate or reduce the incidence of instructional practices that create disinterest, poor comprehension, poor study habits, and general frustration on the part of so many pupils. More specifically

1. each school system needs a blueprint and long-range plan for developing the reading, language arts, and study skills of every student, in every subject, from kindergarten to grade 12;
2. this plan must be formulated and continuously updated by a team of persons including the reading–language arts specialist, teachers, administrators, librarians, and curriculum and psychological specialists; and
3. the goal of the plan must be the continuous professional development of all staff members.

THE CLASSROOM TEACHER IS THE KEY

There is considerable evidence to support the idea that working with and stimulating teachers is the most productive way to reach the pupils. For one thing, the almost inevitable "Hawthorne effect" in experiments strongly suggests that when changes are made in a program, the staff responds and is more productive. At some point, however, the Hawthorne effect undoubtedly begins to wane. More recently a new phrase has been added to our vocabularies—the "Pygmalion effect." This term comes from the title of a book which reported an experiment in south San Francisco.[2,3] In this study, teachers were told that a random sample of the pupils in the school had greater potential than the others. In subsequent months, these pupils scored higher in intelligence tests and achievement tests than a control group. This study seemed to indicate that, if teachers are enthusiastic about their methods and believe that each pupil can blossom, the resulting achievement of the pupils will probably be greater than that normally found.

The Cooperative Reading Studies[4] seem to provide further support for the

---

[2] R. Rosenthal and L. F. Jacobson, *Pygmalion in the Classroom* (New York: Holt, Rinehart and Winston, Inc., 1968).

[3] Two reviews of this study have found serious flaws in the data presented and in the conclusions drawn from them. See R. Snow, "Unfinished Pygmalion," *Contemporary Psychology* (1969), vol. 24, no. 4, pp. 197–99 and R. L. Thorndike, "A Critical Review of *Pygmalion in the Classroom* by Rosenthal and Jacobson," *American Educational Research Journal* (November, 1968), vol. 5, no. 4, pp. 708–11. At this time, the Pygmalion effect can be regarded as a very attractive theory.

[4] R. Dykstra, *Final Report. Continuation of the Coordinating Center for First-Grade*

idea that the teacher factor is central to improving instruction. These studies compared a number of reading methodologies. Only a few slight differences between and among methods were found, but there was a great variation in achievement within a given method. In other words, given the same method and equivalent groups of children, teachers varied widely in the results they achieved.

In view of these and other findings, the role of the reading specialist should undoubtedly center around (1) the expressed needs and interests of teachers, and (2) the development of teacher understanding and interest in instructional configurations, child development, and the psychology of learning.

It is not possible to specify precisely how to staff a school system to develop and implement a plan for reading improvement. Certainly, if there is to be *only one person* appointed to a position in reading, his major concern should be working with the staff on their professional development.

ROLE AND RESPONSIBILITIES OF THE SPECIALIST

The role of such a reading–language arts specialist should be primarily one of leadership in helping teachers continue their professional development.[5] Some of the responsibilities of the specialist which fulfill this objective are listed below.

1. Coordinating of the reading and language arts professional development program.
2. Responding to teacher requests for assistance.
3. Helping teachers in all subject areas to determine the instructional levels of their pupils and the reading levels of the textbooks used in their classes.
4. Helping to adjust materials and methods in the light of pupil differences.
5. Helping teachers develop competency in teaching directed reading lessons in all subjects.
6. Helping teachers find alternative instructional strategies for teaching subject matter when textbooks are too difficult for some or all of their pupils, and demonstrating effective classroom techniques.
7. Setting up procedures for identifying and diagnosing pupils who need special remedial help.
8. Coordinating the evaluation and selection of reading and language arts textbooks, tests, and other media.

Reading Instruction Programs (Washington, D.C.: U.S. Department of Health, Education, and Welfare, 1967).

[5] Another helpful view of the role, responsibilities, and qualifications of reading specialists has been prepared by the Professional Standards and Ethics committee of the IRA, and will be found in Appendix 3.2.

9. Organizing a reading materials resource center.
10. Supervising the work of special reading teachers.
11. Helping parents understand their role in influencing their children's language and reading development.
12. Initiating and supervising pilot, experimental, and innovative instructional strategies.
13. Orienting new teachers in the program.
14. Keeping the staff informed regarding research findings and new theories and helping teachers implement them.

It is clear from the nature of the work described that the reading–language arts specialist must not be responsible for the evaluation of teachers. If teachers believe that they are being judged by the specialist and that these judgments are being reported to the administration, they will almost surely refrain from admitting their weaknesses, concerns, and needs. The success of the program depends upon the willingness of the staff to admit that they have much to learn and to make proper changes in their teaching activities.

THE READING COMMITTEE

Specific activities and responsibilities of the reading specialist should be reviewed by a reading committee. The chairman of this committee might be a teacher, curriculum director, or principal.

This committee should have an advisory and liaison function. Its members review the reading specialist's proposals for enhancing the objectives of the reading program, lending its suggestions and support.

Proposals

Seven examples of such proposals follow. These are representative of the kinds of ideas, strategies, and practices that are found in outstanding classrooms. Each proposal cuts across several of the responsibilities of the specialist enumerated above. It must be kept in mind that these proposals involve all who are concerned with the improvement of the reading program. They are not formulas to be handed down from above and to be implemented by the specialist. At the same time, the Reading Committee is not just a debating society. It should be expected to suggest precise ways to implement suggested proposals.

Furthermore, it must be obvious that such proposals and their implementation do not necessarily depend upon having a reading specialist on the staff. Often principals, curriculum specialists, and master teachers have the skills necessary to bring about these and other desirable outcomes.

MATCHING CHILDREN AND BOOKS

It is essential from both a psychological and linguistic point of view that pupils be given books which they can read fluently and with a high degree of comprehension. Psychologically, we know that pupils who are successful are more likely to have the motivation to continue to make efforts toward an objective. And from a linguistic point of view, fluent reading makes it possible for a pupil to more closely relate printed ideas to their oral counterparts. Pupils who are wrongly placed in materials in which they are not fluent develop symptoms of frustration which signal their underlying inability to cope with the materials.

Flora Arnstein describes the overriding central symptom of frustration-discouragement and its antidote, success, in these well-chosen observations:

> For some two years I conducted an office for remedial study for children who were having difficulties in their school work. I was surprised to find that all the children, no matter what their specific problem in any subject, had one attribute in common—they were all more or less discouraged. What this discouragement stemmed from I was not in a position to determine, though in some instances the parents' attitude toward the child suggested the cause. I found that what these children needed as much as, perhaps more than, help in subject matter was a buildup of confidence in themselves and in their own ability. Surprisingly, this buildup did not require too much time to establish. Given a graduated program involving a series of small successes, the children were able to achieve the confidence that is often manifested in their slightly scornful comment "Oh! That's easy!" Arrival at this point is the beginning of clear sailing and ultimate accomplishment.[6]

In order to increase the likelihood that pupils will be reading appropriate materials that assure success, the following steps are proposed:

1. Teachers should determine the independent, instructional, and frustration levels of pupils in the materials they are using. The independent level is defined as that range of reading difficulty in which a pupil can read a book easily on his own; the instructional level is that range in which a pupil can read a book with some guidance; the frustration level is that range in which a pupil cannot read a book with reasonable comprehension (at least 70 to 75 percent) without the continued presence of the teacher. These levels are delineated in Table 3.1. One way to determine these levels is to have pupils read, both orally and silently, samples of the graded books in the series they are using to informally determine which of these books is most appropriate for instruction. Another is to test pupils on commercially prepared informal reading inventories such as the Botel[7] or McCracken[8] to estimate these levels. This

---

[6] Flora J. Arnstein, *Poetry in the Elementary Classroom* (New York: Appleton-Century-Crofts, 1962), p. 18, 19.

[7] M. Botel, *The Botel Reading Inventory* (Chicago: Follett Educational Corporation, 1966).

[8] R. McCracken, *The Standard Reading Inventory* (Bellingham, Wash.: Pioneer Publishing Co., 1966).

TABLE 3.1

Performance in Context[a]

Levels	Oral Fluency	Comprehension
Independent	99–100%	95–100%
Instructional	95–98%	75–94%
Frustration or Overplacement	less than 95%	less than 75%

[a] The criteria for the percentages in this table are based on those levels first proposed by Emmett Betts and his students in *Foundations of Reading Instruction* (New York: American Book Company, 1946). A critical position with respect to these criteria is taken by William R. Powell "Reappraising the Criteria for Interpreting Informal Inventories," *Reading Diagnosis and Evaluation,* vol. 13, Part 4, Proceedings of 13th Annual Convention (Newark, Del.: International Reading Association, 1970).

should be done following an orientation period of two to six weeks at the beginning of each school year. Findings should be discussed with the reading–language arts specialist before groups are formally organized.

2. Pupils who complete their readers should be tested for fluency and comprehension in selected stories in the completed book by the specialist, principal, or a master teacher before proceeding to the next book in the series.[9]

3. In the subject fields, members of the department aided by the consultant should prepare an informal reading inventory for each textbook. Each inventory should be taken early in the school term. Pupils who are frustrated by a certain textbook should be given alternative assignments in more suitable materials or with other modes of learning and subsequently should be encouraged to contribute to the class discussions.

Recording the chapter on tape cartridges so that poor readers can get the material aurally should be considered as one such alternative. In addition, the reading specialist will help the departmental teachers determine the reading difficulty of the textbooks and will suggest others more suitable for poor readers.

4. Graded newspapers should be ordered on the basis of the instructional or independent reading levels of the students rather than on the basis of chronological grade level placement.

5. Summer workshops should be arranged so that teachers of content subjects can locate and identify suitable texts, supplementary books, and other instructional media; determine the reading level of their textbooks and rewrite certain textbooks at lower levels of difficulty; write original material to provide

[9] A detailed discussion of this procedure entitled "The Cooperative Checkout" may be found in M. Botel, *How to Teach Reading* (Chicago: Follett Educational Corporation, 1969).

for the range of reading levels in the classroom; and determine effective methods of helping pupils understand these materials.

6. Letters should be sent to parents, informing them each time a pupil advances from one reading level to another and explaining the level of fluency and comprehension the child achieved. Standard letters such as the one below can be developed.

[10]

Dear _____

    I am happy to report that _____ has been advanced to the _____ reader. This means that he has <u>mastered</u> the _____ reader. Research and experience have shown that a child has mastered one level and is ready for a higher level when he can:

    1. recognize 95 to 100 percent of the running words;
    2. understand 75 to 100 percent of the content.

    The reader your child has mastered is being sent home so that he can share with you some of the stories we enjoyed so much the past few months.

    Be a good listener. Sit down with your child. Let him pick the stories or parts of stories he wants to read. Discuss the stories with him. Be generous with your praise.

    If occasionally he is troubled by a word, ask him to read the rest of the sentence and see what word would make sense. Then, if he still is unable to get it, supply the word without comment and go on.

    Look over the workbook together, too. You will be interested in the kinds of practice experience your child is getting.

    I would appreciate your comments and questions at any time concerning your child's reading. Thank you for your cooperation.

                  Sincerely,

                  _____

[10] Ibid., p. 20.

DEVELOPING COMPREHENSION, CRITICAL INTERPRETATION, AND APPRECIATION IN READING

History was once defined as "One . . . thing after another." Indeed, a number of textbooks are written in such a way that readers are likely to get identical notions from its explication. To make matters worse, many teachers, following the pattern of most of their former teachers, pose strictly factual questions that further emphasize such linear fragmentation of the subject. With this approach, even literature is likely to suffer from such deadly sameness.

To be informed, enlightened, and challenged to feel and to think are among the major purposes of learning to read. If these objectives are to be implemented, a major and continuous effort must be made to help teachers pose questions that provoke diverse thinking and lively discussions.

To accomplish diversity and evaluative discussion, recurrent in-service meetings should be scheduled which focus on a piece of written material— a challenging sentence or paragraph, a story, a poem, or an entire chapter— which pupils are reading. Faculty discussion in groups of six to twelve should focus upon the principal alternative feelings and ideas portrayed in the material and indicate how these feelings and ideas can be generated by pupils in a dialogue with their teacher and classmates. Questions for guiding discussions and directed reading activities suggested in manuals should be analyzed for their values and limitations. But no formula for teaching a lesson and no list of questions formulated by authors, editors, or other teachers can produce the spontaneity, relevance, and involvement that understanding requires. Each teacher must devise questions based on his knowledge of the pupils and objectives in reading. His ability to do this can be enhanced by regular opportunities to share his approaches with his colleagues and to benefit from their ideas.

ESTABLISHING A SCHOOLWIDE PROGRAM OF STUDY SKILLS INSTRUCTION

Students must become increasingly self-directive in their study if they are to mature fully as learners. Study skills are demanded in such activities as previewing, turning headings into questions, taking notes, immediate and delayed recall, adjusting rate, planning time and place of study, writing a report, using the library, and preparing for or taking exams. Lecturing to pupils regarding these skills is not too helpful for most students. They must learn to study by performing these tasks under supervision and be helped to improve their skills while actually studying. The following are suggested for the improvement of study skills instruction:

1. Gear an entire year's professional development program to improving the study skills. Begin with a week-long preschool workshop in which the faculty (working at grade level in the elementary schools and in departments at the secondary level) studies good books and manuals on the improvement

of study. Specific habits, skills, and activities to be taught should be identified and listed.

2. The teaching of the study skills should be appropriate to the grade and subject and scheduled in connection with actual study activities and assignments in regular classrooms.

3. Throughout the year, periodic workshops should be held to share experiences and analyze progress and to make revisions. Live demonstrations and video-tape recordings of actual skills sessions will enhance the process.

CULTIVATING THE LIFETIME HABIT OF READING

No goal of reading instruction is more important than that of cultivating the love of books and the habit of turning to books for enlightenment and for sheer joy. The chief values of reading include the extending of one's own experience, enabling one to live vicariously, being confronted with human problems similar to the reader's experiences as well as to those which he does not himself experience. In other words, through reading one can crawl inside another's skin and see the world through eyes other than his own.

For most children, the habit of reading does not just happen. It is not enough to teach pupils the skills of reading and study in their readers and in their textbooks. Training lessons, as such, do not foster the love of books and the habit of turning to books when leisure offers the choices available today. Hoping for joy in reading will not do it. Instead, teachers must actively cultivate among pupils this lifetime habit. Certain practices have been found to be especially effective, among them are

1. Daily reading or telling a good story or poem to pupils.
2. Acting out stories which have been read and discussed.
3. Reading poems frequently to the group, and occasionally making choral arrangements.
4. Providing class time for browsing, self-selection of books, and independent reading.
5. Using trade books in connection with units in the content areas as a complement to textbooks.
6. Encouraging book-club memberships.
7. Inviting authors and illustrators of children's books to discuss their work with the pupils.
8. Encouraging parents to take their children to libraries and book stores so that they may browse and purchase books of their own choosing. (Several studies have shown that books selected by adults for children are not the same as those children would choose for themselves.[11,12])

[11] Marie Rankin, *Children's Interests in Library Books of Fiction, Teachers College Contributions to Education,* no. 906 (New York: Bureau of Publications, Teachers College, Columbia University, 1944).

[12] C. J. Kolson, R. E. Robinson, and W. C. Zimmerman, "Children's Preferences in Publishers," *Education* (November 1962) vol. 83, pp. 155–57.

9. Building a large and attractive classroom library.
10. Using individual incentive charts to encourage independent reading (one of least effective in inducing permanent love for books and reading).

ORIENTING NEW TEACHERS TO THE READING–LANGUAGE ARTS PROGRAM

As the reading–language arts program develops and matures, it is important that new staff members be systematially oriented to the evolving instructional program. The following practices will aid in accomplishing this purpose:

1. All new teachers should be brought in a week or two earlier than the rest of the staff for an orientation program. Following general meetings, master teachers at all grade levels and in the various subject areas can meet with small groups of new teachers to discuss, illustrate, and demonstrate with pupils, procedures for giving an informal reading inventory, teaching a directed reading activity, and teaching study skills.
2. Monthly meetings should be planned with new teachers to discuss their problems in implementing the program.
3. New teachers should be helped and supported by regular visits from the reading specialist throughout the first year.

ESTABLISHING A TUTORIAL PROGRAM

Many parents and other members of the lay public and university and high school students are eager to participate in and contribute to the instructional process. With careful training and supervision, such persons will be able to help problem readers in significant ways. The following ideas may be helpful in establishing such a program

1. Parent-teacher organizations, women's clubs, and student associations should be contacted to enlist their aid for the project.
2. In-service training sessions should be held for the volunteers. These sessions should emphasize the importance of (a) the child's need for a sympathetic supportive relationship with the tutor, (b) materials at the independent or easy instructional level of the child, and (c) a modified directed reading activity in which guided silent reading is followed by discussion of the story and oral reading.
3. In-school and after-school schedules should be worked out. Some of the volunteers might work as coordinators.
4. To maintain morale, tutors need to be helped to understand that the ethics of their relationships require that they do not discuss or criticize the behavior of school personnel outside of the school setting.

HELPING INNOVATIVE TEACHERS ESTABLISH
ALTERNATIVE INSTRUCTIONAL CONFIGURATIONS

Although good management requires that a school system have a specified minimal instructional configuration for the teaching of reading and language arts, provision should be made for any teacher who prefers an alternative but productive instructional strategy. To accomplish this

1. any teacher who prefers an alternative configuration should present an outline of the plan to the reading–language arts specialist and committee for their consideration;
2. every assistance should be provided the teacher to help in teaching the program efficiently; and
3. such teachers should report to their colleagues from time to time on the progress and problems of the program.

Conclusion

This discussion has centered on the leadership role of the reading specialist working with his colleagues to develop an all-school approach to the improvement of reading and language arts. The changes that they initiate should help every student in the school system improve in his skills and appreciations. More specifically, from a child development standpoint the objective is to help each pupil develop his reading, language arts, and study skills by gearing instruction to his level of ability and achievement, his rate of reading, interests and emerging needs. From the point of view of the content subjects, the objective is to develop each pupil's skills in word attack, vocabulary, comprehension and interpretation, study skills, oral reading, and oral and written expression in every subject and at every grade level. These objectives are most effectively accomplished in a program that is committed to the continuous development of the competence of each faculty member

Appendix 3.1

CASE STUDY: A STAFF IN ACTION

A case study of the Carl Sandburg Junior High School[13] Reading Term is presented below to illustrate one of many possible variations of the staff organization proposal discussed in this chapter. The program, which is supported by ESEA Title III funds, is an exemplary one. The entire staff is in-

---

[13] In the Neshaminy School System, Levittown, Pa.

volved in its activities and shares the responsibility for pupils' continued improvement in reading.

Mrs. Clara Milner, program coordinator, has prepared the following report summarizing the program's evolution, structure, and growth.

The Neshaminy Reading Team Program

An in-service training program designed to provide teachers of science, social studies, math and English with continuous professional development in reading–language arts was initiated six years ago (1963–64) in the Neshaminy School District.

Since 1966 the program in operation at the Carl Sandburg Junior High School in Levittown, Pennsylvania, has been Federally funded under a Title III, ESEA grant.

ORIGINS OF THE PROGRAM

The need for the Neshaminy Reading Team Program was first recognized by concerned content area teachers who were confronted in their classroom-teaching with the noticeable and handicapping skill deficiencies of many of their students, including academically talented students.

Because content area teachers are generally unable to identify the specific nature of skill deficiencies, or are not oriented to the sequential nature of skill development, they attempt through trial and error, and in a haphazard manner, to teach skills essential for learning in the discipline. Through such procedures teachers meet only minimal success in skill development. Skill deficiencies result in more talented students becoming only superficially involved in learning; handicapped readers are overplaced in instructional materials that they cannot read. Classroom teaching is too often done through language that students cannot comprehend.

Concerned teachers at the Carl Sandburg Junior High School wanted more than superficial learning for their better students and they wanted to teach less competent students to read and write. They therefore explored with the reading teacher how the talents and knowledge of the reading teacher could be directed toward the professional development of classroom teachers. A program was designed that would provide in-service training for the professional development of teachers and simultaneously provide the basis for a developmental program of reading–language arts instruction for students assigned to teachers participating in the program.

ESTABLISHMENT OF THE PROGRAM

A committee composed of the Director of Curriculum of Neshaminy School District, the Supervising Principal of the junior high schools, the involved reading teacher and the county reading consultant met to consider the proposal and to discuss plans for its implementation.

Inherent in the organization plans for in-service training was a recognition of the uniqueness of individual pupils, the varying levels of student achievement and the importance of skill mastery in learning the subject content in each academic discipline. The established practice within the school of homogeneous grouping lent itself to a realistic program for ultimate extension of reading–language arts instruction in grades 7, 8 and 9. The initial organization and the subsequent growth of the program are outlined below to illustrate the need for continuous professional development of teachers.

ORGANIZATIONAL STRUCTURE FOR THE INITIAL PROGRAM

1. The reading teacher was appointed coordinator of the newly structured program and was relieved of other responsibilities.
2. Structure for in-service training
   a. *Teacher participation:*
      Four seventh-grade teachers representing science, social studies, math and English were assigned to a team to teach the same four classes of students.
   b. *Student participation:*
      Students in the "top" two classes and in the "lowest" two classes were selected for assignment to the program to provide the widest possible range of reading–language arts ability.
   c. *Scheduling of workshop-meetings for in-service training:*
      1. A five-day summer workshop.
      2. Two class periods per week were designated as workshop meetings for team teachers. The scheduling of students provided for their availability for workshop meetings for teaching demonstrations.
3. Sessions for parents of handicapped readers
   Six evening sessions were scheduled to acquaint parents with the specific word-attack problems of their children and to prepare them to work with their children in specific reading material provided by the program.

EXTENSION OF SERVICES UNDER FEDERAL FUNDING

1. The summer workshop was extended from five to ten days.
2. Three class periods a week were scheduled for teachers for workshop-type meetings.
   a. One period to coordinate instructional approaches within a team group.
   b. Two periods for content area workshop meetings to:
      1. Identify the reading–language arts and study skills essential for the discipline.
      2. Develop a sequential program of reading–language arts instruction in each discipline for students representing varying levels of skill mastery and academic achievement.

3. Select and prepare appropriate materials for instruction of seriously handicapped readers.

4. Observe teaching demonstrations.

3. A specified number of one-day workshops were scheduled throughout the school year to permit essential in-service training and the formulation of developmental plans for the program to accommodate the needs of students representing varying levels of ability and achievement.

4. Teacher aides were employed to assist classroom teachers and to provide tutorial assistance for seriously handicapped readers.

5. Consultative services were provided.

6. Parent sessions were extended to include additional parents.

7. In 1968–69 two reading specialists were added to the staff.

GROWTH OF THE PROGRAM

Educational growth

1. Identification by content area teachers of specific reading–language arts and study skills essential for learning in the discipline.

2. A testing program developed by teachers in each discipline to determine students level of mastery in reading–language arts and study skills specific for the discipline.

3. The development of a sequential program of instruction in reading–language arts and study skills in each discipline for

    a. Academically talented students

    b. Average students

    c. Handicapped readers

Numerical growth

Year of program	Number of teachers involved	Number of teacher teams	Approximate number of students	Grades
1st (1963—64)	4	1	120	7
2nd	8	2	240	7 & 8
3rd	8	2	240	7 & 8
4th[a]	12	3	360	7, 8 & 9
5th	16	4 (2 teams in 7th gr.)	480	7, 8 & 9
6th	20	5 (2 teams in 7th gr. 2 teams in 8th gr.)	600	7, 8 & 9

[a] Federal funding began in the fourth year.

The effectiveness of the program is measurable through a testing program. It is reflected also by teachers in multiple ways, some of which are the following:

1. The emphasis that teachers place on teaching students *how to learn*.
2. The emphasis that teachers place on the selection of instructional materials and on the development of classroom libraries.
3. The emphasis that teachers place on independent thinking and evaluation of information or knowledge acquired.
4. The involvement of students in the inquiry approach to learning.
5. The emphasis placed upon word-attack skills, vocabulary development, and reading and writing experiences for handicapped readers.

These changes in emphasis come about only through teachers' active involvement with reading as a learning process in workshop experiences and in classroom and workshop teaching demonstrations.

Teachers trained in the program are able to identify the instructional needs of all of their students and are able to meet their instructional needs so that children learn how to learn.

Appendix 3.2

ROLES, RESPONSIBILITIES, AND QUALIFICATIONS OF READING SPECIALISTS
by The Professional Standards and Ethics Committee of the IRA

Definition of Roles

Reading personnel can be divided into two categories: those who work directly with children either as reading teachers or reading clinicians; and those who work directly with teachers as consultants or supervisors with prime responsibility for staff and program.

    A. Special Teacher of Reading

       A Special Teacher of Reading has major responsibility for remedial and corrective and/or developmental reading instruction.

    B. Reading Clinician

       A Reading Clinician provides diagnosis, remediation, or the planning of remediation for the more complex and severe reading disability cases.

    C. Reading Consultant

       A Reading Consultant works directly with teachers, administrators, and other professionals within a school to develop and implement the reading program under the direction of a supervisor with special training in reading.

    D. Reading Supervisor (Coordinator or Director)

       A Reading Supervisor provides leadership in all phases of the reading program in a school system.

Responsibilities of Each Reading Specialist

    A. Special Teacher of Reading

       Should identify students needing diagnosis and/or remediation.

       Should plan a program of remediation from data gathered through diagnosis.

       Should implement such a program of remediation.

       Should evaluate student progress in remediation.

       Should interpret student needs and progress in remediation to the classroom teacher and the parents.

Should plan and implement a developmental or advanced program as necessary.

B. Reading Clinician

Should demonstrate all the skills expected of the Special Teacher of Reading and, by virtue of additional training and experience, diagnose and treat the more complex and severe reading disability cases.

Should demonstrate proficiency in providing internship training for prospective clinicians and/or Special Teachers of Reading.

C. Reading Consultant

Should survey and evaluate the ongoing program and make suggestions for needed changes.

Should translate the district philosophy of reading with the help of the principal of each school into a working program consistent with the needs of the students, the teachers, and the community.

Should work with classroom teachers and others in improving the developmental and corrective aspects of the reading program.

D. Reading Supervisor

Should develop a systemwide reading philosophy and curriculum, and interpret this to the school administration, staff, and public.

Should exercise leadership with all personnel in carrying out good reading practices.

Should evaluate reading personnel and personnel needs in all phases of a schoolwide reading program.

Should make recommendations to the administration regarding the reading budget.

Qualifications

A. General (Applicable to all Reading Specialists)

Demonstrate proficiency in evaluating and implementing research.

Demonstrate a willingness to make a meaningful contribution to professional organizations related to reading.

Demonstrate a willingness to assume leadership in improving the reading program.

B. Special Teacher of Reading

Complete a minimum of three years of successful classroom teaching in which the teaching of reading is an important responsibility of the position.

Complete a planned program for the Masters Degree from an accredited institution, to include

1. A minimum of twelve semester hours in graduate level reading courses with at least one course in each of the following:

   a. Foundations or survey of reading

   A basic course whose content is related exclusively to reading instruction or the psychology of reading. Such a course ordinarily would be first in a sequence of reading courses.

   b. Diagnosis and correction of reading disabilities

   The content of this course or courses includes the following: causes of reading disabilities; observation and interview procedures; diagnostic instruments; standard and informal tests; report writing; materials and methods of instruction.

   c. Clinical or laboratory practicum in reading

A clinical or laboratory experience which might be an integral part of a course or courses in the diagnosis and correction of reading disabilities. Students diagnose and treat reading disability cases under supervision.

2. Complete at undergraduate or graduate level, study in each of the following areas:
   a. Measurement and/or evaluation.
   b. Child and/or adolescent psychology.
   c. Psychology, including such aspects as personality cognition, and learning behaviors.
   d. Literature for children and/or adolescents.
3. Fulfill remaining portions of the program from related areas of study.

C. Reading Clinician

Meet the qualifications as stipulated for the Special Teacner ot Reading.

Complete, in addition to the above, a sixth year of graduate work, including

1. An advanced course or courses in the diagnosis and remediation of reading and learning problems.
2. A course or courses in individual testing.
3. An advanced clinical or laboratory practicum in the diagnosis and remediation of reading difficulties.
4. Field experiences under the direction of a qualified Reading Clinician.

D. Reading Consultant

Meet the qualifications as stipulated for the Special Teacher of Reading.

Complete, in addition to the above, a sixth year of graduate work including

1. An advanced course in the remediation and diagnosis of reading and learning problems.
2. An advanced course in the developmental aspects of a reading program.
3. A course or courses in curriculum development and supervision.
4. A course and/or experience in public relations.
5. Field experiences under a qualified Reading Consultant or Supervisor in a school setting.

E. Reading Supervisor

Meet the qualifications as stipulated for the Special Teacher of Reading.

Complete in addition to the above, a sixth year of graduate work including

1. Courses listed as 1, 2, 3, and 4 under Reading Consultant.
2. A course or courses in administrative procedures.
3. Field experiences under a qualified Reading Supervisor.

BIBLIOGRAPHY

Arnstein, Flora J., *Poetry in the Elementary Classroom* (New York: Appleton-Century-Crofts, 1962).

Botel, M., *The Botel Reading Inventory* (Chicago: Follett Educational Corporation, 1966).

Botel, M., *How to Teach Reading.* (Chicago: Follett Educational Corporation, 1969).

Dykstra, R., *Final Report: Continuation of the Coordinating Center for First-Grade Reading Instruction Programs* (Washington, D.C.: U.S. Department of Health, Education, and Welfare, 1967).

McCracken, R., *The Standard Reading Inventory* (Bellingham, Wash.: Pioneer Publishing Co., 1966).

Rosenthal, R., and Lenore F. Jacobson, *Pygmalion in the Classroom* (New York: Holt, Rinehart and Winston, Inc., 1968).

Snow, R., "Unfinished Pygmalion," *Contemporary Psychology* (1969), vol. 24, no. 4, pp. 197–99.

Thorndike, R.L., "A Critical Review of *Pygmalion in the Classroom* by Rosenthal and Jacobson," *American Educational Research Journal* (November, 1968), vol. 5, no. 4, pp. 708–11.

Rankin, Marie, *Children's Interests in Library Books of Fiction*, Teachers College Contributions to Education, No. 906 (New York: Bureau of Publications, Teachers College, Columbia University, 1944).

Kolson, C.J., R.E. Robinson, and W.C. Zimmerman, "Children's Preferences in Publishers," *Education* (November, 1962), vol. 83, pp. 155–57.

4

Organizational Relationships
with Outside Agencies

George Brain

Strong public interest in the reading process, especially on the part of many organizations and agencies, has significantly contributed to the development of resources for the teaching of reading. To distinguish them from in-school instructional programs and resources, they will be referred to as the nonschool resources for the teaching of reading. This identification does not in any way suggest that the schools do not have the central responsibility for reading instruction.

Types of Nonschool Resources in Reading

Nonschool resources for the teaching of reading may be identified in several areas: (1) the academic community—including research centers, training centers for reading specialists, and laboratory schools; (2) nonschool reading centers and clinics; (3) nonprofit groups and agencies, including foundations; (4) instructional technology research and development corporations; (5) product resources; (6) the Federal government; and (7) information services. Obviously there will be some overlapping from one category to another and, therefore, the classification scheme used merely aids in sifting out and organizing the information. Nor will any attempt be made to list all the possible entries in each category. Instead, examples will be selected in each area which are representative of the kind and extent of the resources available. A more complete listing of available nonschool resources for reading can be found in the appendix to this chapter

COLLEGE- AND UNIVERSITY-SPONSORED
READING PROGRAMS

There are many college- and university-sponsored centers with excellent programs in reading. Some of these are better known than others, but all make significant contributions, and many play major roles in publishing and distributing project reports, papers, conference proceedings, and other publications. Some have adjunct reading clinics, laboratory schools, and specialized reference collections. Knowledge of the activities of these institutions provides investigators, specialists, supervisors, teachers, and administrators direct access to first-hand information on current reading studies and reading programs. Among the universities currently engaged in noteworthy reading research and development activities are: Columbia, Cornell, Harvard, Hofstra, Lehigh, Rochester, Stanford, Syracuse, Chicago, Georgia, Minnesota, and Pittsburgh. This is only a partial listing of institutions where major efforts are taking place. A more complete listing appears in an *Inventory of Projects and Activities in Reading and English,*[1] compiled by the Center for Applied Linguistics in Washington, D.C.

Further reading research and development efforts in higher education grow out of programs of colleges and universities in a local region. For example, metropolitan Baltimore has three nearby schools offering graduate programs for reading specialists, two schools operating laboratory schools, several sponsored basic and applied research projects, and one institution using the Edison Responsive Environment to develop communication skills in autistic children.

In some cases, public school personnel are aware of and understand what goes on in college and university laboratories, training centers, and research centers. But often they are uninformed about the extramural activities which provide academic and clinical aid and conduct school-oriented research. To compensate for this lack, questions need to be raised which are of interest to school staffs and which are answerable by materials and services provided by the college or university across town, across the state, or even across the country.

Who are the researchers in the field who are available and capable of assisting schools in solving their reading problems? What problems are being investigated? What are they discovering? In other words, how is the ongoing study actually taking shape in the research setting? While there often is no immediate assistance in solving classroom problems, contact with the research centers does generate interest, increase mutual understanding and appreciation, and provide a basis for exchanging points of view.

To illustrate, school personnel should endeavor to learn what the new reading demonstration program being tested by a laboratory school or educational laboratory is all about. What is being discovered, as the program pro-

[1] Center for Applied Linguistics, *Inventory of Projects and Activities in Reading and English* (Washington, D.C.: The Center, 1968), 74 pp.

ceeds, that suggests the possibility of improved school practice? Could the school program's effectiveness in other areas be tested at the same time? The research center might help to answer questions such as these: What are the trends in the education and training of teachers and specialists? What courses are being recommended or required? What reading lists are recommended or required?

There is, of course, the question of how to organize and structure activities which would promote exchanges of this kind. In-service courses, workshops, institutes, and working conferences are possibilities. If these devices are used, it is suggested that those who participate should be rewarded by stipend, or by compensatory or released time.

NONSCHOOL READING RESOURCE CENTERS TO AID READING DISABILITIES

Nonschool reading centers constitute another large category of resources for reading. The very existence of such centers is an indication that the special problems of children who cannot learn to read in the usual classroom setting are not being met by the public schools. It should be pointed out, however, that children with reading disabilities come from private as well as public schools, and the clinics and centers are called on to provide services for children of all backgrounds.

A Directory of Reading Clinics,[2] published in 1964 and compiled with the help of the International Reading Association, is avaliable from Educational Developmental Laboratories, Inc. This directory lists, by state, the centers which meet the following criteria: (1) the organization must be concerned primarily with the diagnosis of reading problems and special instruction in reading; (2) the reading center must have a minimum staff of three professionally trained personnel; and (3) the center must grant admission to the general public. Thus remedial reading classes serving only a single school or institution are not included.

Another directory of agencies providing diagnostic and remedial services in reading is included in *The Shadow Children*[3] by Careth Ellingson. The information in this directory, gathered by the market research firm of Rome Arnold and Company in Chicago, is more up to date and more descriptive. Public and private school agencies are described on the basis of a questionnaire survey which elicited information about the sponsoring organization, diagnostic facilities, faculty, and special requirements or special information.

As in the case of the research centers and laboratories, school administrators would find it helpful to know what centers or clinics exist in the local area or region. A wide range of services could be available as is demonstrated by the

---

[2] Educational Developmental Laboratories, *Directory of Reading Clinics,* 1964 edition, EDL Research and Information Bulletin No. 4 (Huntington, N. Y.: EDL., 1964), 14 pp.
[3] Careth Ellingson, *The Shadow Children* (Chicago: Topaz Books, 1967), pp. 104 ff.

following instance. In one metropolitan community, there are six facilities offering diagnostic testing or instructional services or a combination of these. Sponsoring groups include a state college, the state university, two hospitals, and two private schools. The majority of centers listed have a waiting period of from two to three months, which indicates that such services are in high demand.

Hospital-sponsored facilities concentrate on providing diagnostic services in such areas as minimal brain damage syndromes, the aphasias, and hearing and speech disorders. Professional and consultative services are available in neurology, psychology, audiometry, pediatrics, ophthalmology, visual training, optometry, psychiatry, and endocrinology. Referral sources are physicians, parents, clinics, and public and private school systems. A comprehensive profile is developed for each case on the basis of observations of the referral sources, past medical history, and new data collected from a multidiscipline approach. However, far too few children with serious learning and reading disabilities receive such complete evaluation.

Although the chapter later treats the subject of Federal assistance for reading clinics and centers, it should be mentioned here that a substantial number of reading centers have been funded under Title III of the Elementary and Secondary Education Act. These centers provide comprehensive diagnostic, testing, and instructional services for public and private school children and in some cases for out-of-school youth. The centers, which serve urban neighborhoods or extra-urban school districts or regions, have potential for providing for children with serious reading disabilities.

ASSISTANCE FROM NONPROFIT GROUPS AND AGENCIES

Those Specializing in Reading. Among the nonprofit groups and agencies there are many interested exclusively in reading. The activities of the largest and most active of these is the International Reading Association. Working in conjunction with the IRA are local association councils and affiliates organized by educators who are directly interested in the teaching of reading. Such councils and affiliates are formed by ten or more active members in localities, states, regions, or nations. They are chartered by the Association and organized to further the general purposes of the Association. The *International Reading Association Directory*[4] for 1969–70 lists approximately 590 councils representing every state in the Union, several United States territories, Canadian provinces, and eleven other countries around the world.

Other organizations exclusively concerned with reading and reading instruction include the Committee on Diagnostic Reading Tests, Inc., the National Reading Foundation, and the Reading Reform Foundation. The

[4] International Reading Association, *1969–1970 Directory* (Newark, Del.: The Association, 1970).

Committee on Diagnostic Reading Tests was organized in 1945 to promote individualized reading instruction by developing and distributing diagnostic tests as well as exercises and practice materials. In addition, the Committee sponsors many other activities contributing to the improvement of reading instruction. These include seminars, work conferences, home study units for reading teachers, and study sessions at the Committee Headquarters in Hendersonville, North Carolina. Information on current and upcoming programs and services is provided in a newsletter published twice yearly.

Established in 1961, the Reading Reform Foundation has as its major aim the improvement of reading instruction through promoting the intensive teaching of phonics. Its declared bias favors "intensive phonics" as opposed to other methods such as "look-and-guess." Its activities include sponsoring an annual meeting; publishing and distributing conference proceedings, articles, and papers; and informing parents, teachers, and the public about the presumed value of intensive phonics in reading instruction.

Those Including Reading in a Diversified Program. In addition to the groups concentrating on reading and reading instruction, there are a number of other organizations with concerns only partially devoted to reading. Such organizations are the American Educational Research Association, American Montessori Society, Association for Supervision and Curriculum Development, Council for Basic Education, Phi Delta Kappa, National Council of Teachers of English, National Society for the Study of Education, and similar curriculum-oriented professional organizations. Just as with the reading-centered groups, they carry on their work by sponsoring research projects and conventions, by issuing publications, including books, journals, and newsletters, and by enlisting the active support of members.

A case in point is the American Montessori Society established in 1960 to foster interest in the educational principles of Maria Montessori as they apply to early childhood education. Growing interest and increasing membership are bringing much support. Thus the Society is enabled to disseminate pamphlets and publications on Montessori teaching strategies, to establish and supervise Montessori schools and classes, to establish teacher training programs, to prepare teaching materials, and to support research and the development of new approaches to early childhood education.

The Montessori system is founded on the idea that a child's early growth and development are advanced by "freedom within limits," and a carefully "prepared environment." This environment provides special materials and experiences which help to develop the child's fundamental intellectual and physical abilities. Although the system was introduced to this country in 1912, it did not begin to flourish until the founding in 1958 of the Whitby School in Greenwich, Connecticut. Since that time about 400 Montessori schools have been established and four Montessori Teacher Training Centers have been set up in various parts of the country. The resurgence of interest in the Montessori method parallels current thought in education and psychology in respect to (1) the considerable early childhood learning capabilities and (2) the now more widely recognized view of readiness for learning as a function both of maturation and environmental factors.

The professional organizations listed in Appendix 4.1, along with those described in the preceding paragraphs, have been identified as sponsoring significant activities or programs to improve reading and reading instruction. Undoubtedly this list is not complete. Other organizations may also be making contributions in this area and, when identified by the reader, should be added to the inventory of resources.

READING ASSISTANCE FROM PHILANTHROPIC FOUNDATIONS

Philanthropic foundations do not as a rule initiate, direct, or develop reading projects or programs. Instead they provide financial support and aid or contribute to the support structure of such programs. Foundations have been included because they play a vital role in helping professional groups, agencies, and schools carry on their work. Several foundations have contributed handsomely to education in general and to reading research and special programs in particular. A review of foundation grants listed in *Foundation News,* the bulletin of the Foundation Library Center, New York City, indicated that for the period 1965 to 1968 the Fund for the Advancement of Education, the Ford Foundation, and the Carnegie Corporation of New York together supported special projects in reading costing more than $3,000,000. Funds were used to sponsor interdisciplinary study committees, to test programmed learning materials, to encourage preschool reading programs, and to research reading habits of adults in the United States. In addition, funds were granted to develop techniques for teaching visual perception, to develop instructional materials using the augmented Roman alphabet, to support teacher training programs, and to purchase collections of paperback books for mobile libraries or for free distribution to children in disadvantaged areas.

A comparison of the funding practices of such foundations for the same three-year period reveals some interesting patterns. For example, a special interest of the Fund for the Advancement of Education appears to have been to provide books and library services for children in disadvantaged areas. Special concerns of the Ford Foundation have been the sponsorship of reading research as well as the introduction and testing of innovative learning materials. During the same three-year period, Carnegie Corporation, in addition to supporting research studies, made funds available to expand teacher training programs in reading at several educational institutions.

Not only do patterns of foundation support reveal particular concerns or interests in reading improvement, they may also suggest an interest in certain regions or locales. Thus the Fund for the Advancement of Education has shown an interest in urban and rural areas in the Southeast where there are disproportionate numbers of disadvantaged children. Similarly, the Old Dominion Foundation has supported several reading improvement programs in Washington, D.C.

Of particular interest to educators in local regions who may be seeking support for special, limited programs are those foundations which, by and large, restrict their grants to projects in their home areas. For example, the Rosenberg Foundation in California has granted funds to colleges, school systems, and community tutorial centers—all in areas of California. Accordingly, one approach to marshaling wider support for modest innovative programs in reading would be to engage the interest and backing of local foundations. *The Foundation Directory,*[5] a volume containing descriptive information on nearly 7000 foundations arranged by state, and *Foundation News,* a periodical, published bimonthly, which includes articles on philanthropy and reports on grants for various programs and projects, are very useful in identifying foundations, including their areas of interest and geographical locations.

The importance of the role of foundations in supporting basic research and other projects, as pointed out by Weaver in *Foundation News,*[6] is not in the amounts of money they make available (compared to government spending the amounts are relatively inconsequential) but in their ability to pursue excellence in ways that are more daring than those used by the government.

> Among sources of Government funds there is a certain inevitable tendency toward conformity. The moment you try to become venturesome in Government you're sticking your neck out in the direction of the other end of Pennsylvania Avenue and that's a very dangerous direction in which to stick your neck out if you're getting your money from the Government.

> Look at what is happening to the recently established National Foundation for the Support of Research in the Humanities. They made a grant to have somebody study comic books and somebody on the Hill in Washington learned about this and immediately sounds off and says, "Can you imagine using Federal funds to support research in comic books? How perfectly ridiculous!"

> But, you see, anybody who thinks that comic books are not a significant element in our culture just isn't in touch with things. If you don't know what Charlie Brown is doing you are just unaware of what a majority of the people in this country live and think and what they are interested in.[7]

[5] Marianna O. Lewis, ed., *The Foundation Directory,* Edition 3 (New York: The Foundation Library Center, 1967), 1198 pp.

[6] Warren Weaver, "Matter of Opinion," *Foundation News,* vol. 8 (November, 1967), pp. 111–13.

[7] Ibid., p. 111.

READING ASSISTANCE FROM CORPORATIONS

Instructional technology research and development corporations also provide important resources for improving reading instruction. Various factors and considerations will determine the immediate and long-term values of these resources for reading specialists and school systems. One of the most important of these involves the question of whether we should be more concerned with curriculum and content than innovations in hardware. Harmin and Simon in the *Harvard Educational Review*[8] illustrate our extraordinary concern with technology in a fiction entitled "The Year the Schools Began Teaching the Telephone Directory." They describe the strategies teachers used to motivate their students, the objectives, activities, and assignments that were developed, and the textbooks and teaching manuals that were supplied by publishers. In addition, someone applied to a

> . . . foundation for a general school-improvement grant, which was given after extended negotiations. The extra money was promptly used to establish team-teaching. . . . A teaching machine corporation constructed programmed materials to help the students learn names and addresses in small, carefully sequenced steps with immediate reinforcement. Educational television brought some of the most dynamic teachers into all of the classrooms.

> When the national government officially declared its war on poverty, disadvantaged pupils were discovered within the school system. While most children were able to get through the H's by fifth grade, the disadvantaged child was still on the C's and was about five letters behind in his directory work. The school began to focus on this problem. A variety of programs was instituted to compensate for deficiencies of experience in "deprived" children.[9]

In their recent book, *The Disadvantaged: Challenge to Education,*[10] Fantini and Weinstein, discussing the Harmin and Simon article, maintain that

> . . . this curriculum may not seem quite so absurd when we consider that much of what is taught in schools today has about as much rationale in the curriculum as the contents of the telephone directory. Most conversation in education today concerns innovations and hardware aimed at increasing the efficiency of "directory-type" teaching and curriculum. The majority of teaching energies are devoted to developing a technology to get pupils to learn things for which they have little use or concern.[11]

Fantini and Weinstein make a strong case for a more relevant curriculum for all children—those from deprived backgrounds as well as those from

---

[8] M. Harmin and S. Simon, "The Year the Schools Began Teaching the Telephone Directory," *Harvard Educational Review,* vol. 35 (Summer 1965), pp. 326–31.

[9] Ibid.

[10] Mario D. Fantini and Gerald Weinstein, *The Disadvantaged: Challenge to Education* (New York: Harper and Row, 1968). 455 pp.

[11] Ibid. p. 340.

middle and upper class backgrounds. What constitutes the relevant curriculum "is the correspondence of the curriculum to the 'condition and pattern of experience' of the learner. The closer they are, the more relevant the curriculum."[12]

Thus, in these terms, perhaps reform in reading should take place in the domain of curriculum and content rather than in the domain of technology. Moreover, the challenge in the substantive area of reading is to ensure that the material used as a vehicle for teaching corresponds more directly to the real conditions and experiences of life. As Fantini and Weinstein maintain, we must abolish "phony" content.

It can be argued that, while there is a need for relevant content in reading material, reading is a process requiring certain fundamental skills which are developed slowly through practice. For the teaching of these skills, software articles such as charts, cards, kits, workbooks, basal tests, programmed texts, and hardware articles such as overhead projectors, recorders, film loop projectors, and desk-top teaching machines, have become important aids.

What may eventually turn out to be a reasonable application of modern technology to the teaching of reading is demonstrated by two large-scale projects involving millions of dollars in corporation research and development funds, one on the West Coast and one on the East Coast. In a joint venture the School District of Philadelphia and Philco-Ford Corporation have developed a computer-assisted instructional system for teaching biology and remedial reading. Hardware includes on-line school computers, computer classrooms containing student consoles in several junior and senior high schools, and a central computer installation which collects and monitors student progress and sends out new lessons as required. Student consoles consist of a small electric typing unit and a television display unit. The lessons, including words and pictures, appear on a television screen. The student responds either by typing the answer or by using an electronic pen to point to the answer on the screen. The computer not only sends out the lessons but also provides real time evaluation of student progress so that special drill is available as required, or enrichment material is made available if appropriate. After the lesson, the master computer analyzes all responses, enters a score on the student's record, and arranges for the next day's lesson.

Observations on the teacher's role and the computer's role are provided in a brochure prepared by Philco-Ford and the Philadelphia School District.

> No computer will ever replace a teacher. Teachers with warmth, humor, compassion and understanding are as essential to a child's development as loving parents. Rather than deprive children of the personal relationship of a teacher, the computer can take over many of the routine tasks that sap the time and energies of our already over-burdened teachers, and permit them to give more of themselves to each student.
>
> The computer relieves the teachers of the chores which a machine can

[12] Ibid., p. 340.

handle better, such as counting heads, keeping records of progress, and filing reports. Having more time and more information about each student, the teachers can be free to observe the characteristics of each individual and take care of his needs. They'll spend their time doing things the computer can't do.

Freed by the computer, the teacher has more time to lead bright students toward full fulfillment of their potentials, and to help slow learners and difficult children over the hurdles.

Guided by the computer's detailed analysis of the individual student progress, the teacher may call into play all other teaching aids at his command in order to further enrich the learning process. The teacher thus becomes the manager of learning resources and counselor to the child in need—his most effective role.

In the computer-assisted system, the computer is a private tutor for each student. It has limitless patience, an elephant-like memory, and is totally free of prejudice or favoritism. It can teach a child to read, to count, to spell, to speak French, Spanish, or English—in an atmosphere of complete privacy. And it can build the encouragement and confidence that are essential to the learning process.[13]

There would appear to be no reason why programmed instruction could not reflect current developments in reading curriculum and content. Presumably, the reason the School District of Philadelphia joined with Philco-Ford was to help determine what the input to the system would be, that is, what content material and process material would be programmed and how.

A cooperative approach was also used to develop the RCA computer-assisted instructional systems. Early in 1964, Stanford University's Institute for Mathematical Studies in the Social Sciences, headed by Patrick Suppes, joined with RCA Instructional Systems, the schools of Palo Alto, California, and the Federal government in the establishment of the Stanford-Brentwood Computer-Aided Instruction Laboratory. The facilities include a conventional classroom and an adjacent computer classroom holding carrels and teaching terminals generally similar to those used by Philco-Ford (except that lessons may be presented on printout tear sheets which the student takes away with him). The system, which has become part of the instructional program of the Palo Alto, California, schools, uses curriculum materials developed by "leading educational authors and publishers," the traditional source of academic curriculum materials. An elementary arithmetic series is available from L. W. Singer Company, and Harcourt Brace Jovanovich has developed CAI Elementary English and CAI Remedial Reading Programs.

Modeled on the California system is a federally subsidized system in operation in New York City, also designed and installed by RCA. The system pro-

---

[13] Philco-Ford Corporation, Communications and Electronics Division, in Cooperation with the School District of Philadelphia, *A Private Tutor for Every Child* (Willow Grove, Pa.: Philco-Ford Corporation), 8 pp. (Leaflet).

vides daily drill and practice in arithmetic, spelling, and reading for about 6000 school children in 16 of the city's elementary schools. In most of these schools, twelve to fifteen stations are located in a central classroom where students go for daily drill sessions of about ten minutes duration. The computer is capable of servicing up to 192 stations at one time. When it is not being used for instructional purposes, the computer is used for administrative data processing, scheduling tasks, and various other housekeeping functions. The central computer installation is located in midtown Manhattan, 229 East 42 Street (the ground floor of the Charles Pfizer Building) and is open to the public. An information center, staffed by Board of Education personnel, provides the visitor the opportunity to see a film on innovations in educational technology and also to take lessons in arithmetic from the computer.

Commenting on the promise of computer-assisted instruction for education, L. M. Stolurow states that the computer provides "two significant capabilities: memory and logic."[14] No other aid provides the detailed collated memory of students' responses to individual displays of instructional materials in a form that is directly useful for automatic processing. Nor does any other aid provide its logical capability for making the organization of instructional information dependent upon the characteristics of the individual. Likewise, Patrick Suppes points out that the best single reason for using computers for instruction is that "computer technology provides the only serious hope for accommodation of individual differences in subject-matter learning."[15]

Dissenters are Anthony Oettinger and Sema Marks who question the claims of advocates of computer-assisted instruction, at least for the foreseeable future, on several grounds. These include cost, the currently limited programmable modes of computer-assisted instruction, and the limitations on the instructional sequences in various subjects that can be made available at any one time.[16]

TECHNOLOGICAL AIDS AND RESOURCES

The concept of educational technology as a "collection of 'know how' information" or a "set of systematic techniques" with or without the use of hardware is ably demonstrated by Vicore, Incorporated, an educational firm, which offers reading improvement courses. Vicore has contracted with numerous governmental and educational agencies to operate reading improvement courses and workshops. Contractors have been the Navy Department, the State Department, Agency for International Development, National Institutes of Health, Office of Education, World Bank, Cardozo Model School Program (Washington, D.C.), Howard Law School, Alexandria (Virginia) Public

[14] L. M. Stolurow, "What Is Computer Assisted Instruction?" *Educational Technology*, vol. 8 (August 15, 1968), pp. 10–11.

[15] Patrick Suppes, "Computer-Based Instruction," *Electronic Age* (Summer 1967), p. 4.

[16] Anthony Oettinger and Sema Marks, "Educational Technology: New Myths and Old Realities," *Harvard Educational Review*, vol. 38 (Fall 1968), pp. 714–15.

Schools Adult Education, MENSA, and Winchester (Virginia) Public Schools, to mention only a few.

Among the benefits claimed for the program are improved reading speed, greater comprehension, increased efficiency on technical and work-related material, improved study techniques and skills, increased vocabulary, and increased reading enjoyment. A refund of tuition, less $12.50 for materials, will be made for any student who has not tripled his reading efficiency (reading rate times percentage of comprehension) provided that the student attends all classes and completes the assigned homework. Statistics drawn from classes of students in industry, government, and education indicate remarkable gains in reading skills after completion of the Vicore course. The company, which is the largest reading improvement contractor to the Federal government, makes a point of the fact that these courses use no machines or "gimmicks."

Vicore is prepared to contract with the public schools to teach reading on a guaranteed improvement basis. A letter requesting information brought the following offer: "Upon request we will be pleased to submit a proposal for a pilot program in your schools." Whether the school should delegate such responsibility by contract is open to question. Yet, the possibilities as pointed out by James Coleman in an article on open schools in *The Public Interest*[17] are intriguing to consider.

> In an open school, the teaching of elementary-level reading and arithmetic would be opened up to entrepreneurs outside the school, under contract with the school system to teach only reading or only arithmetic, and paid on the basis of increased performance by the child on standardized tests. . . . The payment-by-results would quickly eliminate the unsuccessful contractors, and the contractors would provide testing grounds for innovations that could subsequently be used by the school. . . . Each parent would have the choice of sending his child to any of the reading or arithmetic programs outside the school, on released time, or leaving him wholly within the school to learn his reading and arithmetic there. The school would find it necessary to compete with the system's external contractors to provide better education, and the parent could, for the first time in education, have the full privileges of consumer's choice.[18]

In another category of resources, educational products, there are a number of new devices and instruments that could be used for the teaching of reading. They will be briefly listed, but no attempt to describe or evaluate them will be made. Instead, a list of manufacturers and a list of information resources helpful in identifying and evaluating products is provided on page 86 in Appendix 4.1. The following items of equipment have recently appeared on the market and are becoming popular: (1) light-weight 8 mm. cartridge-loading sound movie projector, also called film loop projector; (2) wireless classroom language laboratory suitable for easy installation in any classroom; (3)

[17] James S. Coleman, "Toward Open Schools," *The Public Interest,* vol. 9 (Fall 1967), p. 25.
[18] Ibid.

cassette recorder for individual listen-respond-compare instructional technique; (4) desk-top automatic reading training instrument; (5) cordless headset; (6) portable audiovisual programmed-instruction cartridge teaching machine; and (7) closed circuit television and video-tape recording hookups. Descriptive literature on these and other teaching devices may be obtained from the manufacturers.

For assistance in keeping up with these and other new products, the Educational Products Information Exchange in New York City publishes *Educational Product Report* which contains articles on product selection methods and practices and also provides descriptions of texts, kits, and other software in particular areas. In addition, mention should be made of two ERIC/CRIER information sources in reading which are available through the ERIC Document Reproduction Service, the National Cash Register Company. The first, *Guide to Materials for Reading Instruction,* includes basal reading materials, materials for teaching specific reading skills, workbooks, programmed texts for developmental or remedial reading, and high-interest, low-difficulty materials for poor readers. The forthcoming *Guide to Tests and Measuring Instruments* will classify tests and measuring instruments in reading. It will also identify tests used in reading research reported in the literature.

FEDERAL SUPPORT FOR READING PROGRAMS

Directly Sponsored Programs. The federal government has greatly increased support for basic and applied research and development programs in the field of education through the Research and Development Centers, established in 1963 under the Cooperative Research Act, and through the Regional Educational Laboratories, established in 1965 under the Elementary and Secondary Education Act. Both programs are designed to bring together academic talent and other resources for a coordinated program of research, development, and dissemination. They reflect three major concerns in educational research and development efforts: (1) previous efforts tended to be small and fragmentary and, consequently, the results were neither conclusive nor cumulative; (2) there was a wide gap between research and practice. Research results were not being used as a basis for developing new educational materials or practices. Few schools had put into practice the available research findings, and research communication between universities and teacher education institutions, state departments of education, and local school systems was poor; and (3) the field of education had not attracted the necessary research personnel from the behavioral sciences and other disciplines.

Although both the Research and Development Center program and the Regional Educational Laboratories have a similar rationale, they are somewhat different in organization, orientation, and emphasis. Each Research and Development Center is sponsored by a major university which focuses inquiry on a particular problem area. Generally the Research and Development Centers are more concerned with basic research studies than action programs;

however, pilot tests and field studies are often included in their activities. This is true of the Stanford Center for Research and Development in Teaching at Stanford University, which among other things is piloting a "Community-Centered Teaching Laboratory," located in the community it serves, which allows parents, community leaders, and students to join together to help improve teaching in economically-deprived schools.

The Regional Educational Laboratories, located throughout the United States, relate more closely to public schools. They concentrate on applied research and developmental activities which are aimed at introducing and testing innovative ideas in curriculum, instruction, teacher training, administration, and school-community relations. Their programs are more action oriented.

Both the Centers and the Laboratories are responsible for disseminating information in their problem areas and furnish publications on topics of particular interest. In some cases, information services in the form of replies to specific questions are provided on a limited basis.

Federally Assisted Programs. The final category of nonschool reading resources consists of contributions made by the federal government. Some of these contributions supplement existing programs and some make additional, discrete programs and projects possible. These projects often become an integral part of the school's instructional program and supplement by providing funds for established programs as well as for innovations.

Although Title I programs have been supplementary in design and in implementation, they reflect the governmental strategy for compensatory education in deprived areas. Improvement of reading is a special concern. In fact, improvement in reading scores is one of the easily identifiable effects of compensatory education. The future of federally augmented programs such as those administered under Title I is uncertain.

In making library resources, textbooks, and other instructional materials available to elementary and secondary students, Title II has also furnished increased reading resources for learning. The books and materials made available supplement existing library resources and other instructional materials. The value of good library resources in a modern reading program is no longer an issue for debate. Those who are informed about the purposes of education, the nature of learning processes, and the curriculum and instructional procedures employed in today's schools are agreed upon the important contribution which library service makes to the character and quality of the reading program.

Title III of ESEA has also had a tremendous impact on reading through matching grants to the states, loans to private schools for the strengthening of instruction in designated critical subject areas, and the PACE (Projects to Advance Creativity in Education) Program. The original purpose of the PACE Program was to provide grants for supplementary education centers and services in a variety of subject areas including reading. Under Title III guidelines, a wide variety of cultural and educational agencies—state education agencies, intermediate school districts, public schools, colleges and universities, nonprofit private schools, libraries, museums, artistic and musical organizations, educational television, and industry—were encouraged to work in close collaboration with local educational agencies to submit proposals for demonstration or for operational projects.

The Office of Education announced activities appropriate for PACE projects as including: learning centers for basic subjects, learning resource and materials centers, television course offerings, regional guidance centers, model demonstration schools, performing arts centers, career information centers, mobile planetariums and audiovisual centers, and educational parks.

In the main, projects have focused on establishing local or regional reading clinics or activities centers which provide for diagnosis and treatment of reading problems. Treatment is in the hands of professionally trained personnel who utilize special materials and resources. In some cases, effective use was made of existing nonschool resources for the consultation and planning required to implement programs. Many school systems combined these reading clinics with programs of in-service training for teachers by providing opportunities for observing clinical diagnosis and treatment. Other Title III programs concentrated on identification and screening procedures for students with reading disabilities or on surveying the disabilities and needs of the rural or urban culturally disadvantaged. A number of projects were funded to develop or demonstrate new instructional techniques such as the use of initial teaching alphabet, individualized instruction, ungraded reading groups, color reading, and tachist-o-reading. Other programs established educational media centers through which instructional materials were made more readily available by the use of local service centers, mobile units, and dial-access audiovisual information systems. Also included in ESEA, Title III projects were efforts to improve opportunities for superior readers, which resulted in centers providing or coordinating cultural enrichment activities such as Great Books discussion groups.

As reported in the *First Annual Report of the National Advisory Committee on Adult Basic Education,* there are at least ten federal agencies supporting programs in adult education, many of which have language arts and reading components.[19] Of particular interest are the educational components of the Community Action Programs (CAP) of the Office of Economic Opportunity. OEO has sponsored reading improvement programs, remedial reading programs, and tutoring programs, which have been operated by various community and neighborhood agencies, including public and private schools, interdenominational religious groups, settlement houses, and CAP-created community schools. Although CAP programs are thought to have a significant effect on strategies of education for the poor through the recognition of specific neighborhood and community needs, the future organization, implementation, and, indeed, existence of these and similar programs are in doubt. This uncertainty is caused by budgetary exigencies and a reconsideration, on the

[19] National Advisory Council on Adult Basic Education, *First Annual Report,* pp. 37–40.

national level, of which agency is properly responsible in the areas of education and poverty.

A special program of the Office of Economic Opportunity with great potential for mobilizing human resources for improving basic learning skills, is the support of countrywide tutorial projects and the funding of the Tutorial Assistance Center in Washington, D.C., operated by the United States National Student Association. The Center attempts to join the federal government's efforts to compensate for the effects of poverty on educational achievement with the growing interest of college students in community problems. To this end, the Center provides a number of information and education services including a *Directory of Tutorial Projects,* a newsletter, publications, and articles on establishing and funding tutorial projects, teacher manuals, and materials. In addition, the Center sponsors regional conferences and workshops and maintains a staff of field coordinators who are available for consultation and for training institutes. The Center estimated that there are over 1200 tutorial projects in the United States today and from 200,000 to 250,000 volunteers, primarily college students, working with 350,000 or more children. One of the current projects of the Tutorial Assistance Center involves joining with interested individuals, local groups, and educators in a dialogue on the possibility of establishing neighborhood learning centers. The idea is to use existing tutorial programs as a springboard for developing such centers.

One of the more significant developments on the national level in the area of reading was the formation of the National Advisory Committee on Dyslexia and Related Reading Disorders. The Committee is charged with studying the problem of reading disability with the aim of providing guidance for the teachers of the millions of children with reading problems. The Committee members represent such fields as the medical sciences and the behavioral sciences including psychology, and education. Reporting to the Secretary of HEW, the Committee, headed by Arleigh B. Templeton, President of Sam Houston State College, will:

Examine in detail the areas of research, diagnosis and evaluation, teacher preparation, and corrective education in dyslexia and related reading disorders.

Make recommendations concerning the need for a continuing national program to deal with this problem.

Note gaps to which attention should be directed, recommend priorities for a program to meet the needs of children or adults with these problems, and suggest ways to develop national concern and support for further work.[20]

---

[20] U.S. Department of Health, Education, and Welfare, Office of the Secretary, "Press Release. August 24, 1968. National Advisory Committee on Dyslexia and Related Reading Disorders" (Washington, D.C.: U.S. Department of Health, Education, and Welfare, August, 1968), 3 pp. (Xerox).

The task with which the Committee is faced would seem to be monumental, particularly in the area of gathering the background information and data required for an evaluation of present practices and programs. It appears that much of the information gathering and documentation of practices would best be contracted to a firm with professional expertise in this area—as was done in the case of the National Advisory Committee on Adult Basic Education. The primary role of the Committee would then be to examine and sift the huge collection of data, to evaluate present efforts, and to formulate recommendations. Not the least in importance of these would be recommendations for coordinating the existing programs administered by myriad federal agencies. Many agencies are now involved in programs to improve basic learning skills and in allied programs to guarantee that *equal and effective* educational opportunity is a right for all.

INFORMATION SERVICES

An innovative information handling system has been developed in the area of the behavioral sciences, which has successfully placed specialized information in the hands of users, and which has proved at the same time to be a profit-making venture. This system has great potential for information dissemination in the field of education, especially with the development of computerized storage and retrieval techniques.

The system functions as a kind of current awareness service whereby a user of information, in this case a scientist or clinician in the behavioral sciences, receives on a regular basis an annotated bibliography of recently published articles in his area of interest. The system allows the scientist to scan the annotated bibliography under his subspecialty or topic of interest and to request just those articles he wants. In other words, instead of reading a dozen or so journals, he relies on the information specialists on the journal staff to review the journals that yield articles in his field of specialization. The user can subscribe to an indexing journal from which he chooses only the articles he actually wants to read or wants to own.

The journal which offers this service is *Communications in Behavioral Biology* published by Academic Press. Each issue consists of two parts: Part *A* contains full-length reprint articles and original articles; Part *B* contains abstracts of recent articles covering all the substantive areas in behavioral biology. Many of the abstracts have been culled from journals with a high relevant yield. Users may subscribe to either or both parts. *Communications in Behavioral Biology* has done for the journal literature in behavioral biology what *Research in Education* has done for government research and demonstration project reports in the field of education, with some differences. Reprints are easily ordered with prepaid article request cards; the reprints are of good reproduction quality; and they may be stored in standard loose leaf binders.

If such a service were available to reading specialists, it would allow them to receive only the articles they really want to use. The task of staying abreast of the literature would be much easier if one could zero in on particular areas of interest in this fashion.

Making Use of Nonschool Agencies

This chapter sought answers to the following questions:

1. What are the nonschool resources available for the teaching of reading?
2. What are the information sources for a continuing effort to identify such resources?
3. How may teachers, specialists, supervisors, and school systems, public or private, capitalize on these resources?

Some possibilities for using the resources identified in this chapter and their implications for public school use are surveyed here. A matter of prime importance is the question of how to organize for maximum effective use the existing reading practices, programs, and efforts. Four alternatives for structuring broad-based support for reading are discussed.

At the very least, there should be a campaign aimed at informing all those interested in reading—educators, parents, and interested citizens—about the wide range of programs and resources available. The purpose of such a campaign would be mainly informational; there would be no attempt to structure or organize such resources. An education and information center could be established and maintained by the state educational agency, or there might be close cooperation with intermediate school districts, in which case the intermediate districts would constitute an informational network. This network would help to identify resources throughout the state as well as to disseminate information about these resources. As a result, school personnel in local school districts would be more cognizant of additional resources on which they might draw.

Beyond this, state and local school systems, professional groups and agencies, and organizations of interested citzens might well be encouraged to pool resources in order to avoid unnecessary duplication or overlapping among programs and to make more effective use of talent and material support. Such a concerted effort would no doubt entail adjustments and compromises among the agencies, groups, and programs involved. However, the organizational structure of the schools on the state or intermediate level at once provides a mechanism for consolidating such resources. Educational planners must be willing to take the bold steps required to decentralize organization, responsibility, and planning through broader and freer association with other official public agencies, unofficial groups, and participating citizens.

A second option involves a loose association of public school systems and nonschool organizations with an identifiable coordinating center or unit, which would either offer diagnostic and remedial services, or make referrals for such services. In addition, the center would catalog resources and disseminate the information.

Option three entails a more formal structure. In this case, a consortium of public school and nonschool agencies is suggested as a possibility. Such a consortium would provide diagnostic and instructional services in schools and community learning centers, and would also provide backup support in the form of consultation, in-service training, program evaluation, and informational services.

The fourth and final option could be an extension and refinement of the preceding arrangement which would involve a nonprofit corporation of public school systems and nonschool agencies and groups, perhaps including educational entrepreneurs who contract to provide specific instructional services. Such a nonprofit organization would, as before, provide diagnostic and instructional services in school and community learning centers and would provide for backup support in the form of consultation, in-service training, program planning and evaluation, and informational services. The main additives here would be the provisions for external contractors and the well-defined commitments and responsibilities as well as the flexibility that a corporate structure would allow.

There should be few objections to the first option, but there are significant issues and problems involved in the other alternatives. The schools will have problems of support structure, of control, and of management. There is the danger of irresponsible domination by one organization—whether by the public schools or any other organization. In a more highly structured approach there would also be the danger, inherent in most ambitious programs for the public good, of high expectations and mixed results. These problems, however, are not insuperable.

There is little doubt that the schools must bear ultimate responsibility for the planning and implementation of educational programs, including the reading program. On the face of it, few would disagree with the statement of Carl J. Dolce.

> The responsibility and resources for all formal education—and for "schooling"—should be centered in the school system. Given such specialization of public functions, resources can be clearly earmarked, duplication reduced, and accountability more clearly held.[21]

That school districts and systems across the country are the foci of responsibility and resources in education is a historical and present fact. And schools must continue to be the foci of responsibility.

Boards of education have traditionally served as advocates for allied agencies, interested groups, and laymen. Other approaches to educational

---

[21] Wilson C. Riles, Carl J. Dolce, and Martin Mayer, *What Are the Priorities for City Schools?* Occasional Papers No. 15 (Washington, D.C.: Council for Basic Education, March, 1969), pp. 9–10.

planning can be used in conjunction with the traditional ones. Strategies such as those which have been used on a limited basis for the cooperative planning of a new high school complex and more notably those which have been developed in the Saint Paul Public Schools for the projection of an entire educational system comprising a City Center for Learning as well as Consolidated Community Schools are but two examples of responsible and responsive approaches to educational planning. These ventures and others, including many of the ESEA Title III PACE Reading Projects, have demonstrated the value of combining the resources and talents of interested and knowledgeable laymen, allied agencies, and concerned groups with those of educators through dialogue and through direct participation in planning and activities. What is needed is not "specialization of institutional function," but an opening up of the schools to freer discussion of problems and priorities, to cooperative enterprises involving other agencies whenever there exist shared interests and concerns or overlapping programs. This is precisely what a discussion of cooperative or advisory planning in education has to do with reading instruction. Shared interests and concerns and overlapping programs do exist in the area of reading.

Appendix 4.1

NON-PUBLIC SCHOOL RESOURCES

   I. Academic Community
  II. Nonpublic School Reading Centers and Clinics
 III. Nonprofit Groups and Agencies, Including Foundations
 IV. Instructional Technology Research and Development Corporations
  V. Product Resources
 VI. The Federal Government
VII. Information Services and Sources

   I. *Academic Community*
     A. *Directories:* The following directory is helpful in identifying and describing research centers and programs in reading.
       Hayes, Alfred S. and Hugh W. Buckingham, Jr., comps. *Inventory of Projects and Activities in Reading and English* (Washington, D.C.: Center for Applied Linguistics, 1968). Available from Center for Applied Linguistics, 1717 Massachusetts Avenue, N.W., Washington, D.C. 20036.
     B. *University-Sponsored Research Centers:* The following is a partial list of university-sponsored reading research and development centers intended to give an overview of the kinds of activities presently being conducted. Other university centers, many of which are identified and described in the directories, are also making substantial contributions.

1. Columbia University
   New York, New York 10027
   Studies on the language development of Negro and Puerto Rican speakers and implications for teaching of reading. Comparative study of approaches to teaching reading to disadvantaged children.

2. Cornell University
   Project Literacy
   Ithaca, New York 14850
   Planning conferences to identify problems in the area of reading, establish priorities, design strategies of research, and plan for dissemination of results. Studies on the psychological processes underlying the acquisition and development of reading skills.

3. Harvard University
   Cambridge, Massachusetts 02138
   Development of self-instructional reading programs for use in teaching of beginning reading. Analysis of children's literature in order to establish an appropriate measure of readability.

4. Hofstra University
   Hempstead, New York 11550
   Conferences and symposia on the teaching of reading. Publication of conference proceedings, papers, reports.

5. Illinois Institute of Technology
   Chicago, Illinois 60616
   Prepared jointly with the University of Chicago, a study of the effects of the substandard dialects of American English on the development of reading skills and the preparation of resource materials on this subject for teachers of the culturally disadvantaged.

6. Lehigh University
   Bethlehem, Pennsylvania 18015
   Studies on the relative effectiveness of the initial teaching alphabet for teaching reading. Development of i.t.a. materials for instruction.

7. Stanford University
   Palo Alto, California 94304
   Development of computer-assisted instruction for use in beginning reading in cooperation with the U. S. Office of Education and RCA Instructional Systems.

8. Syracuse University
   Syracuse, New York 13210
   Study on relative effectiveness of three approaches to teaching reading. Study on the early identification of reading disability. Literacy programs, publications, and newspapers for use with older, beginning reader.

9. University of Chicago
   Chicago, Illinois 60637
   Study on the effectiveness of the initial teaching alphabet. Study on the level or range of difficulty which generates maximum interest and provides for maximum information gain. William S. Gray Collection, annual summaries of reading research.

10. University of Georgia
    College of Education
    Athens, Georgia 30601
      Study on the development of basal reading skills (phonetic analysis, structural analysis, dictionary skills, word functions, and comprehension) among intellectually retarded, normal, and superior pupils. Study on the role of certain visual and auditory skills and characteristics in first-grade reading readiness.
11. University of Minnesota
    Minneapolis, Minnesota 55455
      Study on the effectiveness of a combined visual-linguistic approach to teaching first-grade reading. Coordinating Center for Cooperative Reading Research Program involving 27 separate projects comparing effectiveness of instructional methods. Study to determine the effect of associative strength between words on learning to read. Study to develop a measure of reading difficulty. Interdisciplinary curriculum center for English and language arts.
12. University of Pittsburgh
    Pittsburgh, Pennsylvania 15213
      Development of a new beginning reading program based on the regularity of sound-symbol relationships and controlled introduction of elements. Study comparing effectiveness of language experience approach and the basal language arts approach in second and third grade.
C. *Regional Educational Laboratories:* A description of all the Regional Educational Laboratories supported by the U. S. Office of Education is found in the *CEMREL Newsletter* (Summer 1968), pp. 7–8. Available from Central Midwestern Regional Educational Laboratory (CEMREL), 10646 St. Charles Rock Road, St. Ann, Missouri 63074.
   1. Center for Urban Education
      105 Madison Avenue
      New York, New York 10036
        Objective is "to improve educational practice in northern metropolitan school systems through programs that ensure literacy in the early grades, promote teacher competence and morale, and assist schools to integrate their facilities and use mass media more effectively." Provides publications and information services on a limited basis.
   2. Southwestern Cooperative Educational Laboratory
      117 Richmond N. E.
      Albuquerque, New Mexico 87106
        Main purpose is to develop new materials and techniques to improve learning in primary level language arts. In addition to special projects (such as improving the early use of oral language in Mexican American and Indian children), the Laboratory issues a newsletter, publishes papers and reports, and provides consulting services in the Oklahoma, Arizona, west Texas, and New Mexico area.
D. *Research and Development Centers:* A description of all the Research and

Development Centers supported by the U. S. Office of Education is contained in *Southern Education Report* (January–February, 1969), p. 15.

1. Learning Research and Development Center
   University of Pittsburgh
   Pittsburgh, Pennsylvania 15213
      Special projects include development of individually prescribed instruction which is currently being used in elementary mathematics and reading. Disseminates publications, reports, papers.

2. Stanford Center for Research and Development
   770 Welch Road
   Palo Alto, California 94305
      Basic aim is "to improve teaching in American Schools." In addition to special projects, such as a "Community-Centered Teaching Laboratory," the Center publishes and disseminates reports and articles on the variables that influence the "impact of the teacher on his students in the classroom."

3. Wisconsin Research and Development Center for Cognitive Learning
   University of Wisconsin
   Madison, Wisconsin 53706
      Long-range effort to identify and describe the specific language skills required in the reading process and to gain an understanding of the kinds of skills children bring to the reading situation. Disseminates publications, papers, reports.

E. *Other Research or Research Dissemination Centers*
   1. ERIC Clearinghouse on Reading
      Indiana University
      204 Pine Hall
      Bloomington, Indiana 47401
         The ERIC Clearinghouse on Retrieval of Information and Evaluation of Reading (ERIC/CRIER) is one of the 19 clearinghouses in the ERIC system. ERIC/CRIER acquires, analyzes, and disseminates "research reports, materials and information related to all aspects of reading behavior with emphasis on the physiology, psychology, sociology, and teaching of reading." A description of products and services is available on request.

   2. Institutes for the Achievement of Human Potential
      8801 Stenton Avenue
      Chestnut Hill
      Philadelphia, Pennsylvania 19118
         Research and teaching programs in the area of neurological organization. Promote an approach to reading and language problems based on the Doman-Delacato theory of neurological development.

F. *Schools for Reading Specialists*
   1. "Directory of Colleges and Universities Offering Graduate Programs for the Preparation of Reading Specialists." Available from International Reading Association, Professional Standards Committee, Six Tyre Avenue, Newark. Delaware 19711

2. The best sources of up to date information on specific programs and courses are yearly catalogs and direct inquiries to the schools themselves.

II. *Nonpublic School Reading Centers and Clinics*

    A. Directories: The following publications list, by state, centers which meet specified criteria.

    Educational Developmental Laboratories, *Directory of Reading Clinics,* 1964 Edition, EDL Research and Information Bulletin No. 4 (Huntington, N.Y.: E. D. L., 1964).

    Ellingson, Careth, *The Shadow Children* (Chicago: Topaz Books, 1967).

    B. The most up to date information on services provided by local centers and clinics is available from the agencies themselves.

    C. Information on reading centers funded under ESEA, Title III, is available from the U.S. Office of Education, Division of Plans and Supplementary Centers.

III. *Nonprofit Groups and Agencies, Including Foundations*

    A. *Groups Interested Exclusively in Reading*

        1. Committee on Diagnostic Reading Tests, Inc.
        Mountain Home
        North Carolina 28758

        The primary objective of the Committee, organized in 1945, is to promote individualized reading instruction by developing and distributing diagnostic tests. Also sponsors other activities including workshops, seminars, working conferences, and study sessions.

        2. International Reading Association
        Six Tyre Avenue
        Newark, Delaware 19711

        Founded in 1955 through the merger of the International Council for the Improvement of Reading Instruction and the National Association for Remedial Teaching. Main purposes are:

        a. "To improve the quality of reading instruction at all levels.

        b. "To develop an awareness in our citizenry of the impact of reading.

        c. "To sponsor conferences and meetings planned to implement the purposes of the Association.

        d. "To promote the development among all peoples of a level of reading proficiency that is commensurate with each individual's unique capacity."

        The International Reading Association Directory for 1968–69 lists approximately 590 councils representing every state in the union, several United States possessions, and eleven countries around the world.

        3. Reading Reform Foundation
        36 West 44 Street
        New York, New York 10036

        "The Reading Reform Foundation was established in October, 1961, to restore the alphabet (phonetics) to its proper place as the basis of elementary reading instruction in English." Primary objectives are "to enlighten teachers, parents, public authorities, and the nation generally on the nature and extent of the reading crisis, its cause and cure; to coordinate and encourage the numerous local reform movements already active; and to create an informed national public opinion in favor of quickly eradicating from all our schools, the cancer of configurationism . . ."

The Reading Reform Foundation has organized a 250-member National Advisory Committee of authorities on phonics and education and has established Committees of the Foundation in 38 states.

B. *Groups Which Include Reading As One of a Number of Interests*

    1. American Educational Research Association
       1126 Sixteenth Street, N.W.
       Washington, D.C. 20036

       Support for the dissemination of research literature in reading through publications and special interest sessions held at AERA Annual Meeting.

    2. American Montessori Society
       175 Fifth Avenue
       New York, New York 10010

       Primary purpose is to foster interest in the educational principles of Maria Montessori as they apply to early childhood education by providing pamphlets and publications, establishing and supervising Montessori schools and classes, establishing teacher training programs, preparing and distributing teaching materials.

    3. Association for Supervision and Curriculum Development
       1201 Sixteenth Street, N.W.
       Washington, D.C. 20036

       ASCD commissions and councils are primarily concerned with current problems of curriculum workers. These groups attempt to keep educators informed of current developments and seek to predict future trends in curriculum and instruction. More generally the organization, through research on the broad problems of elementary and secondary education, publishes specific material helpful to improvement of reading instruction.

    4. Council for Basic Education
       725 Fifteenth Street, N.W.
       Washington, D.C. 20003

       Primary objective is to strengthen the teaching of basic subjects in public schools through supporting and publishing studies in basic education, through public discussion and dialogue, and through an information and education service.

    5. Educational Developmental Laboratories, Inc.
       Huntington, New York 11743

       A division of McGraw-Hill devoted to developing "reading improvement techniques and instructional approaches." Maintains an education and information service.

    6. National Council of Teachers of English
       508 South 6 Street
       Champaign, Illinois 61820

Primary purpose is to strengthen the teaching of English, but special attention is directed through some published materials to development of reading techniques and abilities. Offers recommendations based on investigation for developing such abilities.

7. Phi Delta Kappa, Inc.
Bloomington, Indiana
Sponsors special projects in reading such as the ESEA Title IV project: "Application of the Convergence Technique to Basic Studies of the Reading Process."

C. *Foundation Support for Reading*
The following information services of the Foundation Library Center are useful for investigating foundation support for special projects in reading.

1. Libraries of reports, books, pamphlets, and file materials on foundation grants and activities.
The Foundation Library Center
444 Madison Avenue
New York, New York 10022
Branch Office
1001 Connecticut Avenue, N.W.
Washington, D.C. 20036

2. Lewis, Marianna O., ed., *The Foundation Directory*, Edition 3 (New York: Russell Sage Foundation, 1967), 1198 pp.
Directory of foundations arranged by state which "possess assets of at least $200,000 or distribute annually $10,000 or more in grants or for programs." Information includes name, address, data on establishment, donor, purpose, activities, financial information, officers. and trustees.

3. Foundation Library Center, *Foundation News,* Bulletin of the Foundation Library Center (Baltimore, Md.: The Foundation Library Center).
Bimonthly periodical which includes articles on philanthropy and reports on grants for various programs and projects.

IV. *Instructional Technology Research and Development in Computer-Assisted Instruction*

A. Philco-Ford Corporation
Communications and Electronics Division
Willow Grove, Pennsylvania 19090
In cooperation with the School District of Philadelphia, Philco-Ford has developed computer-assisted instruction for teaching remedial reading and biology.

B. RCA Instructional Systems
530 University Avenue, Dept. QA
Palo Alto, California 94301
In cooperation with Stanford University and the Palo Alto schools, RCA has developed computer-assisted instruction for teaching elementary arithmetic, elementary English, and remedial reading. Curriculum materials in arithmetic developed by L. W. Singer Company; curriculum materials in reading and English developed by Harcourt Brace Jovanovich, Inc.

C. New York City Board of Education
Computer Center
229 East 42 Street
New York, New York 10001

Modeled on the RCA system in use in Palo Alto, California, New York's system provides drill and practice in arithmetic, spelling, and reading for about 6000 school children. The Computer Center houses the central computer hardware and an information and display center manned by Board of Education personnel. Open to the public.

V. *Product Resources*

A. *Items of Equipment*

The following is a partial list of devices and instruments of potential use for the teaching of reading intended to give an overview of the kinds of products available. No evaluation or endorsement is given or intended. For help in product selection see Section "C" following: *Educational Media and Products Information Sources.*

1. CBS Laboratories/Viewex Inc.
Holbrook, New York 11741
Portable audiovisual program cartridge teaching machine.

2. Concord Electronics Corporation
1935 Armacost Avenue
Los Angeles, California 90025
Closed circuit television and video-tape recording systems.

3. Craig Corporation
Education Division
3410 S. LaCienega Blvd.
Los Angeles, California 90016
Craig reading training instrument and reader programs.

4. Dictaphone Business Machines Division
International Headquarters
120 Old Post Road
Rye, New York 10580
Wireless classroom learning laboratory including central tape recorder, small transmitter, wireless headset receiver for each student and instructor, and a simple induction loop. Listen-respond cassette recorder.

5. Dukane Corporation
Communications Systems Division
St. Charles, Illinois 60174
Mobile and permanent installation language and learning laboratories.

6. Electronic Futures, Inc.
57 Dodge Avenue
North Haven, Connecticut
Instructional program in phonics using EFI Audio Flashcard Reader.

7. Graflex, Inc.
3750 Monroe Avenue
Rochester, New York 14603
Low-cost cordless headsets.

8. The Kalart Company, Inc.

   Plainville, Connecticut 06062

   System which shows 16 mm. films at remote locations by closed circuit TV. Also uses video tape.

9. MAST Development Co.

   2212 E. 12 Street

   Davenport, Iowa 52803

   Desk-top programmed instruction cartridge teaching machine.

10. Science Research Associates

    259 E. Erie Street

    Chicago, Illinois 60611

    "Detect"—visual discrimination program. SRA Reading Laboratories.

11. Technicolor

    Commercial and Educational Division

    1300 Frawley Drive

    Costa Mesa, California 92627

    Lightweight 8 mm. cartridge-loading sound movie projector. Publishes Sound Film Loop Source Directory listing films that are cartridged for 8 mm. sound movie projector.

B. *Entrepreneurial Reading Instruction*

   Vicore, Inc.

   1611 E. Kent Street

   Arlington, Virginia 22209

   Contracts with governmental and educational agencies to operate reading improvement courses and workshops on guaranteed progress basis.

C. *Educational Media and Products Information Sources*

1. Educational Products Information Exchange Institute (EPIE)

   386 Park Avenue South

   New York, New York 10016

   Nonprofit information service for educators. Publishes Educational Product Report containing articles on product selection methods and practices and also provides descriptions of texts, kits, other software in particular areas.

2. ERIC at Stanford

   Institute for Communication Research

   Stanford, California 94305

   "Concentrates on research which evaluates the effects of using different modern educational media in different ways." Processes documents for input to the central ERIC system which are listed in *Research in Education* and generally available from the ERIC Document Reproduction Service, The National Cash Register Company, 4936 Fairmont Avenue, Bethesda, Maryland 20014.

3. ERIC Clearinghouse on Reading

   Indiana University

   School of Education

   Bloomington, Indiana 47401

   Available from ERIC Document Reproduction Service: *Guide to Materials for Reading Instruction*, No. 019 528 Microfilm, $1.25; hard copy, $11.16. Includes basal reading materials, materials for teaching specific reading skills, workbooks, programmed texts for developmental or remedial reading, and high-interest low-difficulty materials for poor readers.

1911 Trent Street

Costa Mesa, California 92626

Guide to Tests and Measuring Instruments (forthcoming) will classify tests and measuring instruments in reading and will identify tests used in reading research reported in the literature.

4. International Reading Association

Six Tyre Avenue

Newark, Delaware 19711

Publishes and disseminates literature on reading research and reading instruction in areas of particular interest to teachers. In addition to the Association journals, a number of bibliographies, summaries, articles, proceedings, and monographs are available. Sample titles:

Individualized Reading, Henry Sartain

Sources of Good Books for Poor Readers, George Spache

Corrective Reading in the Elementary Classroom, Roy Kress and Marjorie Johnson

Bold Action Programs for the Disadvantaged: Elementary Reading (1967 Reading Institutes)

Teaching Critical Reading at the Primary Level, Russell Stauffer and Miles R. Cramer

A complete listing of publications is available in "IRA Publications/Membership Information, Winter 1968–69."

5. *The National Information Center for Educational Media* (NICEM)

University of Southern California

University Park

Los Angeles, California 90007

Collecting information on what specific materials are available in nontext media: films, film strips, video tapes, audio tapes, overhead transparencies, slide sets.

6. Reading Reform Foundation

36 West 44 Street

New York, New York 10036

Identifies and provides information on available instructional systems and materials with strong phonics emphasis.

VI. *The Federal Government*

A. *Educational Programs of the Office of Education: Information Sources*

1. Office:

Publications and Information Center

Office of Education

Washington, D.C. 20202

(202) 963-5178

2. Publications:

U.S. Office of Education, *American Education* (Washington, D.C.: Office of Education).

"Official journal of the U.S. Office of Education, published ten times a year. Reports on Office planning and action, legislation and Federal activities, and programs affecting education; includes statistical information of national interest." $3.75 a year.

U.S. Office of Education, *Publications of the Office of Education, 1968,* revised by Bobbie Doud (Washington, D.C.: Office of Education, 1968), (OE-11000F).

Elementary and Secondary Education Act, Title I:

U.S. Office of Education, Division of Compensatory Education, *Profiles in Quality Education,* 150 Outstanding Title I, ESEA Projects (Washington, D.C.: U.S. Office of Education, 1968), 123 pp.

Elementary and Secondary Education Act, Title III:

U.S. Office of Education, Division of Plans and Supplementary Centers, *PACE Reading Projects* (Washington, D.C.: U.S. Office of Education, November, 1967), 38 pp., (Mimeo).

B. *Research Programs of the Office of Education: Information Sources*

   1. Office:

Publications and Information Center
Office of Education
Washington, D.C. 20202
(202) 963-5178

   2. Publications:

U.S. Office of Education, Bureau of Research, *Research and Development: Advances in Education* (Washington, D.C.: U.S. Office of Education, November, 1968), 109 pp., (OE 12034). Available from Superintendent of Documents, U.S. Government Printing Office, Washington, D.C. 20402. $1.50.

U.S. Office of Education, Bureau of Research, Division of Educational Laboratories, *Regional Educational Laboratories* (Washington, D.C.: U.S. Office of Education, November, 1968), 20 pp., (OE-12030). Available from U.S. Government Printing Office. $.35.

Center for Applied Linguistics, *Inventory of Projects and Activities in Reading and English* (Washington, D.C.: Center for Applied Linguistics, 1968). Available from Center for Applied Linguistics, 1717 Massachusetts Avenue, N.W., Washington, D.C. 20036.

C. *Programs of the Office of Economic Opportunity*

For information on the Tutorial Assistance Center, Tutorial Programs, and educational components of the Community Action Programs contact:
Public Relations Department
Office of Economic Opportunity
1200 Nineteenth Street, N.W.
Washington, D.C. 20506

D. Information on adult basic education programs with reading components may be obtained from:

National Advisory Committee on Adult Basic Education, *First Annual Report of the National Advisory Committee on Adult Basic Education,* 90th Congress, 2nd Session, House Document No. 384 (Washington, D.C.: U.S. Government Printing Office, 1968).

E. The newly formed National Advisory Committee on Dyslexia and Related Reading Disorders will be issuing information items and reports.
Office of the Secretary
Department of Health, Education, and Welfare
Bethesda, Maryland 20014

F. The National Advisory Committee on the Education of Disadvantaged Children, 1900 E Street, N.W., Washington, D.C. 20415, reviews ESEA Title I programs in an annual report and makes recommendations for program continuation.

BIBLIOGRAPHY

Acker, Ralph S., "Reading Improvement in Government and Business," *Education,* vol. 82 (1962), pp. 428–31.

Adams, Mary L., "Teachers' Instructional Needs in Teaching Reading," *The Reading Teacher,* vol. 17 (1964), pp. 260–64.

Austin, Mary C. et al., *The Torch Lighters* (Cambridge, Mass.: Harvard University Press, 1961), 196 pp.

Ausubel, David P., "The Use of Advance Organizers in the Learning and Retention of Meaningful Verbal Materials," *Journal of Educational Psychology,* vol. 51 (1960), pp. 267–72.

Bailyn, Lotte, "Mass Media and Children: A Study of Exposure Habits and Cognitive Effects," *Psychological Monographs.* vol. 73 (1959), pp. 1–48.

Bogart, Leo, *The Age of Television* (New York: Frederick Ungar, 1956), 348 pp.

Bormuth, John R., "Readability: A New Approach," *Reading Research Quarterly,* vol. 1 (1966), pp. 79–132.

Bormuth, John R. and C. Aker, "Is the Tachistoscope a Worthwhile Teaching Tool?" *The Reading Teacher,* vol. 14 (1961), pp. 172–76.

Buswell, Guy T., *Non-Oral Reading: A Study of Its Use in the Chicago Public Schools* (Chicago: University of Chicago Press, 1945), 56 pp.

Center for Applied Linguistics, *Inventory of Projects and Activities in Reading and English* (Washington, D.C.: The Center, 1968), 74 pp.

Christensen, Clifford M. and K. E. Stordahl, "The Effect of Organizational Aids on Comprehension and Retention," *Journal of Educational Psychology,* vol. 46 (1955), pp. 65–74.

Coleman, James S., "Toward Open Schools," *The Public Interest* (Fall 1967), vol. 9, p. 25.

Dale, Edgar and Jeanne S. Chall, "Developing Readable Materials," *Adult Reading,* 55th Yearbook, Part II, NSSE (Chicago: University of Chicago Press, 1956), pp. 218–50.

Deutsch, Martin, "The Role of Social Class in Language Development and Cognition," *American Journal of Orthopsychiatry,* vol. 35, pp. 78–88.

Educational Developmental Laboratories, *Directory of Reading Clinics,* 1964 Edition, EDL Research and Information Bulletin No. 4 (Huntington, N.Y.: EDL, 1964), 14 pp.

Ellingson, Careth, *The Shadow Children* (Chicago: Topaz Books, 1967), pp. 104 ff.

Fantini, Mario D. and Gerald Weinstein, *The Disadvantaged: Challenge to Education* (New York: Harper and Row, 1968), 340 pp.

Fries, Charles C., *Linguistics and Reading* (New York: Holt, Rinehart and Winston, 1963), 265 pp.

Gates, Arthur I. "Sex Differences in Reading Ability," *The Elementary School Journal* vol. 51 (1961), pp. 431–34.

Good, Carter V., *The Supplementary Reading Assignment: A Study of Extensive and Intensive Materials and Methods in Reading* (New York: Appleton-Century-Crofts, 1927), 227 pp.

Harmin, M. and S. Simon, "The Year the Schools Began Teaching the Telephone Directory," *Harvard Educational Review,* vol. 35 (Summer 1965), pp. 326–31.

Herrick, Virgil E., "Basal Instructional Materials in Reading," *Development In and Through Reading.* 60th Yearbook, Part I, NSSE (Chicago: University of Chicago Press, 1961), pp. 165–188.

International Reading Association, *1969–1970 Directory* (Newark, Del.: The Association, 1967), 4 pp. (Mimeo).

Klare, George R. and Byron Buck, *Know Your Reader* (New York: Hermitage House, 1954), 192 pp.

Lewis, Mariana O., ed., *The Foundation Directory,* Edition 3 (New York: The Foundation Library Center, 1967), 1198 pp.

McGrew, J. M., et al., "Branching Program, Text and Lecture: A Comparative Investigation of Instructional Media," *Journal of Applied Psychology,* vol. 50 (1966), pp. 505–8.

McNeil, John D., "Programmed Instruction Versus Usual Classroom Procedures in Teaching Boys to Read," *American Educational Research Journal,* vol. 1 (1964), pp. 113–19.

Marchbanks, Gabrielle and Harry Levin, "Cues by Which Children Recognize Words," *Journal of Educational Psychology,* vol. 56 (1965), pp. 57–61.

National Advisory Council on Adult Basic Education, *First Annual Report,* pp. 37–40.

NSSE, *Adult Reading,* 55th Yearbook, Part II (Chicago: University of Chicago Press, 1956), 279 pp.

NSSE, *Reading in the High School and College,* 47th Yearbook, Part II (Chicago: University of Chicago Press, 1948), 318 pp.

NSSE, *Report of the National Committee on Reading,* 24th Yearbook, Part I, *Public Schools* (Bloomington, Ill.: Public School Publishing Co., 1925), 339 pp.

Norvell, George W., *The Reading Interests of Young People* (Lexington, Mass.: Heath, 1950), 262 pp.

Oettinger, Anthony and Sema Marks, "Educational Technology: New Myths and Old Realities," *Harvard Educational Review* (Fall 1968), vol. 38, pp. 714–15.

Peltola, Bette J., "A Study of Children's Book Choices," *Elementary English,* vol. 40 (1963), pp. 690–95, 702.

Philco-Ford Corporation, Communications and Electronics Division, in Cooperation with the School District of Philadelphia, *A Private Tutor for Every Child* (Willow Grove, Pa.: Philco-Ford Corporation), 8 pp. (Leaflet).

Riles, Wilson C., Carl J. Dolce, and Martin Mayer, *What Are the Priorities for City Schools?* Occasional Papers No. 15 (Washington, D.C.: Council for Basic Education, March, 1969), pp. 9–10.

Roman, Melvin, *Reaching Delinquents Through Reading* (Springfield, Ill.: Thomas, 1957), 125 pp.

Smith, Nila B., *American Reading Instruction* (Newark, Del.: International Reading Association, 1965), 449 pp.

Stolurow, L. M., "What Is Computer Assisted Instruction?" *Educational Technology*, vol. 8 (August 15, 1968), pp. 110–11.

Suppes, Patrick, "Computer-Based Instruction." *Electronic Age* (Summer 1967), p. 4.

Tinker, Miles A., *Bases for Effective Reading* (Minneapolis, Minn.: University of Minnesota Press, 1965), 322 pp.

Traxler, Arthur E. "Research in Reading in the United States," *The Journal of Educational Research*, vol. 42 (1949), pp. 481–99.

Tulvig, Endel and Cecille Gold, "Stimulus Information and Contextual Information as Determinants of Tachistoscopic Recognition of Words," *Journal of Experimental Psychology*, vol. 66 (1963), pp. 319–27.

U.S. Department of Health, Education, and Welfare, Office of the Secretary, "Press Release. August 24, 1968. National Advisory Committee on Dyslexia and Related Reading Disorders" (Washington, D.C.: U.S. Department of Health, Education, and Welfare. August 1968), 3 pp. (Xerox).

Weaver, Warren, "Matter of Opinion," *Foundation News*, vol. 8 (November, 1967), pp. 111–13.

5

Contemporary Problems in Home and Community Relationships

Kenneth E. Oberholtzer

In many communities, there is considerable dissatisfaction with the reading achievement results of both elementary and secondary pupils. Although criticism is not new to schools, some aspects of the current controversy are unusually intense. For example, the performance of the schools has been criticized most sharply by people living in large urban centers, where there are relatively large concentrations of racial and ethnic minorities. The criticism by both organizations and individuals has been heated. Changes are demanded. Added to this dissatisfaction is a growing feeling that the usual channels of communication between school and home and community have been fractured or broken. As a result there has been an increase in community intervention and the creation of new educational institutions outside of the usual school system in an attempt to bring about change.

There are many barriers between the home and community and the school; they vary from school to school, from home to home, and from community to community. However, there are a number of basic problems that need to be explored. Those problems that might be considered as most strategic for administrators to solve are examined in this chapter.

Responsibility of School to Home and Community

UNDERSTANDING AND APPLYING RESEARCH

Administrators must be aware of the research on the learning and development of children in their first six years of life and its implications for schools and their reading programs. Are we placing appropriate emphasis, financial and otherwise, on the period of life where the results can be the most dramatic—the preschool years? Undoubtedly we are not doing so.

In a very readable book, Maya Pines discusses some of the research by cognitive psychologists. Some of her statements summarize current points of view.

> Millions of children are being irreparably damaged by our failure to stimulate them intellectually during their crucial years—from birth to six. Millions of others are being held back from their true potential.[1]

> The scientists who would raise the nation's intelligence through early learning believe that few educators or parents have heard their message.[2]

> The mind-builders see the difference between babies from middle-class homes and those who are born into poverty emerging vividly about the age of one and a half. Until then, standard tests show most normal babies performing in pretty similar fashion.[3]

The role of the home as the principal educational unit for the first six years of life is given new importance by much of recent research. All too few homes and schools take advantage of the basic educational opportunities of these early years. Rarely are schools devising new programs that emphasize intellectual development in very young children.

RECOGNITION AND APPLICATION OF TECHNOLOGY

No generation of youth has been so surrounded by technology, especially radio, television, telephone, and published materials. Private business corporations, including publishers, have become active in the production of "hardware" as well as "software" for both home and school. Individualized and programmed equipment and materials are becoming available on the market in increasing variety.

These technological advances have greatly altered the relationship of the home and community to the school. This fact must be recognized and efforts must be made to use technology more widely and effectively. However, most schools do not reflect changes in children's environment. Although some ideas can be gained more readily through radio and television, our schools continue to rely mainly on reading.

Combinations of technological media such as films and audio tapes with books and other printed matter, give the pupil more options, more variety in his learning opportunities. Such flexibility is needed in today's schools because of the varied backgrounds of learning which pupils bring to school, because of the differences in patterns of learning among pupils and because variety in in-

---

[1] Maya Pines, *Revolution in Learning—The Years from Birth to Six* (New York: Harper and Row, 1967), p. 1.

[2] Ibid., p. 2.

[3] Ibid., p. 34.

structional programs enriches and vitalizes learning. The potential of instructional technology is being studied by several national groups in the profession. Feared by some and favored by others, television, radio, computers, and other components of instructional technology are beginning to make notable changes in educational opportunities.[4]

APPRAISING THE LEARNING ENVIRONMENT

Various groups and many individuals have proposed that we reexamine our views about intelligence and experience in the context of a total learning environment. Perhaps the two most significant subjects for this critical thinking have been the children who come from low-income homes and those from segregated racial or ethnic groups. The retardation of these children in reading has been the subject of several national studies. As a result of these studies there has been a reexamination of the use of the IQ, of life experiences, of achievement standards, and of the materials used, which has been expressed in new reading programs in some cities. In addition, schools now recognize the importance of changing the home and the community as well as the school program. The resulting awareness and the participation of children and parents, as well as the school, in planning for changes in the total learning environment has brought a new hope to many.[5]

SETTING UP PROGRAMS OF JOINT ACTION

Until more school administrators make commitments to act on newly realized concepts, schools will be hampered in their efforts to improve home and community relationships. To achieve this goal, the following suggestions are offered.

First, since preschool language development is crucial, the school and the home must join forces in developing programs of language development. The child's speech may be a dialect or even a foreign language. In any case, reading has to be based on the oral language of the child. Too much of our present school energies are used in "speech correction" after the child enters school. Instead, the instructional program should start where the child is, be ready to utilize the dialect and/or foreign language of the child in the early months of school, and gradually familiarize him with the standard English of the books and technological aids he will be using.

Second, intelligence, or the capability of the child to do school work is not a fixed, unchanging characteristic. That capability can be affected by such things as food, clothing, and lighting. In other words, measured intelligence is

[4] For a more extended discussion, see Sidney G. Tickton, ed., *To Improve Learning: An Evaluation of Instructional Technology* (New York: R. R. Bowker, 1970).

[5] A more detailed treatment is provided by George D. Spache, *Innovation and Change in Reading Instruction*, Sixty-Seventh Yearbook of the National Society for the Study of Education, Part II (Chicago: University of Chicago Press, 1968).

affected by home and community environment as well as by the school environment. Many children are not achieving their potentials in reading because of deficiencies in the environment. Although this has been said many times before, neurologists and psychologists have now provided scientific evidence of its truth. We must use the evidence for new action programs.

Third, positive interaction of the school, the home, and the community in reinforcing desirable reading activities can be very helpful in improving relationships. Simply providing reading materials for the home where materials are absent can be of critical importance. The establishment of school and community study halls, the employment of indigenous teacher aides who understand the language and the use of counseling techniques with parents are other examples of ways in which schools need to meet the problems.

Community Involvement in School Affairs

SCHOOL ORGANIZATION AND CONTROL

Problems of organization and control are of greatest concern in large cities where school boards and administrators have been accustomed to concentrations of authority in the board, central office, and regional administration. Barriers in school-community relationships frequently arise over the budgetary and financial operations, the assignment and transfer of teachers and principals, and the development of curriculum. These are interdependent and reading, as a part of the curriculum, is affected markedly by finance and personnel.

In the past, home and community members have felt that the controlling authority has been too far removed from the school where the instruction occurs. They have also contended that the school has not been responsive to the needs of children, that the teachers and principals have not been sympathetic with the pupils, and that the curriculum has not reflected a proper recognition of the people's cultural heritage.

In an effort to make the schools more relevant, lay citizens are demanding the decentralization of school administration in order to give them a more direct influence on their schools. Generally, modifications have been effected under crisis threats, and the compromises have not been satisfactory to either schools or homes. Occasionally, the demands have been reflected in state legislation. In other situations experimental changes on the local level have resulted. But whatever the results, positive action does take place.

The principle of autonomy in the local school conflicts with the problems of school financing which cannot be satisfactorily solved on a local basis. Still other obstacles, such as teacher tenure in school districts, must be overcome. However, the idea of bringing the individual school into closer and more effective relationships with the home and community remains important. It must be accepted as a problematic situation which requires the best thought of both the professional and the lay citizen. Surely a variety of approaches need to be designed, some much more experimental than those tried to date. Improvement of organization and control relationships will undoubtedly result in better reading instruction.

ASSESSING COMMUNITY ATTITUDES

Since 1950 the Denver Public Schools have conducted triennial opinion surveys of adult Denver citizens. A representative cross section of citizens has been interviewed by trained enumerators employed by Research Services, Inc. of Denver. Data submitted to the Board of Education and the Superintendent have been published and distributed widely in the school and throughout the community.[6] Two questions, among many, have appeared in each survey. One was, "In your words, how would you describe someone who is well-educated?" The response of the majority of people was, "Uses good English; speaks intelligently; expresses himself well; is well-read." In another question, those interviewed were asked to assess school subjects as "very important for all; worthwhile, but not for all; not worthwhile." Comments by parents and citizens generally sustained the statement that English (especially reading) was "very important for all."

School administrators concerned with reading instruction can find strong support in home and community. To do so, administrators must develop public information programs that reinforce the people's belief in the importance of reading. The author's survey of public information activities conducted by large city schools shows a dearth of notable, sustained programs that have relevance to reading.[7] Schools have occasionally published pamphlets that relate to school activities and conditions, but little has been done to interpret and explain modern reading to the community. However, the schools have had more effective programs in other curriculum areas, for example, modern math.

PREVENTING DISRUPTIVE COMMUNITY ACTION

The attitudes of the adults, especially parents, in the community toward the school reading program can be hostile and disruptive. Teachers and administrators, together with boards of education, have to make important choices, sometimes with the opposition of vocal critics in the home and community. Such choices as which basal and supplemental readers should be selected, at which age or time reading should begin, whether special phonics material should be used, whether programmed material should be adopted, and similar alternative choices have caused communities to explode in bitter controversies. To prevent disruptive controversy, the lines of communication between school

[6] Further information may be obtained from the Office of Press Relations and Public Information, Denver Public Schools, 414 Fourteenth St., Denver, Colo. 80202.

[7] See the material in the concluding paragraphs of this chapter.

and home and community must be kept open. The use of newspapers, bulletins, radio, and television can be helpful. Bringing the home and community into the school by means of aides or tutors and by parent-teacher conferences helps. It is also important to take the school into the home and community through the telephone, through home calls, through meetings in community centers, or through cooperation with such community agencies as the public library. Often these efforts make the difference between an effective reading program with community support, and one that is ineffective and the potential cause of a community explosion.

Pressure groups or zealous lay citizens sometimes push for the inclusion or exclusion of specific reading activities and materials. In response, some schools jump on and off each newly emerging band wagon. Relationships with both the professional staff and the community can become strained under such circumstances, and the reading program can suffer. The choice of programs is rarely made by the school administrator alone, although he is frequently asked to do this. Teachers and parents have a legitimate interest in knowing about and participating in making these decisions. Presentation and exploration of the issues and the various viewpoints in the local press can be useful before decision making. But the decisions should be based on research information, general practice, and thoughtful philosophy.[8]

INVOLVING THE COMMUNITY IN THE READING PROGRAM

If reading is accepted by the school, the home, and the community as a high-priority subject, the achievements of children will be relatively high. But if the home and the community feel that reading is the responsibility of the school alone and is of little importance, the achievement of children will be adversely affected. Low expectations and criteria in all relationships beget meager results.

The school must consider not only what to do in the classroom, but how to involve home and the community. Efforts should go beyond the parent-teacher conferences. In some instances, as in low-income areas where parent conferences and school meetings are poorly attended, the reading program has little chance of producing good results. Changes in the home and community environment, including cognitive and affective factors, must become a concern of the school. Remedial and compensatory programs within the school can improve the reading achievement of children, but when they are combined with home and community programs, especially for children of preschool age, the results are generally more impressive.

The necessity for school involvement is emphasized by Levine.

> Our understanding of child growth in general, and of the genesis of educational disadvantage in particular, has been greatly enhanced by the

[8] For a more extended treatment of this subject, see Gordon E. McCloskey, *Education and Public Understanding* (New York: Harper and Row, 1967).

recent work of scholars who have attempted to assess how human development is facilitated and impeded by various environmental conditions. Probably the most significant of these studies was reported by Benjamin Bloom in an influential book published in 1964 under the title *Stability anl Change in Human Characteristics.* Professor Bloom's major conclusion, after marshaling the available research evidence on the mental, emotional, and social development of children, was that the school should intervene earlier and more vigorously to counteract the detrimental effects of disadvantaged environment.[9]

Further, Professor J. McV. Hunt points out the crucial role of the total life experience in the intellectual processes that are important to reading achievement.

> For over half a century, the leading theory of man's nature has been dominated by assumptions of fixed intelligence and predetermined development. These beliefs have played a large role in psychological theorizing and investigation; they have provided a conceptual framework for the measurement of intelligence and for accounting for the development of human abilities, which have been regarded as the unfolding of capacities almost completely predetermined by inheritance. Recently, however, a transformation has been taking place in this traditional conception of intelligence and its relation to experience. Evidence from various sources has been forcing a recognition of central processes in intelligence and of the crucial role of life experience in the development of these central processes.[10]

Total life experiences are vital to child development. If this thesis is accepted—and accept it we must—a considerable portion of the reading program must involve the home and the community.

Understanding the Role of Reading in Early Childhood

IMPORTANCE OF PRESCHOOL INTELLECTUAL ACTIVITIES

Cognitive psychologists, inspired by such scientists as Jean Piaget and his collaborators at the Roussean Institute in Geneva have cast new light on the importance of the early years. Professor Hunt has provided a lucid interpretation of Piaget's writing.

> Many of the principles uncovered by Piaget get at least suggestive support from evidence deriving from quite diverse sources. The principle that the rate of development is a function of variety of stimulation during the early months of life gets support from those studies of the roles of ex-

---

[9] Daniel V. Levine, *Raising Standards in the Inner-City Schools* (Washington, D.C.: Council for Basic Education, 1966), p. 6.

[10] J. McV. Hunt, *Intelligence and Experience* (New York: Ronald Press, 1961), p. v, reprinted with permission of the publisher.

perience in the developments that stem from Helb's theorizing and from the studies of retardation that follows homogeneous stimulation in some orphanages. While there is little doubt that great degrees of retardation can result from the lack of variety in early stimulation, the degree to which such retardation is permanent or can be reversed remains an unsettled question. Similarly, the question of the degree to which the rate of development now characteristic of life in what is considered the best of home-rearing could be increased also remains open, but it is tenable to believe that with better knowledge of the process whereby schemata and central structures are modified by experience, the rate of development might be increased substantially, and with pleasure for the developing child.[11]

Professor Hunt stresses the importance of early development but he also notes that we do not yet know how to achieve full development.

On the other hand, Dr. William Fowler of Yeshiva University predicts that within a generation the world is destined to find itself caring for, and cognitively cultivating, its children from the cradle on. There is no evidence that guided stimulation has ever harmed young children, he states, but there is plenty of evidence that no human being of high ability has ever grown up without it.[12]

Further, confirming the importance of the early years, Arthur I. Gates says:

> The six year old of today who has enjoyed the advantages of both a good home and a good life is vastly superior to the child who has had neither. These facts suggest that certain steps be taken as soon as possible.
>
> The first and most obvious step is to get the school and the home together while the child is still very young. Before a child reaches his first birthday, he is beginning to learn spoken words. He is learning to distinguish word sounds; he is developing a hearing vocabulary; he is beginning to understand phrases, sentences and paragraphs; he is starting to use 'context clues' and to imitate all the other skills required to read printed words. Reading spoken words and reading printed words are basically the same; they involve substantially the same skills, as I tried to explain in an article published forty years ago. (Gates, "Methods and Theories of Teaching Reading Tested by Studies of Deaf Children," *Journal of Educational Research,* XIV, June, 1926, pp. 21–32.)
>
> Reading is largely learned at mother's knee during these early years, which the late Leta Hollingsworth called the 'Golden Age of Intellect'. Children who have been deprived of minimal home care and learning opportunities during these years suffer limitations which the school at present simply cannot overcome. The home and school must combine forces much earlier.[13]

[11] Hunt, *Intelligence and Experience,* p. 306.
[12] Pines, Op. cit., p. 49
[13] Arthur I. Gates, *Reading: Seventy-Five Years of Progress—Proceedings of the*

Searching studies of reading retardation and reading disability supply substantial evidence that, generally speaking, children from homes and neighborhoods in which reading activities are engaged in and are respected and rewarded tend to become successful readers, but children coming from homes and neighborhoods in which reading plays little or no role and is not well understood or approved tend to become retarded readers.[14]

INAUGURATING JOINT SCHOOL-HOME READING PROGRAMS

The school and the home and the community need to take a new look at what each agency can do in the early cognitive development of the child, especially through language development and early beginning reading activities. This is vitally important, for, as Spache says

> Of all the linguistic interpretations of the reading process that have been noted, the only assumption supported by definitive research evidence is that of the significance of the child's comprehension and use of language for his success in beginning reading. The breadth of the child's language experiences, auditory and oral, and the maturity of the sentence structures that he can use in speaking and can listen to comprehendingly are certainly related to early success in reading. Volumes of studies attest to the handicaps imposed by the inadequate language experiences of the bilingual, the culturally deprived, or the foreign-born child. Dozens of contemporary experimental programs are engaged in the exploration of effective ways of strengthening or promoting the language development of such children. Some of these are employing linguistic concepts and materials with favorable results. . . .[15]

Beginning reading activities are described in *Preparing Your Child for Reading,* the report of a Denver program which arose, in part, from the inquiries of mothers who had children who were interested in reading before they could enter school. A series of television lessons was presented and accompanying materials were prepared for the mothers. The results were good.

> Statistically significant gains in achievement, as measured by the evaluative instruments, were made by those who practiced 30 or more minutes per week . . . the best performance on the test was made by children who had both practiced the beginning reading activities more than 30 minutes a week and had been read to more than 60 minutes a week.[16]

Annual Conference on Reading Held at the University of Chicago, Vol. XXVIII (Chicago: University of Chicago Press, 1966), p. 14, reprinted with permission of the publisher.

[14] Ibid., p. 8.

[15] George D. Spache, *Innovation and Change in Reading Instruction,* The Sixty-Seventh Yearbook of the National Society for the Study of Education, Part II (Chicago: University of Chicago Press, 1968), pp. 265–66.

[16] *A Report—The Effectiveness of Parents in Helping Their Preschool Children to Begin Reading* (Denver Public Schools, 1962), pp. 27–28.

Another type of early start was made in Denver in Head Start. Although Head Start is a national program, there are differing views on the emphasis to be given to cognitive and affective activities and to ways of working together with parents. Mrs. Gwen Hurd, Project Coordinator, Child Development Centers, Denver Public Schools, in a letter to the author, provides a brief picture of some of the emphases in the Denver approach to early parent involvement:

> The key to success is the parent. Innovation in preschool education must include teaching a parent his own value; how he may present language arts, number concepts, music, art, social studies, creativity and self identity in the home and mesh it with the work to be presented in the school.
>
> The privacy of the home and the importance of the parent must be foremost in the parental teaching. As an example, when a teacher explains to a parent how he may present basic number concepts to a child, the teacher must be careful to do it when the child is not present. The presentation from the parent to the child must allow the child to feel his parent has always known these facts . . . Parents are helped to understand that preparation for reading occurs during prekindergarten years. The parents and teachers work together on material. . . . It is complex and involved but most important in the educational success.[17]

Strengthening Home-Community Role in School-age Reading

After the child enters school, and especially during the kindergarten and primary years, the supportive action of his home and community is vital. The National Congress of Parents and Teachers has urged programs in harmony with this idea. Elementary school teachers and administrators are familiar with the high degree of parental interest in the young child's activities. Most parents will agree to assist in the reading activities, but not all schools agree on how to use parents. There seems to be little doubt, however, that many parents can help their children show significant improvement in reading and in other subjects. Parent education programs and parent-teacher conferences are two common ways of working together. The parents' interest and encouragement can, by themselves, make a significant difference in children's achievement.

Research has not yet reported evidence of gains in achievement through parent interest and involvement. However, the testimony of teachers and principals shows that parental assistance can make the difference between ordinary and notable achievement. Helene M. Lloyd testifies that the "impact of programs that have successfully included parent involvement has been so marked that New York City, at least, is convinced that parent involvement

---

[17] From a report made to the author when he was superintendent of the Denver Public Schools.

constitutes a vast resource, now barely tapped and worth extensive cultivation."[18] The value of parent participation is further illustrated below.

In January, 1960, the Denver Public Schools and the Institute for Communication Research at Stanford University began a joint research project on the context of instructional television. The object of the project was to learn how educational television could be used in a context of other activities to produce maximum learning with fifth- and sixth-grade children who were studying a foreign language. More than 10,000 children were involved over a four-year period. Direct parent participation was included as one activity to be investigated. The Denver PTA was invited to assist in the project and agreed to handle all administrative aspects directly related to parents. The results of achievement tests (after adjustments for differences in learning potential) clearly demonstrated that parental help increased learning significantly. Although this project was directed primarily at foreign languages, a serendipitous effect was increased achievement in other subjects, including reading.

Lifelong Reading Role of Home, School, and Community

Reading should be an important aspect of lifelong learning, occurring both in school and out of school, and improvement in the practice of reading can be enhanced by the relationships of home and community with the school.

Libraries are provided in both schools and communities as a principal means of encouraging and extending reading to both children and adults. The collections in libraries are growing in size and quality and no contemporary school or college would be without a library or library services. The public library has come to be recognized as an essential service to the entire community. So that these services can be used most advantageously, many useful cooperative arrangements have been worked out between school and public libraries. Councils made up of school and public library personnel have furthered the economical use of available resources as, for example, in Denver, by avoiding duplicate purchases of books and by coordinating their information services related to available books.

The increasing availability of paperback publications, more attractive books, and the appropriation of federal funds for schools and colleges, have all led to expanded reading activities. Book stores, drug stores, department stores, and supermarkets have become common outlets for books for individual ownership.

The provision of optional and newer types of learning experiences in schools and centers, the expansion of reference libraries, the use of discovery and research techniques involving homes and community resources, have all enriched learning and reading. The individualization of instructional materials, the de-

[18] Helene M. Lloyd, "New York City's Program for Developing the Role of Parents in Reading Progress," *The Reading Teacher* (May, 1965), pp. 629–33.

velopment of teaching machines, the programming of instructional materials, the expansion of nonprofessional assistance from the community, have all helped to give much needed variety to the ways reading is learned.

Innovations

In recent years there have been many attempts to innovate, especially in beginning reading. However, Congreve states:

> Innovations are doomed to slow acceptance or rejection if the parents and the community are not somehow involved in the early stages of the planning. Schools can take steps to avoid parental discontent, which can 'torpedo' an innovation as well as make it difficult for other innovations to be introduced into the school. Before initiating the change, the school should describe the innovation as fully as it can to the parents of the children to be involved in the program. The parents should be guided through the same line of argument and discussion the faculty has gone through in coming to a decision to try out the new idea . . . Furthermore, parents can be helped to accept the fact that the results of an innovation cannot be fully predicted until the experiment has been tried out.[19]

Helen Robinson similarly says:

> Increasingly, schools are involving parents in school activities as well as in supportive roles. Furthermore, parents make direct contributions to their children's learning to read.
>
> A few experiments have been reported in which help has been provided for parents so that home and school can work harmoniously. However, only small segments of the total range of possibilities have been examined to date. Innovations in determining the contribution of parents to the reading of their children are urgently needed. Experimentation is needed in all types of schools and with pupils of different ages and levels of achievement.[20]

In short, new instructional practices must have community support if they are to succeed. Efforts must be made to obtain this support and, in addition, ways must be found to allow parents to become directly involved in reading programs.

SOME PROMISING PRACTICES

In response to letter inquiries sent to superintendents of many large city school systems by the author, replies and materials were received which provided a sampling of what such systems are doing. Questions such as the following were

[19] Willard J. Congreve, *Innovation and Change in Reading Instruction*, p. 299.
[20] Helen M. Robinson, *Innovation and Change in Reading Instruction*, p. 409.
National Society for the Study of Education Yearbook, Vol. 67, Part II U.C. Press.

raised. "Do you have programs or studies going on in your system that involve parents in early childhood or regular school years in reading activities?" "What community resources, including persons, have you found to be most useful in the reading program?" "What results have you obtained?" While these responses are from large cities, they are, nevertheless, equally applicable in most instances to smaller communities.

Illustrations of current practice in a number of cities are provided in Appendix 5.1. It is apparent from the reports that most of the school systems have

1. involved parents in the early elementary school years.
2. involved most often the parents of children who have been under-achievers.
3. been experimenting with nonprofessional tutors and aides.
4. been working with public libraries and theaters in many cooperative programs.
5. been enthusiastic about the results of their home and community programs (although few systems have reported evaluation in specific terms).
6. acknowledged the need of developing more effective ways of working with parents of preschool children.
7. not developed public information programs related especially to reading.

Conclusion

The isolation of school from home and community is no longer possible or desirable. An effective reading program is a total community endeavor. Achievement in reading is dependent upon the child's attitudes, information, and general background. Obviously, if the child is deficient in the prerequisites to reading instruction when he enters school, the school is less than totally effective in enabling the child to become an effective reader. Public relations are important, but more important and pervasive are those aspects of home and community relations that will contribute in a positive manner to the total environment so that the child comes to school well-equipped to learn and, also, so that his home provides an environment for on-going learning and encouragement in the learning process.

Appendix 5.1

BALTIMORE—The Parent Volunteer Reading Project has been established. Parents have volunteered to listen to children reading and also to read to the children.

CHICAGO—(1) The public library has arranged for Story Hours for both pre-school and regular school children. A Story Caravan visits special summer schools. Discussion groups have been organized for parents at inner-city branch libraries. And (2) The Goodman Theater of the Chicago Art Institute produces children's plays in cooperation with school reading programs.

DETROIT—(1) School-community agents and school-community assistants have been working with many agencies in developing cooperative efforts. (2) Teacher aides, staff aides, and clerical aides are recruited from the school served. (3) A poetry program for junior high and high schools features poets reading and discussing their poetry.

HOUSTON—A summer program for four year olds, with active parent involvement, has resulted in expanded vocabularies.

KANSAS CITY—(1) The Division of Urban Education has an Inner-City Parent Council which involves parents in reading activities. (2) Earn a Book Program. Books are given to the children for their home libraries after reading a required number of books. This program also involves teacher aides who listen to the children reading the books.

LOS ANGELES—(1) A parent education reading program is offered in Adult Education classes in many schools to show how parents can help their children read. (2) Parental Involvement in Educational Programs utilizes school advisory committees, composed largely of parents. Among other activities, the programs have established Family Centers as an outreach of schools to parents and their pre-school children.

MINNEAPOLIS—(1) A Citizens Committee on Public Education has formed a subcommittee, the Reading Study Committee, which is active in (a) making citizens aware of what the schools are doing in reading, and (b) promoting parent education in reading. (2) Community volunteers with particular knowledge or skills are invited into the schools to stimulate interest in reading.

NEW ORLEANS—(1) The public library conducts a large summer reading program. (2) The Experimental Laboratory Theatre attracts high school students who are encouraged to read widely.

NEW YORK—(1) The Edison Responsive Environmental Typewriter Project includes children in the day and adults in the evening. (2) Project Read developed together with the Behavioral Research Laboratories of Palo Alto, California, relates to a number of community projects.

SAN FRANCISCO—(1) Project Read uses the Sullivan Reading Materials that pupils may bring home to share with their parents. (2) Project Seed provides parent education review committees that assist in determining programs and materials.

SEATTLE—(1) The Council of Jewish Women, working with the schools, has developed two programs, (a) Reading Tutors and (b) the Primary Enrichment Program. (2) Student Volunteers from nearby colleges assist as reading tutors.

TULSA—The Reading Workshop for Parents explains and demonstrates the three major reading series used in the schools.

VANCOUVER—(1) The University of British Columbia and the schools have collaborated in an experimental program of parent education. (2) The National Film Board, the Vancouver School Board, and the public library cooperate in sponsoring the Children's Own Theatre. Children may attend a biweekly showing of children's films related to children's books.

BIBLIOGRAPHY

Congreve, Willard J., *Innovation and Change in Reading Instruction*, Sixty-Seventh Yearbook of the National Society for the Study of Education, Part II (Chicago: The University of Chicago Press, 1968).

Gates, Arthur I., *Reading: Seventy-Five Years of Progress—Proceedings of the Annual Conference on Reading Held at the University of Chicago* (Chicago: University of Chicago Press, 1966).

Hunt, J. McV., *Intelligence and Experience* (New York: Ronald, 1961).

Levine, Daniel V., *Raising Standards in the Inner-City Schools*, Occasional Papers No. 11 (Washington, D.C.: Council for Basic Education, 1966).

Lloyd, Helene M., "New York City's Program for Developing the Role of Parents in Reading Progress," *The Reading Teacher* (May, 1965).

McCloskey, George E., *Education and Public Understanding* (New York: Harper & Row, 1967).

Pines, Maya, *Revolution in Learning—The Years From Birth to Six* (New York: Harper & Row, 1967).

Robinson, Helen M. and George D. Spache, *Innovation and Change in Reading Instruction*, Sixty-Seventh Yearbook of the National Society for the Study of Education, Part II (Chicago: The University of Chicago Press, 1968).

Tickton, Sidney G., *To Improve Learning—An Evaluation of Instructional Technology* (New York: R. R. Bowker Co., 1970).

II

Strategies for Change

6

Assessing the Total Reading Program

Richard Madden

In order to correctly assess the value of the reading programs of their schools, administrators must be familiar with and make full use of evaluative tools such as reading achievement tests. Correct interpretation of these tests will help the administrator determine whether his students have a grasp of the elements of learning to read and if they are developing as mature readers. However, reading achievement (ability) must be defined before it can be evaluated.

It is basically the medium that varies among reading, listening, and viewing as they simulate thinking. Children have developed considerable proficiency in listening and viewing before they learn to use the printed page. The mental process that occurs while listening is essentially the same as the mental process of reading. The elements of reading deal primarily with coping with printed material and include such skills and abilities as word recognition, sentence understanding, analysis of paragraphs, and the comprehension of longer passages.

A distinction must be made between the elements of reading and mature reading (thinking) when measuring and evaluating reading achievement. The measurement of mature reading is concerned more with reading quality than with efficiency. The quality of reading is the ability of the mind to respond innovatively to printed material. Measurement of innovative responses is difficult because test items provide only indicative evidence. However, there is much that can be measured in the early processes of learning to read and in the higher levels that involve both literal, or explicit, and inferential, or implicit, comprehension. The processes of learning to read are the first aspects of reading to be measured.

Reading ability falls short of thinking ability when there are deficiencies in word analysis, in knowledge of sentence structure, and in ability to analyze paragraphs and longer passages. Such shortages are characteristic of beginning readers, but for many they persist throughout life. Such persons think better in nonreading situations than they do in reading situations. A primary purpose in the measurement of reading is to assess this gap between thinking capacity and reading ability so that it may be closed. Normatively, the difference will be greatest at grade 1 and will tend to close by grade 6; that is, comprehension in reading and in listening tends to become equalized at higher grade levels, unless a deficiency exists in reading.[1] At the upper grade levels, because the pupil has mastered the fundamental skills, the advantages of reading over listening become increasingly apparent. As he reads, he can reread to organize and think at his own pace. This advantage is not available in the listening situation.

Three Types of Measurement

Evaluation of reading, and most other subjects, may be classified into three subtypes, namely, *criterion measurement, ranking measurement,* and *diagnostic measurement.*

CRITERION TESTS

Criterion tests (for example, tests which accompany reading textbooks) are essentially tests of mastery. They can help to determine whether pupils (1) have learned the letters of the alphabet; (2) can match words by sounds of the initial consonant; (3) can read individual words without sentence, story, or picture clues; (4) can give the main idea ("headline") of a short passage; and (5) whether pupils read orally with adequate expression.

RANKING TESTS

A ranking measure is less concerned with specific mastery, but seeks to rank pupils from best to poorest, on the basis of items difficult enough for that purpose. Ranking tests should have adequate validity and reliability for comparison of pupil with pupil, school with school, or of either with a norm; also, they are used to measure growth from one year to the next and to compare different instructional programs. The reading tests included in batteries of standardized achievement tests are examples of ranking tests.

DIAGNOSTIC TESTS

Diagnostic tests are similar to criterion tests in purpose, but more like ranking tests in validity and reliability. Diagnostic tests identify specfic weaknesses

---

[1] Donald D. Durrell and Mary T. Hayes, *Durrell Listening Reading Series* (New York: Harcourt Brace Jovanovich, 1969), Manual, Primary Level, Form DE, p. 16.

in each of various aspects of reading, and help teachers plan future instruction for each pupil. There is an increasing use of diagnostic testing to identify relative weaknesses and strengths of all readers.

AN ALTERNATE CLASSIFICATION

Bloom, Hastings, and Madaus use the classification of summative evaluation, evaluation for placement and diagnosis, and formative evaluation.[2] (Summative evaluation refers to the cumulation of learning and formative evaluation is more concerned with the "formation stages" of the processes such as the instruction, and the curriculum.)

Critical Aspects of Evaluation

A complete program of evaluation includes cognitive and affective aspects, and certain physical correlates.

Assessment of growth in the following cognitive aspects is particularly valuable:

> Decoding (word analysis)
> Word recognition
> Sentence structure
> Comprehension of more extended discourse, as of one or more paragraphs
> Evaluation of content from a variety of sources and points of view
> Synthesis of various points of view and arguments

Affective assessment should include:

> Attitudes and self-concepts
> Personal adjustment to current progress in learning to read
> Satisfactions gained from reading

Complete evaluation of a pupil's potential for learning to read must also assess related physical factors. These factors include visual and auditory perception, general health, and nutrition.

A complete, or adequate, clinical analysis of a seriously deficient reader would, of course, include other factors relating to the individual and his environment. Various environmental factors affect reading achievement. For example, an extensive analysis by Hogan has demonstrated a high correlation of reading tests scores and socio-economic factors.[3]

[2] Benjamin J. Bloom, Thomas Hastings, and George F. Madaus, *Handbook on Formative and Summative Evaluation of Learning* (New York: McGraw-Hill, 1971), p. 117.

[3] Thomas P. Hogan, *Stanford Achievement Test: A Supplementary Report on the Norm Group* (New York: Harcourt Brace Jovanovich, 1970).

The Administrator's Strategy and Plan

The school administrator's strategy of evaluation must first determine the place of reading among all the objectives of the school program. He should then compare the results from year to year with past local performance, as well as with performance in similar systems throughout the state and nation. He and his faculty, after considering the nature of their pupil population, should establish reasonable goals of achievement. When establishing goals, the administrator should take into account convictions and attendant priorities which have become school policy regarding objectives for reading and other aspects of the curriculum. Accountability designations (the goals of achievement expressed quantitatively) are then in order.[4]

The *plan* of evaluation should specify the tests to be used, the grades to be tested, time of year for testing, reports to be made, records to be kept, and the proper use of the tests for instruction. A program of criterion testing and diagnosis should also be developed.

Three testing plans are presented in Table 6.1 below. These differ in extent and cost.

The minimum program advocates certain testing to be done every year. Such a program will provide the administrator with only the minimum information needed to assure a reasonable quality of education.

The suggested medium program includes more diagnostic testing than is included in the minimum program, and less frequent general comprehension testing than is suggested for the complete program.

A complete program of evaluation will identify individual pupils who read inefficiently. It should provide a measure of school achievement as distinguished from pupil achievement, inasmuch as some schools are greatly aided by what parents do for their children. A complete program provides frequent diagnostic evaluation.

A measure of reading potential is not listed in Table 6.1, since such a test is not, in itself, a test of reading. Such a measure, however, is very useful. It is desirable to have a measure of comprehension which does not require the pupil to read, but which is, nevertheless, verbal in nature (for example, a test of verbal ability or of listening comprehension). Only then can a teacher appraise instructional needs versus broader developmental needs.

The issue of fall versus spring testing is resolved in the complete plan by diagnostic testing in the fall, and by ranking testing in the spring. Teachers are thereby acquainted with pupil needs in the fall, and with results of their own instruction in the spring. When fall to spring growth is to be measured, as in some performance contracts, ranking measures are usually specified.

[4] The intricacies of such designations are examined in Aaron Wildavsky, "A Program of Accountability for Elementary Schools," *Phi Delta Kappan,* vol. 52, no. 4 (December 1970), pp. 212–16.

TABLE 6.1

Three Testing Plans

(1) Complete	(2) Medium	(3) Minimum	Grade	
*	*	*	all grades	Criterion tests periodically
*			K.2	Letters and sounds, listening, vocabulary, and general information
*	*	*	K.8	Letters and sounds, listening, vocabulary, and general information
*				Superior schools: word reading, readiness
*	*	*	1.1	Same as K.8, if not done at that level
*	*	*	1.5	Repeat above tests as needed.
*	*	*	1.8	Dictated vocabulary, word or sentence comprehension, word analysis skills, aural comprehension
*			2.2	Same as 1.8, if not done at that level
*	*	*	2.5	Check for special instructional needs
*	*	*	2.8	Dictated vocabulary, word or sentence comprehension, word analysis skills, aural comprehension
*			3.1	Same as 2.8, if not done at that level. Diagnostic test
*	*	*	3.8	Same as 2.8
*	*	*	4.1	Diagnostic test. Comprehension, if not done at 3.8
*	*		5.1	Diagnostic test
*			5.8	Comprehension, vocabulary
*	*	*	6.1	Diagnostic test
*	*	*	6.8	Comprehension, vocabulary
*	*	*	7.1	Diagnostic, comprehension, and, if junior high school, vocabulary

TABLE 6.1

Three Testing Plans

(1) Complete	(2) Medium	(3) Minimum	Grade	
*			7.8	Comprehension
*			8.1	Same as 7.1
*	*		8.8	Same as 7.8
*	*	*	9.1	Diagnostic, comprehension, and if first year of high school, vocabulary
*	*	*	9.8	If first year of senior high school, comprehension
*	*	*	10.1	If first year of senior high school, diagnostic, comprehension
*	*	*	10.8	If first year of senior high school, comprehension
*	*	*	11.1	Diagnostic and comprehension for slow readers
*			11.8	Comprehension for slow readers
*			12.1	Same as 11.1
*			12.8	Same as 11.8

Criterion testing is recommended and will be discussed later in greater detail.

Vocabulary should be evaluated by dictation tests throughout the elementary grades. A vocabulary score is adversely affected by the necessity to read the words of the test, until approximately grade 6 or 7. A vocabulary measure used as a test of expectancy should, therefore, be dictated. This type of test, moreover, is quite valid as a vocabulary test.

WHEN IS A TEST SUFFICIENTLY RELIABLE FOR DIAGNOSIS?

The reliability of a test is more critical when judging individual performance than when judging the performance of a group. Moreover, the larger the group, the more reliable the average becomes. Therefore, each subtest of a diagnostic battery should have a reliability of not less than .85. A reliability of this magnitude is difficult to attain with fewer than 30 items.

Therefore, generally speaking, 30 "good" items are needed as a minimum for generalizing for individuals. One item may give specific information, but several items are needed for determining the ability of a class or school system in a specific area. It is extremely unwise to develop individual pupil profiles from the results of tests of ten to fifteen items. With such tests, a difference of one score point may be the equivalent of one year in achievement. A few lucky guesses by the pupil may easily make a difference of two or three grade levels.

This is not to say that a single item on a criterion test cannot contribute useful knowledge. It is instructionally useful to know, for example, that a pupil cannot select a spoken stimulus word from *run, fun,* and *sun,* or recognize the difference between *house* and *horse.* A teacher cannot, however, generalize from performance on these two items that a pupil is either poor or satisfactory in areas as broad as phonics or word recognition.

Use of Results

Three methods of presenting data are very useful to teachers.

THE CLASS LIST

The first is a class list, with test scores in order of magnitude. This is troublesome to produce when a test is a part of a battery of several tests.

STANINE TABULATION

The second method is the stanine tabulation. The stanine arrangement is easy to interpret when teachers are familiar with the stanine statistic. A stanine unit is equivalent of one half of a *sta*ndard deviation, and is presented in *nine* categories. From Table 6.2 one can observe, for example, that a pupil with a stanine of 8 scores better than 89 percent of the group, but is exceeded by 4 percent. A stanine score of 4 is greater than the scores of 23 percent of the group, but poorer than 60 percent. Table 6.2 presents the relationship of stanines to percentiles and shows the percent of the pupils in each of the stanine categories.

The data in Table 6.3 show some possibilities for diagnostic interpretation. The table presents a set of grade equivalent scores for ranking test at grade 5.2 and a set of stanine scores for a diagnostic test. These beginning fifth-grade pupils are from the same school.

From the table, the following information is readily apparent:

1. All pupils are below their chronological grade level of 5.2, most are more than one year below.
2. Vocabulary and paragraph meaning are equal on the achievement test.
3. In vocabulary the pupils' median stanine is 6 as measured by the dictated vocabulary test of the diagnostic battery. The median per-

TABLE 6.2

Meaning of Stanine[a]

Stanine	Percentiles	Percent of Pupils per Stanine	
9	97–100	Best	4%
8	90–96	Next	7%
7	78–89	Next	12%
6	61–77	Next	17%
5	41–60	Middle	20%
4	24–40	Next	17%
3	12–23	Next	12%
2	5–11	Next	7%
1	1–4	Poorest	4%

[a] A more extensive explanation of the stanine score and its use is presented by Durost. He discusses in detail the use of bivariate charts with stanine intervals. See Walter N. Durost, *Manual for Interpreting Metropolitan Achievement Tests* (New York: Harcourt Brace Jovanovich, 1969), pp. 14–16, 48–61.

formance is well above grade level of 5.2. Reading comprehension, however, is below average, as indicated by a median stanine of 4. The comparison of these two medians is very significant. Eight of these fifteen pupils have a reading potential above average, but all are actually below average in comprehension and five pupils are more than a full year below.

Of the eight pupils who are at stanine 6 or higher in dictated vocabulary (potential), all are below stanine 6 in sound discrimination and at or below stanine 6 in recognition of beginning and ending sounds.

Notice particularly the discrepancy between vocabulary (potential) and skills scores for Pupils 2 and 15. Vocabulary is at stanine 7 (seventy-eighth to eighty-ninth percentile), but only one of their other diagnostic measurements is above stanine 3.

Pupils 9 and 13 are capable pupils with unusually fine vocabularies; their stanines of 9 are in the top four percent. On the vocabulary test that requires reading, their grade scores are 4.5 and 3.6, respectively, .7 and 1.6 years below their grade level and even lower when compared with their dictated vocabulary scores. Note by this illustration that diagnostic testing is as important in revealing the reading deficiencies of bright pupils as it is in identifying the reading needs of the less capable pupils. From the last two lines of Table 6.3, it can be seen that only one pupil is at or above stanine 6 and only one is at or below stanine 2 in comprehension. The others, then, are at stanines 3 to 5. The other measurements show similar levels of mediocrity except in vocabulary. Pupils with high vocabulary scores (potential) and average reading scores are all too common in the classrooms.

TABLE 6.3

Scores of Fifteen Pupils in Grade Equivalents on a Ranking Test and in Stanines on a Diagnostic Test (pupils are at grade 5.2)

	Achievement Test (in grade equivalents)		Diagnostic Test (in stanines)						
Pupil Number	Paragraph Meaning	Vocabulary (read by pupil)	Reading Comprehension	Vocabulary (dictated)	Auditory Discrimination	Syllabication	Beginning and Ending Sounds	Blending	Sound Discrimination
1	3.4	4.1	4	4	3	5	3	5	3
2	3.6	3.0	2	7	3	2	3	2	3
3	3.5	3.7	4	2	3	7	3	4	2
4	4.8	3.7	7	8	5	4	4	4	5
5	4.5	4.6	3	4	4	1	5	8	4
6	2.8	4.7	3	4	1	3	6	6	5
7	3.4	3.3	4	4	3	1	2	2	1
8	3.9	3.6	3	5	4	2	1	2	1
9	3.9	4.5	3	9	5	6	4	5	4
10	3.4	2.5	4	6	4	4	3	3	5
11	3.8	2.6	3	2	4	3	3	3	5
12	4.6	4.4	5	6	7	5	6	5	2
13	3.9	3.6	5	9	7	5	6	6	5
14	—	—	5	8	1	5	5	5	1
15	3.2	2.5	3	7	4	3	3	2	1
Median	3.6	3.6	4	6	4	4	3	4	3
Number less than 3 →			1	2	2	4	2	4	6
Number at 6 or higher →			1	8	2	2	3	3	0

THE CLASS ANALYSIS CHART

The class analysis chart is a third useful method of presenting test results. Stanine charts can be used at all grade levels. Grade equivalent charts are less subject to misinterpretation in the early grades than in the later grades. If stanines are used, the national stanines give the most complete picture. However, stanines based on local groups are particularly useful for presenting relative standings of slower readers, who might tend to be concentrated in stanines 1, 2, and 3 of a national population.

Twenty-nine pupils are included in the class analysis in Table 6.4. The asterisks in each column indicate the middle score point in each subject test. The numbers refer to individual pupils. For example, Pupil 1 is at stanine 9 in

TABLE 6.4
Class Analysis Chart (grade 3.6)

	IQ	Word Meaning	Paragraph Meaning	Science and Social Studies	Spelling	Word Study Skills	Language	Arithmetic Computation	Arithmetic Concepts
9	1 12 ㉖	1	1	1	1 12	12	12		12 ⑮
8	⑲	8 12	8 12 21	24 29	㉘	8 ㉓ 29	8		1 21 29
7	8 ㉘ 10 ㉒	26	4 16 26	16	8	1 3 11 24 26	1 26	12	
6	3 6 15	4 16 21	3 6 14 23 25	4 10 12 19 23 25	3 15 21	6 21	26	3 15 21 22	23 26
5	7 14 23 * 20 25 ⑬ 21	17 24 25 29		6 7 8 9 * 14 17 21 22	4 6 9 10 14 17 23 * 24 25 26 29	9 10 15 16 * 19	3 4 6 14 15 21 29	20 23	6 8 9 10 16 17 22 28 *
4		3 * 19 6 11 23 10 18 28	9 * 19 29 10 17 22 15 18 28	2 3 11 15 18 20 28	11 16 22	4 5 13 14 17 18 22 25	11 13 * 17 18 19 27 28	9 10 17 19 26	3 19 27
3	16 27	7 9 14 15 22 27	7 24 27	5 27	7 13 19 27	20 27	9 10 16 22 23	① 6 * 7 11 14 18 28 29	4 7 11
2	2 11	2	11 13	13	2 5 18 20	2 28	5 7 20 25	4 ⑧ 13 25 27	5 13 18 20 25
1	⑰	5 13 20	2 5 20			7	2 27	2 5 ⑯ 20	2 14 27

English is 2nd Language for Pupils 5, 14, and 20.

the first five tests, stanine 7 in the next two, stanine 3 in Arithmetic Computation, and stanine 7 in Arithmetic Concepts. The numeral has been circled in Arithmetic Computation because it deviates so much from this pupil's general pattern that it warrants careful analysis.

As a whole, the class appears somewhat above average in IQ, but quite weak in Arithmetic Computation. Note that eight pupils are in stanines 7 to 9 in IQ. Only in Word Study Skills is there an equivalent concentration. Pupils 1, 8, and 12 are consistently high in all tests except computation. Pupil 19 is at stanine 8 in IQ, but drops to stanine 4 in reading and mathematics, and does not perform particularly well in other subjects.

It is quite apparent that Pupils 1, 4, 8, 12, 16, 21, and 26 could be included in an individualized, accelerated reading group. All are at stanine 6 or above in both word meaning and paragraph meaning. Pupil 21 drops to stanine 5 in IQ, but is strong in mathematics.

Pupils 2, 5, 13, and 20 constitute a group in need of very basic instruction. Note that English is the second language for Pupils 5 and 20. Pupil 13 has an IQ in stanine 5.

It appears that this class has had intensive instruction in the word study skills, but that this emphasis has not been carried over to the area of paragraph reading. There is an instructional need for better integration of these two aspects of reading.

Observe that arithmetic concepts have been learned very well by all but the eight pupils in stanines 1 and 2. In this group, only Pupil 2 has a low IQ; Pupils 5 and 20 have not taken the intelligence test because of their foreign language background.

This analysis demonstrates the great utility of the class analysis chart. The chart can provide many useful insights about a class and individual pupils.

Interpretation to the Board of Education

School trustees are often concerned with answers to questions such as the following:

> How does achievement compare with that of previous years?
> How do the various areas within the local district compare with the district as a whole?
> How does achievement compare with other school systems in general?
> How does achievement compare with similar school systems?

Comparison with previous years requires that the same test be given at the same time of year over a period of years. The comparison is most effectively revealed by percentile scores at five percentile points, the tenth, twenty-fifth, fiftieth, seventy-fifth, and ninetieth. The twenty-fifth percentile, which is the median of the lower half, indicates how the lower half of a school population is performing; the seventy-fifth percentile can be used for the upper half. The ninetieth and tenth percentiles are useful indices of the achievement of the highest and lowest fifths of the class, school, or district.

National norms may be used for comparison of a district with other school systems. In practice, however, comparison with comparable school systems must usually be made by mutual agreement, or by becoming a member of some group which has as one of its objectives similar evaluative comparisons.

The stanine score, although superior for individuals, is too gross for use in group comparisons. But it may be used, if decimalized, when percentiles are difficult to secure.

Figure 6.1 is a model chart for presenting district or individual school norms. The national percentile scale is provided along the left- and right-hand margins. Notice in the legend that the dots represent the tenth and ninetieth percentiles for the district. This chart is unusual in that the percentile scale is graduated on the stanine scale, giving a truer impression of differences at the various points along the scale than does an ordinary percentile scale. Stanines are equal units, percentiles are unequal units of value, the interpercentile differences being greater toward the extremes of a distribution. Although this chart is in percentiles, distributing them on the stanine scale prevents distortion of differences especially near the middle of the scale. For example, within a school district there may be 100 pupils at the middle of the scale whose test scores are the same. At the ends of the distribution there might be only five or fewer with a given test score. Therefore, a distance of ten points on the percentile scale might be only a point or two in raw score at the middle of the scale and as many as five to ten raw score points near the end of the scale.

A hasty glance at Figure 6.1 reveals no serious learning deficiencies, but a consideration of socio-economic factors and pupils' potential may change this evaluation. If the school population is above average in intelligence there may be sizable deficiencies. On the other hand, if the community is of average ability, the chart evidence may represent significant achievement.

Achievement in reading comprehension, using vocabulary as a measure of potential, is probably satisfactory. This is particularly true at the median. The quartile points are nearly identical. The tenth and ninetieth percentile points suggest, however, that the reading program is not as effective in meeting the needs of either the slow or the gifted pupils.

Mathematics, a relatively "nonreading" subject, may be used as another base for expectancy. Here again, using mathematics as the referent, reading comprehension is generally satisfactory, but the quartile points indicate some cause for concern for the achievement of the less capable pupil.

Spelling is one of the subjects that is usually closest to the national average, whether in a good school or a poor school. Such is the case here. However, since social studies and science correlate so highly with reading at this grade level, one would expect those scores to be higher.

In this school, the most unusual subject bar in the chart is that of mathematics concepts. The dot at the top of the distribution indicates that the dis-

FIGURE 6.1

Chart for Reporting District-wide Achievement

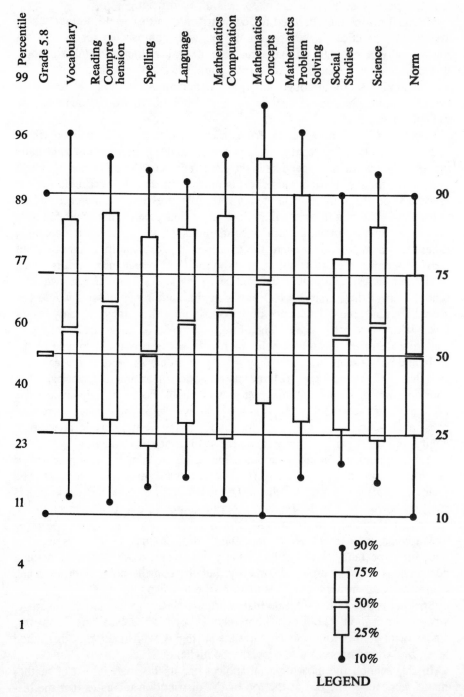

LEGEND

trict is at the ninetieth percentile. The corresponding point on the national percentile scale is approximately the ninety-eighth. Hence, it can be seen that ten percent of the pupils in this school at this grade are in the top two percent of the national population. The same process of analysis using the median of the school shows that almost half are in the top quarter of the pupils of the nation, since the median almost reaches the national seventy-fifth percentile. The lowest score of the district (mathematics concepts) is at the tenth percentile. The district appears to be particularly effective in teaching mathematics concepts to average and above average pupils while the poorest performance in this subject is at the tenth percentile. Is it possible that for the less capable pupils instruction in computation has taken precedence over concepts?

To summarize, in this district reading seems to be taught about as well as other subjects, but the possibility of more effective teaching of reading in social studies and science should be investigated.

THE GRADE EQUIVALENT SCORE

The grade equivalent is the most easily understood score for laymen and for teachers unfamiliar with the stanine. Grade equivalent scores can be used most successfully in grades 1 through 4. However, in later grades or when comparing subject with subject it can be quite misleading.

To say that a pupil is one year ahead of his grade level, or that a class is four months advanced or retarded in terms of grade level appears to have rather specific meaning. However, a grade equivalent score in computation or spelling, subjects in which pupils tend not to be so divergent, is not strictly comparable with grade equivalent scores in reading. For example, the grade equivalent of a reading score at the twentieth percentile for grade 3 would be lower than the grade equivalent of a mathematics computation score. Consequently, a pupil, class, or school achieving at the twentieth percentile in both reading and computation *appears* to be poorer in reading when grade equivalents are compared. As a result, undesirable comparisons are often made which may show reading to be better among superior populations and poorer in disadvantaged populations than it really is. To illustrate, there is very little difference between reading and mathematics computation in Figure 6.1. Yet, presented as grade scores, the differences are as follows:

| District | Grade Equivalent | |
Percentile	Reading	Computation
90	10.0	8.2
75	7.8	6.8
50	6.6	6.2
25	5.2	5.2
10	4.2	4.5

Figure 6.1 shows that computation is slightly better than reading at the ninetieth percentile of this district. Yet the tabulation above shows reading at grade 10.0 and computation at 8.2. This may be true, but it must not be interpreted that, when compared with other districts, this district is doing better in reading than in computation. Also, the inverse situation should be avoided in below average schools, where computation may appear (using grade equivalent scores) to be better than reading.

Expectancy

When can one reasonably expect one child, one class, or one school, to read better, or more poorly, than others? The word *reasonably* compounds the problem. What to expect is fairly simple. Expect children to do what they did the year before. Relative standing for a particular group of children is very stable over a period of several years.[5] Before deciding what one might *reasonably* expect if instruction and pupil effort have been fully analyzed and stimulated, a variety of factors must be considered.

School systems to be compared for efficiency in teaching reading, should be relatively equal in family income, the parents' level of school attainment, the IQs of pupils, and percents of pupils with language handicaps. The composition of the pupil population relative to these factors will affect the school's standing in relation to the national average in achievement.[6]

When considering the individual child, factors such as health problems, sensory defects, and emotional problems must also be taken into account. To define *reasonable* expectation for an individual ultimately requires a clinical analysis. Very perceptive insight, however, may be obtained from scores in dictated vocabulary, computation, listening comprehension, and the IQ.

Although *reasonable* expectation for a class is not easy to define, standardized tests provide sufficient data for action. The following section illustrates the value of criterion measures in assessing pupil learning and in providing guidelines for determining class potential.

Criterion Measures

The term "criterion" is used here to mean the degree of mastery of learning considered adequate to meet the specific instructional objectives at the level being evaluated. The evaluation may indicate continuing progress or a need for reteaching.

[5] Kenneth D. Hopkins and Glenn H. Bracht, "A Longitudinal Study of Constancy of Reading Performance," in Robert E. Liebert, ed., *Diagnostic Viewpoints in Reading* (Newark, Del.: International Reading Association, 1971), pp. 103–12.

[6] Hogan, op. cit.

The two classes whose results are presented in Table 6.5 participated in an experiment designed to teach teachers to use personal systems of instruction, and to assure pupil growth by criterion testing. Figure 6.2 shows the scheme for a personal system of reading instruction.

FIGURE 6.2

Subsystems for Teaching Reading

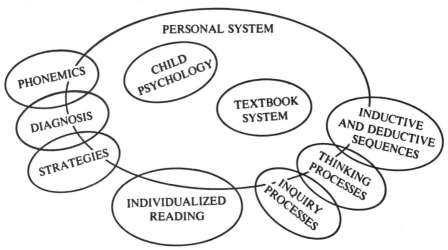

Each teacher was presumed to have had collegiate instruction in child psychology, and each had used her textbook system the previous year. The objective of the experiment was to perfect, at grades 1 through 3, the subsystems for teaching phonics, as well as higher order strategies of word analyses and procedures of individualized reading and diagnosis.

Evaluation was accomplished throughout the project by criterion measures, followed by reteaching where indicated.

Criterion measures, useful from grades 1 through 3, included the following:

1. Naming the letters.
2. Matching words with the same initial consonant sound, the stimulus word being dictated and the pupil's response chosen from three or four printed options.
3. Circling one of three words with minimal phonemic differences (one of the words read by the teacher), such as

rat	sat	cat
bit	bat	bet
may	pay	say
top	tap	tip

4. Circling words with greater differences (one of the words read by the teacher), such as

fed	man	they	help
come	met	fun	want
map	fig	work	said

5. Blending two syllables, and the sounds within one syllable.
6. As a passage is read, occasionally stop for pupils to supply the next word. Similar exercises can be provided in written form, the Cloze-type test.
7. Pupils supply a headline, or main idea, for a passage.
8. Pupils answer questions calling for details from a passage read by them, or to them.
9. Pupils tell what comes next from a passage read by them, or to them.
10. Pupils choose possible implications of a passage.

It should be emphasized that the teachers compiled their own tests. As a result of the test development, the teachers were presumed to have acquired some insight into a set of personal subsystems of instruction appropriate for their respective grades. Such a subsystem of teaching and criterion testing made the teacher independent of any limited system, such as a commercially published phonics system. Discussions and interchanges of practices among the teachers further developed the respective subsystems.

Each teacher developed a system of recording the individual test results. A convenient device is to list the pupil names and provide columns for indicating success or failure, a plus for each success and a zero for each failure (see Figure 6.3).

FIGURE 6.3

Names of Letters

	b	d	p	t	v	z	f	l	m	n	s
Sue	+	+	0	++	0	00					
Tony	0	0	+	++	+	+					
Bob	00	0	+	++	00	00					

The purpose here has been to describe procedures of using test results for improving learning rather than to detail the results of the experiment. The success of the procedure is illustrated, however, by the tabulation in Table 6.5 of results for the two classes. Class A was an experimental class and Class B was a control class of similar initial potential. The two essential differences between the experimental and control treatments were increased criterion testing followed by reteaching and interchange of experiences among a group of teachers from two schools. The pupils were equated on a kindergarten achievement test in October of grade 1. The grade 1 classes of the preceding year, taught by the same teachers, were approximately equal in reading achievement at the end of the year. After the experimental factor was applied, the ability of the two classes, as measured by the dictated vocabulary test in March, was still approximately equal. But observe the difference in reading scores.

TABLE 6.5

Comparison of Two Classes (Grade 1.6)

Class A

	Word Read-ing	Para-graph Read-ing	Dic-tated Vocab-ulary	Spell-ing	Word Study Skills	Arith-metic
+						
4.0						
3.8						
3.6						
3.4						
3.2						
3.0						
2.8			‖			
2.6			‖		‖	‖
2.4	‖		‖		‖	‖
2.2	‖		‖	‖		‖
2.0	‖		‖	‖		‖
1.8	‖		‖		‖	‖
1.6	‖		‖	‖	‖	‖
1.4	‖	‖	‖	‖	‖	‖
1.2	‖	‖		‖	‖	‖
1.0			‖	‖		

Class B

	Word Read-ing	Para-graph Read-ing	Dic-tated Vocab-ulary	Spell-ing	Word Study Skills	Arith-metic	
							+
							4.0
							3.8
							3.6
							3.4
					‖		3.2
					‖		3.0
			‖				2.8
			‖			‖	2.6
‖		‖		‖	‖	2.4
‖	‖	‖	‖	‖	‖	2.2
‖	‖	‖	‖	‖	‖	2.0
‖	‖	‖	‖	‖	‖	1.8
‖	‖	‖	‖	‖	‖	1.6
‖	‖	‖	‖	‖	‖	1.4
	‖		‖	‖	‖	1.2
‖			‖			1.0

Note that Teacher B's pupils, in addition to their standing in vocabulary, are equally good, or better, in mathematics and word study skills; but in word reading, paragraph reading, and spelling they are significantly poorer. A teacher-principal conference may reveal some of the reasons. It is very difficult to pass these differences off casually as normal, or unpreventable, or unrelated to instructional procedures. The children in Class B are somebody's children.

Diagnosis of Instructional Correlates of Poor Reading

Although criterion testing is a limited form of diagnostic testing, the teacher is entitled to the results of better developed tests for diagnosis, tests that have norms for reference. Such diagnostic tests should be provided from those commercially available.

In the early grades, the general achievement test has some diagnostic value. However, it must have subtests that have reliabilities above .85. Suitable subtests are usually designated as tests of word reading, sentence reading, comprehension, and word analysis skills.

DIAGNOSIS OF OTHER CAUSES

Space is too limited to describe a program adequate for diagnosing the causes of poor reading. Ideally, elaborate clinical diagnosis is a multidisciplinary procedure sometimes involving several educational, psychological, and medical specialties. Such services should be critical of pat descriptions, such as nonmotivation, conflict of half learnings, internal refusal by the pupil to learn, and the like, and look first for instructional causes. All pupils should be routinely screened for sensory defects related to reading.

NONTEST INDICATIONS OF ACHIEVEMENT

Anecdotal notes are valuable records for reference. Pupils may assist with their own personal notes. Teacher aides may be helpful in scoring tests and preparing such records. Notes should contain specific and relevant information such as the following:

Tony   Likes animal stories
           Did not like a baseball story
           "That poem wasn't bad."
           Has difficulty syllabicating words for purposes of analysis
Bob   Checks facts in our encyclopedia
           He is our "look it up" boy
           Likes science fiction
           Read three books during Christmas vacation

Have pupils keep lists of books read. Categorize them into mystery stories, poetry, animal stories, science, travel, humor, sports, biography, etc., to encourage diversity in interests. Interest inventories can be helpful in suggesting books for independent reading.

Records of reading activity are helpful in parent conferences. A teacher may show other pupils' reading records (anonymously) in conference with parents. Such information should be used for such purposes as encouraging parent-pupil visits to the public library to read and to secure books.

Note illnesses. Examine health records for evidence of any sensory or other physical problems.

At the high school level, many aspects of "learning to read" can be evaluated by a diagnostic test. Many important qualities of reading, however, are not so easily evaluated.

Mature Reading

Although this chapter deals primarily with the lower level aspects of learning to read, a statement should be made regarding the evaluation of mature reading. Mature reading was defined in the early paragraphs of the chapter as a person's innovative reaction to what is read.

Periodically, pupils should write short summaries of stories, articles, or books. From them the teacher can gain insight into a pupil's level of comprehension, interpretation, and the inferences which come to him. At higher levels of reading ability, the quality of synthesizing and evaluating points of view of various authorities may be assessed by means of a short paper required of the pupil.

Once a pupil has mastered word analysis, achieved a service vocabulary, and is able to differentiate between fact, interpretation, and inference, the printed page, sentence formation, paragraph structure, passage or chapter organization, and basic vocabulary should no longer impede the thinking process. Rather, the process should be improved by such possibilities as re-reading, checking for authenticity, evaluating evidence, and reading contrary opinions.

Accountability and Performance Contracting[7]

Accountability is the concept of holding someone responsible for the results of school instruction. That "someone" could be the principal, the teachers, the

[7] The volume of literature on accountability and performance contracting is increasing rapidly. For a good orientation, see *Phi Delta Kappan*, vol. 52, no. 4 (December 1970), a special issue containing eight articles on accountability.

central administrative staff, the Board of Education, or any combination of these. The aspects of instruction for which someone is held accountable may be the entire curriculum or any part or parts of it.

What constitutes growth in the area of concern must be objectively defined. Currently, the criterion most frequently used is the increase in scores on standardized tests. Various other criteria may be apropos. As evidence of good performance, schools frequently publish data on the performance of their graduates in college or the number of scholarships and honors received.

External auditing of school organization and instructional practice is not new. The school survey, usually conducted by professors of education in graduate schools, dates back a half century. What is relatively new is the performance contract which includes incentive rewards or penalties for superior or inferior performance by the contractor.

A major problem in performance contracts in reading is to measure growth precisely. When the domain to be measured is small, such as learning the letter-sound couplets, or phoneme-grapheme correspondence, such as $\langle ay \rangle \longrightarrow /\bar{a}/$, $\langle c \rangle \longrightarrow /k/$, etc., or the recognition of words taught in the first grade, the measurement task is simple. The measurement of comprehension, on the other hand, is very complex. Reading comprehension involves word meanings, sentence formation, inference, purpose of the author, familiarity with content, and other aspects. Because of the complexity of comprehension, evaluators usually turn to standardized tests. Standardized tests, when used to record a pupil's growth trend over a period of time and when interpreted sagaciously by a teacher, have suitable precision for individual testing.

Performance contracts, however, usually require precise measurement of growth for a period of one year and often for less time. The normal variation in a test score from one time to another produces a situation in which the average gain in reading for an individual may vary by two or three months and yet be very precise for a class group. If contract payments are based upon individual growth, at least two forms of a standardized test should be administered in the pretest and posttest. Care should be taken to select a test that has a sufficient number of items at each pupil's level. Pupils who score at or near the chance level, 25 percent right on a four-option test, have not been adequately measured. Nor can pupils show growth on a test if on the pretest they obtain an almost perfect score.

Conclusion

To recapitulate, measurement assumes an indispensable role in a superior reading program. It provides for essential major comparisons with the achievement of other pupils, other classes, and other schools.

In this chapter, emphasis has been placed upon class analysis charts, diagnostic assessments, and anecdotal records. An experiment has been described to illustrate the use and value of criterion referenced testing. In addition, several specific questions which principals ask are commented upon in Appendix 6.1.

As this chapter is being written, interpretative printouts by textbook publishers are being produced. The use of the computer for assisting teachers in the interpretation of test scores will be developed rapidly.

The school administrator is the key figure in a sound evaluation program, whether he serves as principal, or in the central office of the district. It is his responsibility to devise ways in which teachers can make extensive and sound use of tests.

Appendix 6.1

QUESTIONS ASKED BY ADMINISTRATORS

What do I tell parents about their child's progress?

Parents have a right to know how well their children are learning. A collection of criterion tests can be used to show growth. A good way to inform parents of test results is to report a stanine in a plus 1 and minus 1 band. If the test score is stanine 3, report "probably in stanine 2 to 4."

When during the year should reading be tested?

Educators disagree. Pupils reach a peak in achievement in spring. Teachers prefer spring scores because it indicates how well they have done during the year. For individual diagnostic purposes, fall testing is best. The time lapse between testing and score returns is important. There is little use in testing in the fall if results are not available until February or March.

How soon are commercially scored test results returned?

Two or three major scoring services guarantee a return in three weeks. Testing done in March can then provide useful information for instruction in April and May.

Should teachers score their own tests?

Teachers usually score criterion tests and often standardized tests. Scoring of long tests is a heavy burden. Commercial scoring and use of teacher aides should be explored and is recommended.

What about culture fairness?

"Culture fairness" relates primarily to IQ tests. All reading tests are unfair to children having language handicaps unless the purpose of the test is to ascertain the degree of the handicap. The content of most achievement tests is fair from the standpoint of the school curriculum. Tests should not contain items which "turn off" minority groups, and should contain some items which create rapport. Also, it is very possible that a pupil who speaks and thinks in a dialect may need more time than the normal time limits to render a passage in standard English into the language of his thought.[8]

What can I do to encourage teachers to use the results of the tests they give?

[8] Eric Brown, "The Bases of Reading Acquisition," *Reading Research Quarterly,* vol. 2, no. 4 (Summer 1976), pp. 5–142.

Furnish and encourage the use of a class analysis chart. Have personal conferences with each teacher. Use the chart. Ask questions. Avoid implications of teacher inadequacy; let the record speak. Emphasize helping pupils through the use of tests.

What is the usefulness of item statistics?

It is seldom worthwhile to find the percent of pupils who mark a reading comprehension item correct unless it is used for comparison with the results of the national population. It is more useful to analyze items in word-analysis tests and in word reading. Obviously, formative tests should be analyzed item-by-item.

How can we improve evaluation?

Grow together with your staff. The teaching of reading is complex. Analyze the tests for the school as a whole with the teachers of a single grade.

Should test scores be posted?

No, and class averages should not be circulated among the teachers. Preserve every teacher's self-respect.

Is a nonverbal IQ a good basis for expectancy in reading achievement?

Generally not. If it is lower than the verbal score, it is of no value. If considerably higher, it may show a special ability which needs cultivation, but it still is of doubtful value as a determiner of potential. Reading, after all, is verbal.

Who is a retarded reader?

On the national level, eleven percent of the pupils place in the first and second stanines; these are the retarded readers in the absolute sense. Such pupils generally read two grades, or more, below their peers in age by the time they reach grade 6. Relative to his capability an equally serious case of retardation is the pupil who reads at stanine 5 or below, and is at stanine 7 to 9 in vocabulary, mathematics, and I.Q. He is an average reader, but he could well be two years advanced. Rightful expectancy is a complex concept, so don't overlook the improvement of pupil potential through a better set of circumstances.

Is speed of reading significant?

As an indication of word analysis facility, the answer is yes. Laborious decoding in the higher grades indicates weakness in phoneme-grapheme (sound-symbol) associations, or in blending. Slowness in the middle grades may indicate a continuing necessity for breaking words into smaller units. At the higher levels, slowness may indicate word-by-word reading. On the other hand, some poor and average readers read too rapidly with inadequate attention to context.

How is phonics related to reading?

Phonics and comprehension correlate approximately .70 in grades 2, 3, and 4. This is a significantly high correlation, but a very considerable portion of the comprehension score is unaccounted for by phonics. In other words, there are important strategies other than phonics involved in comprehension.

Is spelling related to reading?

All language arts are quite highly interrelated. Spelling correlates approximately .70 to .75 with reading comprehension in the early grades, and .60 to .65 at the junior high school level. The notion that good readers generally are poor spellers is erroneous.

Can teacher aides score tests?

With proper training, they can score tests as well or better than teachers do.

Can a teacher be judged by her test results?

While the objective test scores of successive classes taught by a given teacher may add something to a principal's total judgment, test scores can be very unfair when used as the sole basis for evaluation. Many factors affect reading achievement.

How are socio-economic factors related to reading?

Census data show the following approximate correlations between socio-economic factors and scores in paragraph comprehension:[9]

Income of family	.45 to .50
Education level reached by adults	approx. .55
Adequacy of the dwelling	approx. .40

Factors of nonschool input may affect reading achievement more than does teacher competency.

BIBLIOGRAPHY

Anastasi, Anne, ed., *Testing Problems in Perspective* (Washington, D.C., American Council on Education, 1966).

Bloom, Benjamin, ed., *Taxonomy of Educational Objectives* (New York: Longmans, Green & Co., 1956).

Benjamin J. Bloom, Thomas Hastings, and George F. Madaus, *Handbook on Formative and Summative Evaluation of Learning* (New York: McGraw-Hill, 1971), p. 117.

Bond, Guy L., and Robert Dykstra, "The Cooperative Research Program in First-Grade Reading Instruction," *Reading Research Quarterly,* vol. 2, no. 4 (Summer 1967), pp. 5–142.

Brown, Eric, "The Bases of Reading Acquisition," *Reading Research Quarterly,* vol. 6, no. 1 (Fall 1970), pp. 49–74.

De Boer, Dorothy L., ed., *Reading Diagnosis and Evaluation* (Newark, Del.: International Reading Association, 1970).

Durrell, Donald D., and Mary T. Hayes, *Durrell Listening-Reading Series* (New York: Harcourt Brace Jovanovich, 1969), Manual, Primary Level, Form DE, p. 16.

Durost, Walter N., "Accountability: The Task, the Tools, and the Pitfalls," *Reading Teacher,* vol. 24, no. 4 (January 1971), pp. 291–304.

Durost, Walter N., *Manual for Interpreting Metropolitan Achievement Tests* (New York: Harcourt Brace Jovanovich, 1962), pp. 14–19, 48–61.

Farr, Roger, and Nicholas Anastasion, *Tests of Reading Achievement: A Review and Evaluation* (Newark, Del.: International Reading Association, 1969).

Farr, Roger, and V.L. Brown, "Evaluation and Decision Making," *Reading Teacher,* vol. 24, no. 4 (January 1971), pp. 341–46.

Goodman, K.S., "Promises, Promises," *Reading Teacher,* vol. 24, no. 4 (January 1971), pp. 365–67.

Hanson, Earl, and H. Alan Robinson, "Reading Readiness and Achievement of

[9] Hogan, op. cit.

Primary Grade Children of Different Socio-Economic Strata," *Reading Teacher,* vol. 21, no. 1 (October 1967), pp. 52–56.

Hogan, Thomas P., *Stanford Achievement Test: A Supplementary Report on the Norm Group* (New York: Harcourt Brace Jovanovich, 1970).

Hopkins, Kenneth D., and Glenn H. Bracht, "A Longitudinal Study of Constancy of Reading Performance," in Robert E. Liebert, ed., *Diagnostic Viewpoints in Reading* (Newark, Del.: International Reading Association, 1971), pp. 103–12.

Kender, Joseph P., "How Useful Are Informal Reading Tests?" *Journal of Reading,* vol. II, no. 5 (February 1968), pp. 337–42.

Morris, Joyce M., *Standards and Progress in Reading* (London: National Foundation for Educational Research in England and Wales, 1966). Reviewed by Donald E.P. Smith in Amer. Ed. Res. Jr., vol. 4, no. 4 (November 1967), pp. 401–3.

Phi Delta Kappan, special issue, "8 Articles on Accountability," vol. 52, no. 4 (December 1970).

Wildavsky, Aaron, "A Program of Accountability for Elementary Schools," *Phi Delta Kappan,* vol. 52, no. 4 (December 1970), pp. 212–16.

7

The Role of Libraries, Media Centers, and Technology in the Reading Program

Margaret Chisholm

Introduction

The fundamental premise of this chapter is that reading students must have access to a great diversity of materials in order to foster their love of reading, to stimulate their interest, to broaden their horizons, to meet individual reading abilities, and to fulfill their informational and recreational needs. This program of support can be provided most effectively through an organized library or media center service. A school library or media center program is indispensable to an exemplary reading program.

To develop a comprehensive and contemporary perspective on the relationship to reading programs of libraries, media centers, and technology, one must consider these basic factors; the teacher, the student, the materials, the equipment, and the process. Finally, one must analyze the interaction of these components.

To assess the relationship between the reading program and the support programs (found in libraries and media centers, and the latest technological developments), it is necessary to be cognizant of the levels of sophistication found in both programs. For example, it is possible to have effective utilization of reading materials by students in a very unsophisticated organizational arrangement such as a classroom collection of materials. At the other end of the continuum, students may be developing reading skills through technology in a sophisticated individualized program of computer-assisted instruction.

One approach to the assessment of the relationship between media and technology and reading is to consider various levels of support in a hierarchical structure, noting that certain schools and certain school districts have greater success than others in their utilization of materials and equipment in relation to their reading programs.

Teachers of reading, supervisors of reading programs, librarians, media center directors, and administrators are encouraged to work cooperatively in analyzing their school's present status with respect to the support of the reading program and then to develop short-range and long-range objectives in moving toward more adequate levels of support.

For purposes of assessment and analysis, to identify advantages and disadvantages, and to determine strengths and weaknesses, these objectives might be expressed as the following levels of development: classroom collections of materials; centralized traditional libraries; media centers including Reading Resource Centers; computer-based instruction; total instructional systems based on technology.

Levels of Support

It is important to note that each of the above programs is able to make some contribution to the reading program, although, the more sophisticated the level of support, the greater the probability that the support will be appropriate and significant. Varying levels of support will require varying degrees of financial and personnel allocations.

CLASSROOM COLLECTIONS OF MATERIALS

The development of classroom collections of materials is the level at which most schools are able to begin a program which supports reading instruction. Authorities in reading agree that for the adequate teaching of reading it is essential to provide materials to meet the individual needs, interests, and abilities of each student. It is impossible to have a program of individualized reading without the provision of a broad diversity of materials. Stauffer states "No longer can reading competency be acquired in a single book, or in a series of books that at best represent an extremely low-level abridgement of a library."[1]

The major advantage of a classroom collection is accessibility. Empirical evidence demonstrates that the more accessible the materials the greater the utilization by students. Although this statement is reasonable and logical, many schools still have not implemented this basic level of support for the reading program.

If there is no centralized school library with a trained librarian to provide guidance and assistance in the selection of materials, the classroom teacher should be encouraged to use recognized selection tools compiled by authorities to provide guidelines for the purchase of materials. The publications in

---

[1] Russel G. Stauffer. "A Reading Teacher's Dream Come True," *Wilson Library Bulletin* (November, 1970), vol. 45, no. 3, p. 285.

Appendix 7.1 would provide information that would assist classroom teachers in acquiring classroom collections of appropriate books and materials of outstanding quality.

One major disadvantage of a classroom collection is that it is not feasible to provide a collection of books and materials for each classroom which will adequately meet the diversity of interests and abilities of the students within that classroom. Usually classroom collections are very limited in size, and, therefore, correspondingly limited in usefulness.

One means of capitalizing on the factor of accessibility is to house in each classroom a limited number of books from the centralized library collection. The continuous exchange of collections would allow each classroom the advantage of having books immediately accessible and also provide the diversity of a much more extensive collection.

A CENTRALIZED LIBRARY

A fine library and an outstanding reading program are so mutually involved in achieving identical goals with respect to student objectives that it is inconceivable to consider one without the other. A school library provides both the means and the end for a reading program. The library provides a variety of books to stimulate the desire to read and, at the same time, it is the embodiment of the *raison d'etre* of the reading program. The library contains both the motivational materials to use in developing skills in reading and the informational and the recreational sources that make the acquired reading skills worthwhile.

The centralized school library offers many advantages over a classroom collection. It contains a far greater number of books and, therefore, is better equipped to meet individual needs, interests and abilities.

A trained librarian must be considered a vital member of the team responsible for teaching a child to read and to improve his reading skills. A librarian can provide motivation and reading guidance and assist in teaching location and reference skills.

As a team, the reading teacher and the librarian must work cooperatively. The reading teacher has the responsibility for keeping the librarian informed of the reading level and the reading problems of the students, while the librarian can supply the reading teacher with information about the student's reading interests, books read, problems encountered, and special skills demonstrated.

An additional advantage of a centralized library is that the materials are arranged in an organized fashion. Students have the opportunity to learn location skills which they will be able to transfer to all school, university, and public libraries which they may use in the future.

The diversity of books in a school library enables the student to practice using reference tools, to read for information, to read for enjoyment, to read for aesthetic appreciation, to read for counseling and insight in solving problems, to read for vocational guidance, and even to read for escape from everyday pressures.

A comfortable, colorful, inviting library helps to provide an atmosphere of relaxation and enjoyment conducive to reading. Here, a student may observe his peers and teachers reading for information and pleasure. Undoubtedly, this can play a vital role in stimulating his desire to read.

It is also important that the student and parent take advantage of the public library. Both the reading teacher and the school librarian should make every attempt to encourage parents to take their children to public libraries for the story hours, book talks, films, puppet shows, summer reading programs, and other activities, and, most importantly, for the selection of books. These books can be chosen for independent reading, or for parents to read aloud to their children. Authorities agree that reading aloud to a child is a vitally important factor in developing a readiness for reading and a desire to read. As soon as children are able to visit the public libraries by themselves they should be encouraged to do so. A parent's enthusiasm for books and his participation in visits to libraries and in reading have immeasurable influence on the reading habits of the child.

MEDIA CENTERS AND READING RESOURCE CENTERS

Probably the finest level of support for reading programs that is within reach of most schools at the present time is a comprehensive media center in every school with additional support at the district level. In the *Standards for School Media Programs* a media center is defined as "a learning center in a school where a full range of print and audiovisual media, necessary equipment, and services from media specialists are accessible to students and teachers."[2]

The major advantage of a media center over a traditional library is that a media center makes every kind of print and nonprint material available to students. Print materials include books, magazines, newspapers, pamphlets, clippings, maps, posters, charts, and graphs. Nonprint materials would include filmstrips, 8 mm. films, 16 mm. films, tape and disc recordings, art prints, study prints, globes, microform materials, realia, models, games, kits, art objects, video-tape recordings, programmed instructional materials and resource files.

A media center furnishes a reading teacher with a wealth of resources which can provide motivation and enhance learning opportunities for reading students at all levels. The following are examples of activities in which nonprint materials might be used:

Show films and filmstrips to reading classes or have students view them independently to assist in developing concepts about which they are reading.

Provide phonograph records for story hours to help children develop a

    [2] American Library Association and National Education Association, *Standards for School Media Programs* (Chicago: American Library Association, 1969), p. xv.

background of folk tales, myths, and legends as well as stimulate reading interest.

Provide audio-tapes of books so that students can follow the printed words and listen to the spoken words simultaneously.

Use magazines and newspapers in reading classes to keep students up to date on current events.

Use charts and graphs in reading classes to teach students styles of reading necessary to interpret special forms of information.

Use art prints and study prints for assisting students to be ready to read.

Use 8 mm. films and film clips to stimulate students to write their own narratives to be used as stories to be read by themselves and other students. In some schools, elementary students are filming their own movies for these purposes.

Make audio-tapes of children's oral reading so they can hear themselves as they read aloud.

Record a variety of exercises on audio-tapes to be presented to individual children through head phones. These exercises could be in listening comprehension, dictation, auditory discrimination, and following directions. Children who have problems with articulation can record their voices on tape and have immediate feedback.

Check out cassettes and tape cartridges with books, so that students can take them home to hear the words on tape and see the words in the book. This is an excellent means of involving parents in the learning-to-read process.

Acquire and utilize the numerous filmstrips, films, tapes, and records which have been made from outstanding books for children. The use of these materials can stimulate children's interests in reading the books.

Use teaching machines with appropriate programmed materials to develop basic skills of structural analysis, context clues, and dictionary and study skills.

If students and teachers are creative, endless numbers of other stimulating activities can be developed.

Cooperative planning between the reading teacher and the library media center director is essential in planning these activities, preparing the materials and making the materials and equipment readily available to the students. These activities could take place in the classroom or in the media center.

READING RESOURCE CENTERS

There are many possible organizational arrangements, in addition to those normally used in all programs, by which to incorporate all of the equipment and machines used specifically to support the teaching of reading. One such arrangement, which can be utilized with maximum effectiveness, is a reading resource center in which all equipment and special materials particularly related to reading are housed. This is often a special room located adjacent to the reading classrooms. Usually, the most feasible plan is to have this facility function under the administrative responsibility of the media center. The rationale for this arrangement is that the materials can be organized in a plan that is coordinated with the central collection of materials. For example, if the books in the central collection are classified by the Dewey Decimal Classification system, it would be logical to have the materials in the reading resource center classified in the same manner. This would permit the records of the holdings of the reading resource center to be interfiled with the main card catalog of the media center with an indication of their location. Students could then readily locate all materials, even though they are housed in the reading resource center rather than in the main collection. This correlated plan also permits materials to be exchanged with the main collection for more efficient use of shelving space, according to specific student needs in the reading resource center.

Another justification of this organizational pattern is that acquisition of materials and equipment can be more economical if it is done on a large scale, incorporated with other purchases, rather than by each resource center independently. This organizational plan is often used for establishing resource centers for subject areas such as English, social studies, math, and science. Less common are resource centers for home economics, industrial arts, and foreign languages. For most efficient operation, resource centers should be under the administration of one director with special personnel to staff each center.

The most effective staffing pattern for a reading resource center would be a full-time staff member in charge of and located in the reading center. To be of greatest service to the students and faculty, this person should have educational background and experience in the field of reading.

The value of the reading resource center is that all of the equipment and materials which the student needs to use are in one place and are readily obtainable. Normally, this center would be located close to the reading classrooms to provide maximum accessibility of materials at all times. The person or persons staffing the center would be available to give personal assistance to each student. In addition, in junior and senior high schools, the reading center normally would be located close to the offices of reading teachers, so that students could readily contact them for assistance.

The most obvious disadvantage of a reading resource center is its cost. Not all school districts will give priority to the development of such a reading resource center equipped and staffed to provide optimum service.

The following is a list of some of the equipment one might expect to find in a reading center.

16 mm. sound film projectors
8 mm. projectors
2 × 2 slide projectors
filmstrip projectors

overhead projectors
opaque projectors
individual filmstrip viewers
record players
audio-tape recorders
8 mm. cameras

In addition, the following devices are needed for the teaching of reading skills including speed and comprehension: Card source audiovisual equipment, tachistoscopes and pacing devices. (See Appendix 7.2 for a list of manufacturers.)

Card Source Audiovisual Devices can be used for prereading exercises in associating sounds, words and images, and for teaching reading skills. To activate this type of device, the students use cards, similar in size and shape to a computer punch card. Each card contains a sound track, a strip of magnetic tape which the machine plays back over a speaker or head set. The card also contains a drawing or picture to illustrate the sound, word, or phrase. Half of the sound track is available for the student's response and comparison. The machine can also record sound tracks on blank cards. Devices of this type are the Bell and Howell Language Master and Electronic Future's Audio Flash-card System. Both companies have produced prepared lesson series in prereading and reading drills and also furnish blank cards on which teachers may prepare their own materials to accommodate special needs of the students.

Tachistoscopes are machines designed for the purpose of increasing a student's reading speed and improving his retention rate. Words, letters, numbers, symbols, phrases or sentences are presented to the student for a brief period of time. These speeds of presentation range from 1½ seconds to 1/1000 of a second. Although conclusive evidence has not yet been presented, it is believed that speed of reading and retention rate can be increased by gradually increasing the segments of information presented, or by reducing the presentation time, or by a combination of both.

Tachistoscopes use several methods for quick presentation. For machines using projection techniques, a shutter method similar to the shutter and lens on a camera is used. Another method used is that in which light falls on a target (a page or a card) for the desired interval.

One machine developed for individual use uses a design in which a film is projected on the small screen of a desk-top unit. In some models the entire slide is projected briefly, in others a word or line of print is picked out and displayed briefly. For group work, tachistoscope adaptors can be purchased to fit over the lens system of slide or filmstrip projectors. Such adaptors are usually activated by a shutter release.

Reading Pacers can also be nonprojecting and include many varieties of design. To indicate pace, some models use a light beam, beads of light, or mechanical rods with which speeds can be varied from 10 to 2500 words per minute. Controlled reading devices for group use usually project single lines of film using filmstrips with automatic built-in filmstrip advance mechanisms and have speed ranges from 0 to 1000 words per minute.

There must be careful assessment before decisions are made to purchase these kinds of equipment. These devices can serve many useful purposes but should not be purchased in any large number until the schools have a rich supply of books and other resource materials.

These pieces of equipment serve primarily as motivational or supplementary devices and must not be considered as first purchases. "Software" is of more vital importance than "hardware." It would be more desirable to purchase a small number of each model rather than concentrate on any one model. This plan provides variety in approach and utilization which is in itself a motivational factor with students.

Answers to the following questions would help to ensure the selection of the most appropriate equipment:

> Is the equipment to be used by individual students or by groups?
> What materials or programs can be purchased to use with the equipment?
> Are these materials appropriate for student needs?
> Does the machine lend itself to the use of teacher-designed materials to meet special student needs?
> Is the machine simple enough for children to operate independently?
> Can the machine be used as a pacer and as a tachistoscope, if both purposes are required?
> Is the machine sturdy and dependable?
> Are new parts and repair services readily available?
> Have teachers been surveyed as to their needs and recommendations?
> Has provision been made for training of teachers and students in the use of equipment?

In his book *Teach Them All To Read,* Cohen[3] presents practical and perceptive assessments of specific types of equipment and recommendations for use, particularly for use with the disadvantaged or retarded reader.

In addition to the equipment to be housed in a reading center or laboratory, it would be desirable to have tremendous variety of materials to teach all aspects of reading. Included would be prereading materials, perceptual training materials, materials for beginning readers, materials for developing vocabulary and for spelling and word-attack skills, materials for developing comprehension, and materials to develop work and study skills. Among the devices included might be tracing boards, templates, balance boards, walking rails, eye-hand coordination kits, spatial-pattern boards, workbooks containing ac-

---

[3] S. Alan Cohen, *Teach Them All to Read: Theory Methods and Materials for Teaching the Disadvantaged* (New York: Random House, 1970), p. 316.

tivities in shape identification, picture portfolios and photograph albums to be used for concept development, letter form boards, programmed reading books, workbooks, handbooks of activities, special reading series, word lists, workbooks in phonics and spelling, word games such as "Word Lotto," "Phonics Fish," "Scrabble" and "Scrabble Jr.," word wheels, flash cards, spelling wheels, word analysis cards, kits of reading materials containing reading cards, pamphlets and paperback books, units made up of exercises, quizzes, writing assignments and reading guides, basal and special reading series, and materials of high interest, low vocabulary in many subject fields. These materials would not duplicate those housed in the media center, but the entire collection would give support to all facets of the teaching of reading.

Reading resource centers can also make effective use of the many forms of programmed instruction which have been developed. These vary from book form to highly complex computer-based programmed instruction. Interesting combinations of audio-tapes with books, workbooks, or work sheets have been developed. Still other programs are being developed which combine the visual and auditory presentation of words with workbooks or work sheets. These programmed materials permit students to work at their own speed to satisfy individual needs.

The total reading resource center can be adapted to be a smaller or more limited version, usually called a skills center or station. A skills center can be set up in a classroom in the form of stations to be utilized by single or small groups of students. Each station can focus on the teaching or improvement of some specific skill, usually utilizing simple combinations of materials and equipment which students use independently. Students can be scheduled to use a specific skills center, or they can be allowed free choice at any time they are not working with a teacher.

Daniels summarized the values of skills centers as follows: ". . . learning stations for reading skills are helpful as they allow a teacher to teach those things for which she is essential. Secondly, they offer her help in classroom management. Thirdly, they provide independent learnings that do not require a teacher. Fourthly, they foster individual learning."[4]

Organizationally, these skills centers could be set up and operated under the direction of the classroom teacher, the special reading teacher, or by the staff of the media center. If the media center accepts this responsibility there would be the opportunity for the utilization of a much greater variety of materials and equipment than normally found in a classroom.

Criteria for selection of materials to be used in the reading resource center or reading skills center differ in many respects from criteria used to evaluate books and materials purchased for the media center. The materials purchased for the reading resource center must meet specific objectives as teaching materials.

[4] Paul R. Daniels, "Learning Centers and Stations: A Different Concept," *Audio-Visual Instruction*, vol. 15, no. 9 (November 1970), p. 29.

The most effective way to select materials for use in a reading resource center is to base the decision for purchase on the findings of pilot projects, demonstrations, clinics, or summer experimental programs. Recommendations of teachers and supervisors who have had personal experience with the materials are invaluable in applying the criteria for selection. First, can the materials be used effectively to accomplish the teaching-learning objectives? Second, are the materials easy to handle, and can students use them independently or with a minimum of instruction? Third, is the degree of difficulty of the materials appropriate to the needs of the students? Fourth, can the materials be readily adapted? Fifth, will the materials contribute to the overall effectiveness of the reading program, and to the specific needs of individual students? Sixth, will the materials assist in moving toward individualized instruction? Seventh, is the format attractive and sturdy enough to be a worthwhile investment?

COMPUTER-BASED INSTRUCTION

The use of the computer for teaching reading appears to have vast potential, which is only partially substantiated by research at present. Currently, of course, the cost is prohibitive for many schools, but cost-sharing plans are being considered by many schools. Experimental programs claim impressive results and several universities have beginning reading programs as their major emphasis in computer-based programs, for example, the projects at Stanford with Patrick Suppes and Richard C. Atkinson, at the University of Pittsburgh directed by Robert Glaser, and the project at Harvard directed by Larry Stoluron. The Stanford program in east Palo Alto, California, has generated much interest. The children work in one of the 16 computer terminals, and all 16 may be working simultaneously, but on different materials and at different rates. The student can respond in three ways—on the picture screen with a light-projection pen, on the typewriter or orally. Computer programs can be used to good advantage in teaching word recognition, phonics elements, prefixes and suffixes, generalizations concerning phonics, syllabication, and comprehension of literal meaning.

A special adaptation of the computer has been made by Omar Khayyam Moore with a device he developed in 1962 called the talking typewriter. This device resembles an ordinary typewriter with a large keyboard. Both verbal and visual presentations are possible through a screen and microphone above the typewriter. Coordinated verbal and visual directions are given to the student to locate letters or to spell simple words on the typewriter. For example, if the word "cat" appears on the screen and is sounded by the speaker, the child can depress only the correct letters in order, as the typewriter keys are color coded and lock in such a manner that only the correct keys can be activated by the student. The manufacturer describes this device as a multisensory (sight, sound, tactile) multimedia, fully synchronized, computer-based learning system, for teaching the language arts (reading, writing, spelling, and speech).

Currently research is being conducted in which the talking typewriter is being used in an effort to discriminate between an analytic and a synthetic approach to easy word recognition. Instead of producing a single letter when a key is depressed, the typewriter will respond with an entire word.[5] In experimental programs, three and four year olds have used the talking typewriters in learning to read, and several public schools have programs using the device with nursery school children and remedial students. Teachers report substantial gains made by remedial students, but there has been much debate about the values of the talking typewriter. Unfortunately, there is no definitive research on its efficiency.

When using programmed materials in computer-assisted instruction, it is possible to tabulate the errors of the student, select corrective steps, and reinstruct the student. Spache[6] points out that because of these capabilities, programmed instruction could be used advantageously in teaching such skills as word recognition.

Fry[7] has made a comparative assessment of programmed instruction and automation in teaching beginning reading and concludes that there is ample evidence that programmed instruction, computer-assisted instruction, and talking typewriters can teach beginning reading. However, as yet there is no conclusive evidence that technology can teach beginning reading any better than regular classroom teaching or human tutoring. Fry does recommend that the classroom teacher be encouraged to use programmed instruction or automated procedures which allow students to work individually and without constant teacher supervision and therefore free the teacher to give other students the personal attention they need.

Smith[8] states that the value of the computer for teaching interpretation and critical reading is questionable. Socratic dialogue and mental interaction of human beings are necessary in teaching deeper meaning in reading. Smith summarizes her conclusions by stating that a skillful teacher will always be needed to stimulate and guide the thinking processes in reading.

Knezevich[9] predicts that computer-assisted tutorial systems, particularly in the well-structured subjects such as reading and mathematics, will eventually carry the main load of teaching those subjects. The teacher's responsibility will be to help students who are not proceeding properly or progressing successfully.

[5] Donald Ross Green and Richard L. Henderson, *A Comparison of Two Approaches to Initial Reading Instruction Using Computer-Assisted Instruction* (Atlanta: Division of Teaching Education, Emory University, 1966).

[6] George D. Spache, "Reading Technology," paper presented at the International Reading Association Annual Convention (Seattle, Wash.: May 4–5, 1967), p. 2.

[7] Edward Fry, "Programmed Instruction," paper presented at the International Reading Association Annual Convention. (Seattle, Wash.: May 4–5, 1967), p. 20.

[8] Nila Banton Smith, "Reading and Technology in the Seventies," *Audiovisual Instruction,* vol. 15, no. 9 (November 1970), p. 23.

[9] Stephen J. Knezevich, *Instructional Technology and the School Administrator* (Washington, D.C.: American Association of School Administrators, 1970), p. 133.

TOTAL INSTRUCTIONAL SYSTEMS BASED ON TECHNOLOGY

In the analysis of the hierarchical levels of support of the reading program, this level of total instructional systems based on technology is undoubtedly the most sophisticated and the most demanding in financial and staff requirements.

Educational technology has been defined as "a systematic way of designing, carrying out, and evaluating the total process of learning and teaching in terms of specific objectives, based on findings from research in human learning and communication, and employing a combination of human and nonhuman resources to bring about more effective instruction."[10]

Educational technology involves more than electronic and mechanical equipment; it includes the teacher, the methods, the materials, and the facilities which must be integrated in order to achieve the teaching-learning objectives.

The proposal of utilizing a total instructional system for the teaching of reading presents a vision of potential achievement that is overwhelming in its implications. A total instructional system would require research, design of curriculum, production of appropriate equipment and materials, evaluation of methodology, supply of materials, the training of special teachers and the evolvement of appropriate techniques. Theoretically, this approach could radically transform the character of instruction and revolutionize its effectiveness.

Knezevich, in *Instructional Technology and the School Administrator* delineates the technological potentials for instruction.

> Technology can contribute many things to the instructional process.   . .
>
> Technology may force reexamination of goals. This reexamination can at the same time refocus attention on the processes of goal attainment and the evidence of goal realization. . . .
>
> Technology may automate learning with development of a more orderly sequence for the elements of work. It may help teachers diagnose learning difficulties more quickly. . . . Machines are far more patient in presenting concepts over and over again to the slow learner than are teachers.
>
> Technology may do certain things which are not possible in any other way. Technology may provide for self-instruction. . . .
>
> Technology may strengthen research by enabling researchers to perform a whole series of computations that could be done no other way.
>
> Technology may help in the management of instructional detail. This includes facilitating testing and measurement of pupil progress. Some devices provide almost immediate feedback on the amount learned.

[10] "To Improve Learning: A Report to the President and Congress of the United States by the Commission on Instructional Technology" (Washington, D.C.: August, 1969).

Technology may have an impact on educational counseling.

The limitations of technology are that it cannot determine values or goals nor define purposes. It cannot overcome bad utilization of its potential. Its effectiveness rests on the adequacy of human and fiscal resources.[11]

It may be another decade before a definitive statement can be made on how technology will affect education, but, on the basis of initial studies, experts in the field are predicting that application of technology to the field of education is the only reasonable solution to the problems which education currently faces.

The application of educational technology to the teaching of reading will be greatly dependent on the competent leadership provided by school administrators and authorities in the field of reading. Educational technology has unprecedented potential for changing the reading programs of the future as well as the total educational system and visionary educators must consider it a potent force.

General Comments on Related Aspects

Among the major concerns of reading teachers and administrators should be the planning of facilities to house such support services as media centers, reading resource centers, and individual skills centers. Consideration should be given to the following basic principles.

Media centers and reading resource centers should be located where they are most readily accessible to students.

The space should be planned to allow for maximum flexibility, so that facilities could be rearranged as curriculum needs change and as the programs and collections expand.

Space needs to be provided for students, or students and teachers to work together in groups.

Media centers and reading resource centers should be designed to accommodate a multiplicity of activities.

The media center and reading resource center must have sufficient electrical outlets for maximum utilization of equipment.

The facilities should have adequate acoustical control.

The facilities should be attractive, colorful, comfortable, and inviting.

For help in planning specific details, one of the most helpful recent publications is published by Educational Facilities Laboratories entitled *Instructional*

[11] Knezevich, Op. cit., pp. 27, 28.

Hardware/A Guide to Architectural Requirements. It provides explicit information on various electronic teaching systems including space requirements, costs, and installation and operation information for audio equipment, visual display equipment, television-based teaching systems, computer-assisted instruction, and student response systems. Also included are a glossary and a list of major manufacturers of electronic teaching equipment.[12]

The following organizations provide additional assistance in planning facilities, guidelines for installation of electronic equipment, and guidance in evaluating materials and equipment.

> American Association of School Librarians
> American Library Association
> 50 E. Huron Street
> Chicago, Ill. 60611

> Association for Educational Communication and Technology
> 1201 Sixteenth Street, N.W.
> Washington, D.C. 20036

Many administrators assume, erroneously, that if equipment is purchased it will automatically be used effectively. It is necessary to provide pre-service and in-service training for teachers who are expected to use new teaching equipment or new teaching methods. In order to interact effectively with students, teachers must be given time to become familiar with new techniques and they must feel comfortable and self-confident in using them. The human factor is still the most vital element in successful teaching.

Although there has been impressive and extensive research in the teaching of reading and also in the area of educational technology,[13] comprehensive research has not been done in the utilization of audiovisual materials and instruments and auto-instructional devices in the teaching of reading.

In their discussion of emerging problems in research on teaching reading Russell and Fea state:

> Research on teaching reading . . . has a certain dynamic character which suggests that new ideas are being tested continuously. As in other curricular areas, much of the frontier activity occurs in the classrooms of capable, creative teachers, and the try-outs of novel procedures must be labeled "operational" or "action" research rather than rigorous experimentation. Such try-outs of new ideas, in turn, may stem from advances outside the classroom, such as improved technology of audiovisual teaching devices. Detailed, definitive research on these and other devices and methods nec-

---

[12] Educational Facilities Laboratories, *Instructional Hardware/A Guide to Architectural Requirements* (New York: Educational Facilities Laboratories, Inc., 1970).

[13] A. A. Lumsdaine, "Instruments and Media of Instruction" and David H. Russell and Henry R. Fea, "Research on Teaching Reading" in N. L. Gage, ed., *Handbook of Research in Teaching* (Chicago: Rand McNally and Co., 1963), pp. 583–682, pp. 865–928. Reviews of current research related to each field can be found in professional journals such as *Reading Teacher* and *Audio-Visual Communication Review*.

essarily lags behind initial utilization, but many new problems recon-
sidered, face the teacher and research worker in reading instruction
today.[14]

Expanding technology offers a challenge to the creative, innovative classroom teacher to develop more dynamic and effective ways to teach reading.
There is an even greater challenge to the researcher to engage in imaginative
and definitive research which will give direction to future developments in the
teaching of reading.

Conclusion

To be effective, a reading program must be supported by appropriate materials
and equipment. Administrators and personnel involved in the development of
reading programs are responsible for assessing the level of support which their
instructional system now provides for the reading program through libraries,
media centers, and reading resource centers) and they must work toward increasing the quality and effectiveness of the support.

The hierarchical levels of support range from classroom collections of
materials, which require a minimum of fiscal support but have limited usefulness, to the comprehensive media centers providing a full range of print and
nonprint materials with equipment for its utilization, to, finally, the total instructional system provided by educational technology.

Inevitably, the effectiveness of the support of the reading program is dependent upon the allocation and efficient utilization of fiscal and human resources.
But for a reading program to have optimum effectiveness, optimum support
services must be provided.

Appendix 7.1

ELEMENTARY LEVEL

Adventuring with Books: A Book List for Elementary Schools, Elizabeth Guilfoile
and Jeannette Veatch, eds. A classified bibliography of over 1250 titles, 256
pp., rev. ed., 1966. Natl. Council of Teachers of English, 508 S. Sixth St.,
Champaign, Ill. 61820   75¢.
A Basic Book Collection for Elementary Grades, by Miriam Snow Mathes et al.
eds. An annotated bibliography of about 1000 books and magazines for grades
K–8, arranged by Dewey Decimal Classification with author, title and subject

[14] David H. Russell and Henry R. Fea, "Research in Teaching Reading" in N. L. Gage,
ed., *Handbook of Research in Teaching* (Chicago: Rand McNally and Co., 1963), p.
915.

index, 144 pp., 3rd ed., 1960. Amer. Library Assn., 50 E. Huron St., Chicago, Ill. 60611 $2.

Books for Children. 1960–1965, ALA Committee ed. A compilation of 3086 books with detailed annotations, recommended in *The Booklist* and arranged according to a modified Dewey Decimal Classification with subject, author and short title index, 447 pp., 1966. Amer. Library Assn., 50 E. Huron St., Chicago, Ill. 60611 $10.

Books for Children 1965–1966, 128 pp., $2.

Books for Children 1966–1967, 136 pp., $2.25.

Books for Children 1967–1968, 154 pp., $2.50. Annotated, classified and indexed bibliographies of books reviewed by *The Booklist* from Sept. through Aug. of the years indicated and ranging from preschool to grade 9. All are available from Amer. Library Assn., 50 E. Huron St., Chicago, Ill. 60611.

Children's Catalog, by Rachel Shor and Estelle A. Fidell, eds. A classified annotated guide to 4274 books for grades K–6, 1024 pp., 11th ed., 1966. H. W. Wilson Co., 950 University Ave., Bronx, N.Y. 10452 $17.

Children's Catalog, 1970 Supplement to the 11th ed., 1966, Estelle A. Fidell and Charlotte J. Bunker eds. A classified annotated guide to 473 books for grades K–6, 120 pp., H. W. Wilson Co., 1970. This supplement comes as part of the annual service provided when the *Children's Catalog* is purchased.

Elementary School Library Collection, by Mary V. Gaver ed. 7420 titles, plus professional and audiovisual materials arranged by Dewey Decimal Classification and indexed by subject, author and title, 625 pp., 4th ed., 1968. Bro-Dart Foundation, 113 Frelinghuysen Ave., Newark, N.J. 07114 $20.

Good Books for Children, by Mary K. Eakin ed. A selection of over 1400 books for K–12, reviewed in *The Bulletin of the Center for Children's Books* from 1950–1965, 362 pp., 3rd ed., 1966. University of Chicago Press, 5750 Ellis Ave., Chicago, Ill. 60637 $7.95, hardback: $2.95, paperback.

Good Reading for Poor Readers, George E. Spache, Garrard Press, Champaign, Ill.

JUNIOR HIGH SCHOOL LEVEL

A Basic Book Collection for Junior High Schools, Margaret V. Spengler, et al. eds. An annotated bibliography of about 1000 books and magazines for grades 7–9, arranged by Dewey Decimal Classification with author, title and subject index, 144 pp., 3rd ed., 1960. Amer. Library Assn., 50 E. Huron St., Chicago, Ill. 60611 $2.

Junior High School Library Catalog, Rachel Shor and Estelle Fidell eds. A classified annotated guide to 3310 books for junior high, 768 pp., 1965. H. W. Wilson Co., 950 University Ave., Bronx, N.Y. 10452 $20.

SENIOR HIGH SCHOOL LEVEL

Senior High School Library Catalog, Rachel Shor and Estelle Fidell eds. A classified annotated guide to 4231 books for grades 10–12, 1038 pp., 9th ed. H. W. Wilson Co., 950 University Ave. Bronx, New York, 10452. Revised edition, 1969 $25.00.

Senior High School Library Catalog, 1970 Supplement, Estelle Fidell ed. A classified annotated guide to 615 books for grades 10–12, 160 pp., 1970. H. W. Wilson Co., 950 University Ave., Bronx, New York, 10452. Revised edition, when the *Senior High School Library Catalog* is ordered.

PERIODICALS WHICH REVIEW MEDIA (PRINT AND NON-PRINT)

Audiovisual Instruction, published monthly, Sept. through June. Department of Audiovisual Instruction, NEA, 1201 Sixteenth Street, NW, Washington, D.C., 20036 $8.00 per year.

The Booklist, published bimonthly, Sept. through July, and once in Aug. Amer. Library Assn., 50 E. Huron St., Chicago, Ill. 60611 $8.00 per year; 50¢ a copy.

Bulletin of the Center for Children's Books, published monthly except Aug. University of Chicago Press, 5750 Ellis Ave., Chicago, Ill. 60637 $4.50 a year; quantity rates; 75¢ a copy.

Elementary English, published monthly Oct. through May. Natl. Council of Teachers of English, 508 S. Sixth St., Champaign, Ill. 61820 $7 a year; $1 a copy.

Grade Teacher. Published monthly except July and Aug. (May–June combined issue). Grade Teacher, 23 Leroy Ave., Darien, Conn. 06820 $6.50 per year.

The Horn Book Magazine, published bimonthly. The Horn Book, Inc., 585 Boylston St., Boston, Mass. 02116 $6 per year; $1.25 a copy.

The Instructor, published monthly (June–July and Aug.–Sept. combined issues). The Instructor, Dansville, New York 14437 $7 per year; $1 a copy.

Saturday Review, published weekly. Children's book reviews appear monthly with two major children's book issues a year. Saturday Review, Inc., 380 Madison Ave., New York, New York 10017 $8 per year; 35¢ a copy.

School Library Journal, published monthly Sept. through May. R. R. Bowker Co., 1180 Ave. of the Americas, New York, New York 10036 $5 per year; 60¢ a copy.

The value of these selection tools is that the books and materials recommended have been evaluated by authorities with extensive experience in using these materials. On each instructional level, numerous additional selection tools covering special subject areas are available. They fall into two major categories; (1) those which cover the classics and outstanding books published in past years and (2) periodicals which review current publications.

For further information about lists of selection tools and current evaluations contact the following organizations:

> The Children's Book Council, Inc.
> 175 Fifth Avenue
> New York, N.Y. 10010

> National Council of Teachers of English
> 508 S. Sixth Street
> Champaign, Ill. 61820

American Library Association
50 East Huron Street
Chicago, Ill. 60611

Appendix 7.2

For up to date information on devices designed to increase speed and comprehension in reading, it is advisable to contact the representatives of the manufacturer. Major manufacturers of reading-related devices are listed below. These manufacturers list their products in the *Audio-Visual Equipment Directory* compiled by the National Audio-Visual Association, Inc.

Americana Interstate Corporation
Mundelein, Ill. 60060

Audio-Visual Research
1509 Eighth Street, S.E.
Waseca, Minn. 56093

Bell and Howell
7100 McCormick Road
Chicago, Ill. 60645

Craig Corporation
2302 E. Fifteenth
Los Angeles, Calif. 90021

DASA Corporation
15 Stevens Street
Andover, Mass. 01810

Educational Developmental Laboratories, Inc.
285 E. Pulaski Road
Huntington, N.Y. 11743

Electronic Futures
301 State Street
New Haven, Conn. 06473

Graflex Inc.
3750 Monroe Avenue
Rochester, N.Y. 14603

Hudson Photographic Industries, Inc.
So. Buckhout and Station Roads
Irvington-on-Hudson, N.Y. 10533

Ken-A-Vision Manufacturing Co., Inc.
5615 Raytown Road
Raytown, Mo. 64133

Lafayette Instrument Company
Box 1279
Lafayette, Ind. 47902

Learning Through Seeing, Inc
8138 Foothill Boulevard
Sunland, Calif. 91040

Psychotechnics, Inc.
1900 Pickwick Avenue
Glenview, Ill. 60025

Rheem-Califone Corp.
5922 Boncraft Street
Los Angeles, Calif. 90016

Standard Projector and Equipment Co., Inc.
1911 Pickwick Avenue
Glenview, Ill. 60025

Teaching Technology Corporation
P. O. 3817
6837 Hayvenhurst Avenue
Van Nuys, Calif. 91407

The source of this information is a comprehensive guide to equipment which is compiled and published annually by the National Audio-Visual Association, Inc. This guide contains pictures of the equipment, the model identification, the price, a description of the operation, a description of the component parts, the weight, electronic information, and notes about uses and/or limitations of the product. It also includes names and addresses of manufacturers. The sixteenth edition was published in 1970 and the cost is $8.50. It contains very complete information and is easy to use. The order information is as follows:

> *The Audio-Visual Equipment Directory*
> National Audio-Visual Association, Inc.
> 3150 Spring Street
> Fairfax, Va. 22030

BIBLIOGRAPHY

American Library Association and National Education Association, *Standards for School Media Programs* (Chicago: American Library Association, 1969).

Cohen, Alan S., *Teach Them All to Read: Theory Methods and Materials for Teaching the Disadvantaged* (New York: Random House, 1969).

Daniels, Paul R., "Learning Centers and Stations: A Different Concept," *Audio-Visual Instruction,* vol. 15, no. 9 (November 1970), p. 29.

Educational Facilities Laboratories, *Instructional Hardware/A Guide to Architectural Requirements* (New York: Educational Facilities Laboratories, Inc., 1970).

Fry, Edward, "Programmed Instruction," paper presented at the International Reading Association Annual Convention (Seattle, Wash., May 4–5, 1967).

Gage, N. L., ed., *Handbook of Research on Teaching* (Chicago: Rand McNally and Co., 1963).

Green, Donald Ross, and Richard L. Henderson, *A Comparison of Two Approaches to Initial Reading Instruction Using Computer Assisted Instruction* (Atlanta: Division of Teaching Education, Emory University, 1966).

Knezevich, Stephen J., *Instructional Technology and the School Administrator* (Washington, D.C.: American Association of School Administrators, 1970).

Smith, Nila Banton, "Reading and Technology in the Seventies," *Audio-Visual Instruction*, vol. 45, no. 3 (November 1970), pp. 22–23.

Spache, George D., "Reading Technology," paper presented at the International Reading Association Annual Convention (Seattle, Wash., May 4–5, 1967).

Stauffer, Russel G., "A Reading Teacher's Dream Come True," *Wilson Library Bulletin*, vol. 45, no. 3 (November 1970), pp. 285–91.

"To Improve Learning: A Report to the President and Congress of the United States by the Commission on Instruction Technology" (Washington, D.C., August, 1969).

8

Stimulating Professional Staff Development

Walter J. McHugh

In recent years, there has been a demand for accountability in terms of reading performance. As an answer to this demand, top-echelon administrators in one of the largest school systems in the United States have seriously considered making each principal responsible for the reading scores of pupils of his school. Principals whose pupils evidence low achievement and slow progress will be subject to replacement. These dictums are a definite threat; the principal is accountable not only for his own performance, but for the performance of his entire staff as well. Yet, what does he know about reading? Does he know more than a third-year teacher? Is he able to evaluate primary-grade reading instruction?

Another form of accountability is being forced upon schools by irate school boards and central office leadership. Publishers of reading programs now must show evidence of success of their programs. Money-back guarantees and reimbursements for failure to produce and achieve are being demanded. Whether healthy or not, this trend is a reality.

How does an administrator cope with these problems? How does his staff react? Under such conditions, what happens to the children and to the curriculum? How do administrators, not faced with this type of coercion, do an honest and professional job of improving reading instruction in their schools?

How much help is there in the literature? Many professional administrators are at a loss to find new strategies for effecting improvements in pre-service and in-service education in reading. When these conscientious and professionally motivated administrators search professional journals, they find little assistance. There is a great scarcity of research on how to provide both pre- and in-service education in reading. What little is reported in the journals is rather general, quite vague, theoretical, and redundant. The blunt fact is, we have been talking the same line for twenty years. The truly great, exciting, and

155

effective teacher education programs rarely are described in print; their carrier, for the most part, has been word of mouth. Why are so few effective programs and strategies reported in the literature? Why are there so few new designs of successful programs? Administrators and teachers subscribe to professional journals to upgrade their competencies, yet these prime sources of aid lack substance in reporting on teacher training.

There are, however, exceptions. Reviewing the literature one finds that Berg and George[1] report on goals, and components; Weiss[2] describes a three-year program for interested teachers involving issues, diagnosis, special services, methods and materials, and evaluations. He outlines a strategy and provides a systematic approach for both elementary and secondary schools. Local bulletins and reports of information as well as principles underlying in-service training programs are detailed by Gray.[3] The sequential development of reading abilities and the administrator's role in the reading program is highlighted by Robinson[4] and others. Textbooks present minimal coverage of in-service education. Heilman,[5] Hester,[6] Strang and Bracken,[7] Harris,[8] Gans,[9] and Brogan and Fox[10] all offer suggestions for conducting such programs. Although their efforts are considerable and their ideas are applicable to many situations, they fall short of describing current progams, reporting mostly general overviews and principles. Robinson has written and edited considerable material on the subject. Robinson and Rauch[11] suggest specific guides for con-

---

[1] Paul C. Berg and John E. George, *Highlights of the 1967 Pre-Convention Institutes* (Newark, Del.: International Reading Association, 1967).

[2] M. Jerry Weiss, "Developing a Dynamic In-Service Teacher Training Program," in Albert J. Mazurkiewiz, ed., *The Wide World of Reading Instruction,* vol. 5 (Bethlehem, Pa.: The Reading and Study Clinic School of Education, Lehigh University, April 1966), pp. 177–82.

[3] William S. Gray, "Development In and Through Reading," *The Sixteenth Yearbook of the National Society for the Study of Education* (Chicago: University of Chicago Press, 1961), pp. 154–58.

[4] Adalene Drew Hoke, "In Word Perception," in Helen M. Robinson, ed., *Sequential Development of Reading Abilities,* no. 90 (Chicago: University of Chicago Press, December 1960), pp. 180–201.

[5] Arthur W. Heilman, *Principles and Practice of Teaching Reading* (Columbus, Ohio: Charles E. Merrill, 1961), pp. 428–37.

[6] Kathleen B. Hester, *Teaching Every Child to Read* (New York: Harper and Row, 1964), pp. 341–51.

[7] Ruth Strang and Dorothy Kendall Bracken, *Making Better Readers* (Boston: D.C. Heath and Company, 1957), pp. 336–37.

[8] Albert J. Harris, *Readings on Reading Instruction* (New York: David McKay and Company, Inc., 1963), p. 361.

[9] Roma Gans, *Common Sense in Teaching Reading* (Indianapolis: Bobbs-Merrill Company, Inc., 1963), pp. 362–63.

[10] Peggy Brogan and Lorene K. Fox, *Helping Children Read* (New York: Holt, Rinehart and Winston, Inc., 1961), pp. 74–75.

[11] H. Alan Robinson and Sidney J. Rauch, *Guiding the Reading Program* (Chicago: Science Research Associates, Inc., 1965), pp. 47–56.

ducting successful in-service programs, and offer tips for discussions, workshops, conferences, bulletins, observations, course work, research, use of television, and ways to establish professional libraries. The University of Chicago Annual Reading Conference Report, another Robinson contribution, reflects his efforts to upgrade in-service programs. Programs in this series are described by Winkly,[12] Dinkel,[13] Janes,[14] and Komarek.[15] Of particular interest to administrators should be the article by Komarek. She cites inadequate as well as successful practices at all levels of school hierarchy and the three major factors influencing the success of in-service training.

Publications of the International Reading Association provide a variety of approaches to different aspects of in-service education. Lloyd[16] describes a program for large urban areas; de Carlo and Cleland[17] examine a program and meeting schedule encompassing the first sixteen weeks of school; Gray[18] explains a program designed primarily for secondary pre-service student teachers. A more general overview of what is needed in in-service education is presented by Hahn.[19] Durkin[20] describes and recommends two courses in reading for teachers: the first course is a specific study of the possible content of reading instruction and how this content may be taught, and the second (the first course is a prerequisite) is a course emphasizing choices a teacher must make about what to teach and how to teach it. It is quite clear that Durkin advocates that the teachers first know what they are attempting to teach before they set out to do it.

[12] Carol K. Winkly, "An In-Service Program Focused on Motivating Students to Read," in H. Alan Robinson, ed., *Meeting Individualized Differences in Reading,* vol. 26, no. 94 (Chicago: The University of Chicago Press, December 1964), pp. 192–96.

[13] Virginia G. Dinkel, "An In-Service Program: All Vocabularies," in H. Alan Robinson, ed., *Reading and the Language Arts,* vol. 25, no. 93 (Chicago: The University of Chicago Press, December 1963), pp. 232–36.

[14] Edith Janes, "An In-Service Program Directed Toward Helping Teachers Motivate Reluctant Readers" in H. Alan Robinson, ed., *Reading: Seventy-Five Years of Progress,* vol. 28, no. 96 (Chicago: The University of Chicago Press, December 1966).

[15] Henrietta Komarek, "In-Service Training to Help Teachers Meet the Need of the Retarded Reader," in H. Alan Robinson, ed., *The Underachiever in Reading,* no. 92 (Chicago: University of Chicago Press, December 1962), pp. 162–66.

[16] Helene M. Lloyd, "The Big City In-Service Story," *Reading and Inquiry,* vol. 10 (1965), pp. 386–89.

[17] Mary Rossini de Carlo and Donald L. Cleland, "A Reading In-Service Education Program for Teachers," *The Reading Teacher,* vol. 22, no. 2 (November 1968), pp. 163–69.

[18] Mary Jane Gray, "Why Not a Pre-In-Service Reading Program?" *Journal of Reading,* vol. 10, no. 1 (October 1966), pp. 33–35.

[19] Harry T. Hahn, "What is Needed in an In-Service Education?" in Paul C. Berg and John E. George, eds., *Highlights of the 1967 Pre-Convention Institutes* (Newark, Del.: International Reading Association, 1967), pp. 16–23.

[20] Dolores Durkin, "In-Service Education That Makes a Difference," in J. Allen Figurel, ed., *Forging Ahead in Reading,* Vol. 12, Part I (Newark, Del.: International Reading Association, 1968), pp. 307–12.

The Pre-Service Preparation of Teachers

Typically, administrators have no voice in recommending the content or influencing the conduct of college programs to prepare teachers of reading. Criticisms they level at the teachers of teachers usually fall on deaf ears. Unfortunately, most principals are resigned to the fact that a new teacher will know little about the teaching of reading. With help from the principal and fellow teachers, the typical new teacher will learn to teach reading on the job. Unfortunately, much of this learning process is by trial and error at the expense of the children. This appears to be a clear indictment of how our colleges prepare teachers. Moreover, it highlights the inability or lack of interest of professional organizations of administrators in presenting strong cases for reform and in influencing teacher training institutions. Although they are largely to blame for poorly trained teachers, colleges are not totally responsible for ineffective teacher training programs.

PROBLEMS IN TEACHER PREPARATION

Little or no change has resulted from Austin's[21] study (already more than a decade old) showing that the professional training of elementary teachers is grossly inadequate. She reported that some teachers had no single course in the teaching of reading; many had only fragmentary preparation in courses combining other areas of language arts; and reading instruction for teachers of middle grades received little attention. Most courses emphasized primary-grade reading instruction.

There are many deterrents to improving pre-service preparation. Perhaps the most critical problem is the inadequate preparation of college instructors. Few meet the minimum qualifications and standards established by the International Reading Association for reading specialists, yet, they remain trainers of teachers. More importantly, most of the universities turning out college teachers offer little or no preparation in dealing with the low achiever in reading. Some of our best-known institutions offer no remedial reading courses, and worse, many do not have or require clinical training in reading. Is it any wonder that the typical college instructor gears his courses exclusively to developmental reading? It should, therefore, come as no surprise to administrators that the new teacher has no hope of understanding and planning a solid program of instruction for the bottom third of his class. Even in colleges where instructors are highly competent in teaching remedial reading, they may have little opportunity to offer more than a basic course in reading instruction to pre-service teachers because they are limited by laws, credentialing agencies, or by academic restrictions of colleges.

[21] Mary Austin, et al., *The Torch Lighters: Tomorrow's Teachers of Reading* (Cambridge, Mass.: Harvard University Press, 1961).

Another major problem contributing to the lack of quality preparation of teachers is usually a nightmare for college deans and department heads. It is difficult to develop minimum scope and sequence standards for course content while at the same time maintaining academic freedom for instructors when the faculty is a combination of independent individualists. Some have never recovered completely from the biases nurtured in writing a dissertation. In a typical faculty it is not unusual to find any or all of the following: an instructor who believes in a totally individualized reading approach; another who is a strict adherent to a basal reader approach; another who puts faith in programmed instruction; yet another whose course is largely centered on phonics; and finally, an instructor whose main thrust is linguistics. Stir into this conglomeration of talent, strong advocates of language experience approaches, color approaches, "reading in-a-box," synthetic orthographies, toss lightly with intermediate grade types emphasizing reading in content areas as opposed to a formal reading program, and Summerhill proponents. Although there are strengths and weaknesses in all of these approaches, the worrisome question may well be, "Does a student who is subjected to a variety of approaches know how to organize and conduct a balanced reading program?"

In defense of college instructors, one should ask the question, "When, where, and how does any instructor hope to incorporate aspects of all these things into one course?" The answer is, justifiably, an overwhelming and discouraging, "He can't."

In most courses in scientific and mathematical disciplines there exist agreed-upon, organized bodies of knowledge that can be logically and systematically taught. Unfortunately, in the teaching of reading, we have not yet assembled and agreed upon any pattern of course sequence and content. It may be that we do not have enough knowledge at present to so organize a course. As a result, we still operate largely on what we hope is appropriate rather than what we know is good.

STRATEGIES FOR CHANGE

If we are to add efficiency, economy, and relevance to teacher preparation, we must overhaul our current practices. Old, tired programs that perpetuate poor teacher products must be abandoned. These may well include

1. College classroom lectures on principles, foundations, rote learning, memorizing, and verbalizing.
2. Required library reading, class discussions, and writing of term papers that have little or no bearing on actual classroom practices.
3. Examinations that center on textbooks—a chapter-by-chapter regurgitation of facts and pronouncements—as opposed to problem solving, thinking and use of knowledge, and application of theory to practice.
4. Abandonment of "super projects" such as, creative bulletin boards,

off-beat methods of stimulating interest, that innocent students spend hours concocting, yet on which no one in the field would waste valuable time and energy.

No aspect in the preparation of teachers of reading is more prone to criticism than the use of teaching assistants, otherwise known as graduate assistants, fellows, doctoral candidates and the like, as the prime and/or only people a pre-service student encounters in his first course in reading instruction. Of all the talent a university can assemble to launch a young student's interest in teaching reading, they regularly assign this challenging task to the people least prepared to execute it. The usual teaching assistant's prime commitment is to earning a higher degree, with some pre-service teaching literally thrown in, under the guise of gaining experience or, more often, to gain necessary financial remuneration in order to defray expenses of attending the university.

Usually, the teaching assistant is capable of teaching only one of three courses, but is assigned all three. This same instructor gives lectures in campus classrooms and seldom, if ever, has the responsibility for a student's performance in an actual classroom setting. Although our pre-service students tend to pay higher fees for their education than do graduate students, they receive the least experienced and sometimes least qualified of university instructors.

It is indeed sad to report that novice instructors who need the encouragement, supervision, and assistance of senior faculty members receive practically none. It is unusual, in the training of college and university professors of reading instruction, that they are ever supervised or observed by senior faculty members while teaching reading to pre-service students. Again, we fail to capitalize on our greatest opportunity to improve the quality, preparation, and teaching competency and thereby enhance the potential impact of our new instructors on future teachers of reading. These instructors could be the greatest change agents in the teaching of reading. Why should our preoccupation with writing and research (that usually have little impact on public school practice) be allowed to interfere with their development?

It can be argued that pre-service students should receive instruction from the most competent instructors available. This is seldom the case. Do college deans and other administrators actually turn their backs to this situation? Do our more seasoned professors do the same? Are our best professors really disinterested in these people? Why has teaching the pre-service student been relegated to so low a status on the professional ladder? Why are these students subjected to a transient faculty rather than to the best faculty a college can offer? For how much longer can universities get away with this? How soon are students going to insist on and demand the best a university can offer?

Nothing in our current practice at the college level is more despised, deadly dull, or as unpopular among students than the use of group discussion as the major activity in a course in reading instruction. Poorly conceived and planned, students are divided into small groups of five to seven and told to discuss, record, and report on a particular topic. Little instructor direction is given.

Frequently, the end result is that each group of novices, having had little or no instructor guidance, present an end-product which is then reported to the total group. This represents, too often, the sharing of each other's ignorance on a topic agreed upon by the group—then reported, unfortunately, to the entire class. In this way, the instructor is relieved of his responsibilities to research, plan, and prepare a bona fide lecture and to spend time in organizing respectable course content.

Perhaps most damaging to both student and instructor morale and motivation is the course organization in which reading is taught as part of a "block," usually combined with methods of teaching reading, the language arts, and, many times, social studies as well.

Another deceptive practice which must be abandoned is the misuse of the educational film. People in the field of audiovisual education are being held in high disrepute because of instructors who depend, in large measure, on film-showing where relevancy to the actual course is suspect. Such escapes from teaching are disrespectful to the intent and depth represented in many high quality instructional films.

If administrators collectively centered their needs and requirements more effectively on positive changes necessary in teacher preparation, our colleges and universities would be forced to study, evaluate, and hopefully, change their practice.

NEW DESIGNS IN TEACHER PREPARATION

How then, do we replace current practice with better practice? How do we change, not for the sake of change but for the better? How do we change our practice and not just our terms and language? Administrators are prone to accept new groupings and programs so that their school and district be ordained "innovative." Far too often we innovate but fail to improve. How then, do we truly improve?

Perhaps the first major task is the reorganization of course content and experiences. Ivory towers of academic security must be abandoned. College professors must step down, out, and into the reality of teaching reading in actual settings such as ghettos and deprived areas. For years these areas have received little notice or help from college teachers.

The second major task is to move college courses off campus and into the public schools where theory can be tied to practice. Real experiences and practices in teaching reading should be closely woven to lectures. The college instructor must be able and willing to demonstrate—with children—the methods he advocates. Concurrently, he should visit classrooms where his students practice the teaching of reading. Thus, the college instructor must serve as a master teacher. Under the leadership of the school administrator, resident teachers, children, and pre-service students can participate in efforts to improve reading instruction.

There are many advantages to this type of course structure. Assignments and experiences can be closely geared to actual situations. Students respond quickly to the relevancy of such courses. Opportunities can be provided for students to work with high, average, and low achievers. Students can see their mistakes in teaching as well as empathize with children experiencing difficulty in learning one or several reading skills.

Such course design was suggested ten years ago by Durrell,[22] but few colleges appear to have changed from traditional methods of pre-service education. Durrell compared pre-service education to medical education of the 1870's. A medical student attended lectures and read books; he never saw his professor attempt to diagnose patients' illnesses, perform operations, or even see a sick person. Durrell predicted that future teacher training programs will be largely school centered rather than college centered.

> It will begin with children's classrooms, continue with these classrooms, and end with these classrooms, using books and lectures as a means to a practical end. In such a school, the student will see the professor at work applying his principles to the teaching of children in the schools. . . . Professional courses which cannot stand the test of relation to school classrooms, sharing with students the practice of translating principles into action, will be difficult to justify in the teacher education program.[23]

Stimulating In-Service Professional Staff Development

Increasingly, a demand for improved reading instruction for children is being generated by various segments of the community, particularly in urban areas. The genuine concern of the community can, if properly channeled, be a positive influence for new, unique, and substantive changes in reading instruction. Restive members of concerned organizations are interested in concrete results. Long ago they tired of educational verbalism and promises.

These demands penetrate the entire educational organizations—school boards, administrators, and teachers. But, all too often, demands are met with a crash program accompanied by huge expenditures of funds and disappointing results. Most crash programs of this nature have been abandoned.

Knowledgeable school board members tend to rely on administrative knowledge and know-how to upgrade current programs. They are also prone to require that the administration seek the upgrading of reading programs, but at the

[22] Donald D. Durrell, "Challenge and Experiment in Teaching Reading," *Challenge and Experiment in Reading* (Newark, Del.: International Reading Association Conference Proceedings, vol. 7, 1962), pp. 13–22.

[23] Ibid., p. 17.

same time, they offer genuine support and encouragement. The concern of board members should not be underestimated.

COMMITMENT BY SUPERINTENDENT AND SCHOOL BOARD AND COMMUNITY

The foundation of a good in-service program does not necessarily begin with an enthusiastic building administrator. Despite his good intentions, the impetus for initiating such a program can only be implemented by a strong, genuinely committed superintendent. Before implementation, the superintendent must express total commitment and lend high-level support and encouragement for such an endeavor.

School board members must support, encourage and, when necessary, provide financial assistance to upgrade instruction. Without top-level administrative encouragement, including community support, little or no changes are likely to take place. And, beyond support, top-level demand for results adds impetus to the development of in-service programs. With the encouragement of high-level administration and community support, school administrators and teachers are highly motivated to attain stated goals in improving reading instruction.

Before a reading program can be improved, goals and objectives must be established. When an administrator is to embark on a program to upgrade professional staff development, he must first consider the difference between temporary and long-term improvements. A good in-service program in reading requires: (1) stated goals and needs; (2) staff involvement in planning; (3) close administrative involvement and genuine commitment; (4) long-range plans for and continual administration of such a program; and (5) some pre-planned type of evaluation.

OBSTACLES TO COMPETENT LEADERSHIP BY SCHOOL ADMINISTRATORS

Instructional change is both difficult and complex. It cannot be executed effectively by central office personnel and district consultants. The building principal must effect changes because he is the only person close enough to the teacher in daily activities. He initiates, encourages, supports, observes, and evaluates improved service. When new attempts at in-service education are necessary, the principal serves as both catalyst and scapegoat, but his efforts cannot succeed without the support of a superintendent.

The responsibility of the principal to effect positive change far outweighs his competency for such a task. How well equipped is the principal to meet this challenge? This situation may be described as follows:

> In far too many situations, the principal is poorly trained for the emerging school curriculum that is rapidly developing. We gave him the title of "instructional leader" but neither the skills nor breadth and depth

of background in each curriculum area to prepare him for the problems he faces today. For example, he probably has taken only one course in reading as an undergraduate many years ago. His individual efforts at study and reading to "keep up" with curriculum changes are probably too little and too late. How can he possibly keep well informed in every curriculum area? For the position of principal he took course work long before appointment to the principalship. For most principals their course taking ended when their administrative position began. The principal is further handicapped, due to the type of training we in the colleges dispense, in that he has little or no understanding of primary-grade reading —especially beginning reading instruction. He tends to spend less time in primary grades than in intermediate grades. He avoids giving specific help and evaluation in primary reading. He is somewhat fearful and uncomfortable—he considers supervision of primary grade reading programs either too sensitive or too delicate. Yet, few will argue the point that primary-grade reading instruction is by far the most crucial level in a comprehensive reading program.

The principal's plight is not of his own making. If we are to be critical of this situation the last to be blamed might well be the principal.[24]

On writing of the attitudes of administrators toward this problem, Kaluger and Kolson give the following opinion:

The most highly professional educators of all are the public school administrators. . . . They are the ones who provide leadership to the schools. They are the ones who must be the most versatile. Yet, it is possible for a person to become a school administrator without ever exploring the basic foundation of all learning—reading. Few administration programs at college level require a course in reading. What is even more tragic is that even fewer administrators ever take courses in reading. Their sole training in reading many times is confined to observation, hearsay, and an occasional speech they may or may not sleep through. The results are near tragic.[25]

Kaluger and Kolson point out extremes, but they maintain that even a fraction of extreme is bad. Is this really the extreme?

It is quite easy to criticize current practice. It is much more difficult to present suggestions for improved practice. Some administrators pay little heed to critics, and rightly so. One should be equipped to recommend improved practice if one is to criticize current practice. Unfortunately, educators, particularly professors, do a better job of telling what is wrong than in describing what could be better. Very few universities and colleges attempt to offer

[24] Walter J. McHugh, "Successful Practices in In-Service Training for the Administrator and the Reading Teacher," in Paul C. Berg and John E. George, eds., *Highlights of the Pre-Convention Institutes* (Newark, Del.: International Reading Association, 1967), pp. 23–32.

[25] George Kaluger and Clifford J. Kolson, *Reading and Learning Disabilities* (Columbus, Ohio: Charles E. Merrill, 1970), p. 209.

courses specifically designed to upgrade the administrators' competency in reading instruction, supervision, and in-service education. Typically, course offerings in reading are geared primarily to teachers. Occasionally, the enrollment includes an administrator who must apply such a course to his particular situation, oftentimes with minimal effect and impact on his school's instructional program. Courses tailored for administrators, taught by highly competent professionals, are needed. If such courses are relevant, practical, and helpful to administrators, there will be no problem with class enrollments. Administrators will flock to such courses.

DEFINING GOALS AND NEEDS

When an administrator sees the need for professional staff development, his first actions must be directed toward stimulating his staff to see these needs. This can be done in a variety of ways.

1. Analyze test results with a teacher or group of teachers, either by each grade or by all grade levels.
2. Assess the learning needs of the bottom third of each class, again with staff deeply involved.
3. Carefully study the school's reading curriculum (this can be a cooperative staff undertaking).
4. Establish a broadly based committee, which includes community leaders and parents, to assess the school's goals in reading.
5. Restate the goals of the reading program in terms of behavioral objectives. This would involve a more precise method of examining not only the reading program, but how well individual children are attaining desired goals.

STAFF INVOLVEMENT IN PLANNING

After needs and goals are defined by appropriate groups, the leadership role of the administrator is crucial in cooperative planning of a program of in-service education and study. The administrator's role now becomes that of a catalyst to design a program that will effect change. It is of the utmost importance that the administrator obtain genuine staff commitment. A change agent who inflicts an unwanted program upon his staff will have to deal with unmotivated and disinterested teachers. Resistance, partially caused by teachers' insecurities and lack of interest, is often the case when in-service programs are dictated by administrators rather than cooperatively planned. A good administrator realizes that he can move only as far as his teachers are able and want to go; sometimes this progress is less rapid than the principal desires, but it may be more sure-footed.

An unusual example of the process of staff initiated development in reading took place in the Berkeley, California, School District during the 1969–70 school year. The superintendent, administrators, staff, and school board made a commitment to achieve one year's growth in reading for *every* child enrolled in the district. The outcome of this commitment was a series of in-service programs in reading for all administrators and central office personnel. Teacher in-service programs emerged for teachers, teacher aides, parents, and volunteers. Each administrator "adopted" a child who needed help in reading. He visited his "adopted" child in school, at home, took him to his own home as a guest on weekends, shared family outings, visits and cultural events; all this in addition to making a concerted effort to help the child improve his reading ability. This commitment by the district administrative leadership inspired teachers to join in the effort to achieve one year's growth in reading for every child they taught. This type of commitment could be emulated by other school districts, and hopefully, each *teacher* could "adopt" a child needing help in reading.

DETERMINING NEED FOR IN-SERVICE STAFF DEVELOPMENT

Initiating changes in reading programs can take many avenues. Morrison feels that a reading program must be planned by both administrators and teachers if it is to succeed. He lists six considerations for this joint effort:

1. Teachers and administrators must identify mutually acceptable goals of instruction. But they cannot arrive at these mutual goals unless ways are found to stimulate modification of their existing perceptions—of the situation, themselves, and of the probable effects of change.
2. Both teachers and administrators must be acquainted with a knowledge of modern theory and practice concerning reading.
3. They must translate their agreed-upon objectives into pupil behavior consistent with appropriate and effective teaching-learning designs.
4. Strengths and weaknesses of the present program must be identified.
5. Reference materials must be provided to fortify teachers and administrators with background information.
6. Release time must be provided for planning periods.[26]

USE OF QUESTIONNAIRES TO DETERMINE NEED

Sometimes a questionnaire that focuses on areas of concern in instruction can trigger teacher interest in desired improvement. Scribner[27] attempted to analyze and evaluate teacher service to pupil learning. He developed a Subject Service Analysis Rating Scale. Two independent raters interviewed each

[26] Coleman Morrison, "Can Administrators and Teachers Plan the Reading Program Together?" *Forging Ahead in Reading,* Proceedings of the Twelfth Annual Convention of the International Reading Association, vol. 12, Part I (Newark, Del.: International Reading Association, 1968), pp. 256–61.

[27] Harvey B. Scribner, "Differentiated Instruction in the Dedham Schools," *Journal of Education,* vol. 142, no. 2 (December 1959), pp. 11–21.

teacher and asked a standard set of questions. Teacher responses were rated according to four types of service: (1) Uniform Instruction, (2) Minor Service, (3) Partial Service, (4) Superior or Major Service. Each teacher's response was checked against a list of typical teacher answers for types of programs and services for pupil learning. A correlation of the ratings recorded by the two evaluators provided a coefficient of reliability of .93.

This scale was later revised by McHugh and Scribner so that it could be used by either teachers or administrators, or both, to determine current pupil service and to analyze needed improvements in the reading program. The following tables are examples of the evaluation procedure described above. Sample questions are presented below; Table 8.1 shows typical answers, arranged by category. Further refinements of this scale were made by the author and are presented here. These examples may aid administrators and teachers in assessing reading programs.

QUESTIONS TEACHERS COMMONLY ASK ABOUT THEIR SERVICES TO PUPIL LEARNING

READING/LEVEL

1. Do I have a range of different abilities in my classroom in reading?
2. How wide is this range of abilities?
3. What have I done about it?
4. How did I organize my reading program?
  Number of groups
  Levels of texts used
5. What criteria did I use in organizing my groups?
  Use of test results
  Standardized tests
  Informal tests
  Teacher observation and judgment
  Past pupil performance
6. What additional changes have I had to make in my groupings?
  Need for re-grouping
  Flexibility of groups
7. Where are my groups now working?

ANALYZING PUPIL LEARNING NEEDS

Some methods of analyzing learning needs are noted in a previous section, "Defining Goals and Needs." Additional ways will be suggested for determining strengths, weaknesses, instructional level, and special skill needs.

TABLE 8.1

Reading/Level—Teachers' Answers for Types of Programs and Services for Pupil Learning

Minimum Service (1)	Incidental Service (2)	Partial Service (3)	Superior Service (4)
—One or two permanent groups	—Has permanent three-level grouping	—Has three or more groups, flexible in nature	—Groupings highly flexible according to lesson or skill being taught
—Sends work home for slow children	—Uses basal reader materials	—Uses basal reader materials for high and low groups	—Groups according to particular skill needs
—Keeps slow children after school, or gives help during recess and lunch periods	—Follows manual with minor variations	—Follows supplementary program for phonics	—Groups in patterns for particular needs in:
—Uses only texts of one or two levels and follows manual closely	—Uses supplementary basal readers	—Uses standard test results and teacher observation for grouping	—applied phonics
—Groups according to last year's grouping	—Groups according to standard test results	—Uses texts and materials of three or more levels	—word meaning and enrichment
—Helps slow children with difficult words during reading period			—comprehension
—All children on same lesson, taking same amount of work			—recall of material read
			—thinking skills (critical and elaborative thinking)
			—organization and subordination of ideas

Determining Proper Reading Level. This can be done for both silent and oral reading. If the basal-type of reading instruction is being used, the teacher or administrator selects a page and asks the child to read it orally. If the child makes more than one error in 20 running words, or five in 100, or if the reading is very slow and labored, the material is too difficult. If the child is asked four to eight questions, based on the reading, and he errs on more than 20 percent, the material is deemed too difficult.

For checking silent reading level, the child is directed to read silently a similar selection from the same book. Again, if the child asks the examiner what certain words are (more than 5 percent), or if he is unable to answer four to eight (depending on the comprehension level) questions accurately, the level is too difficult for him. In addition, specific word-attack skills, phrasing, punctuation, and other errors can be noted.

Determining Reading Range in a Classroom. The administrator can do this rather easily by asking each teacher to fill in the following form:

GROUPING INFORMATION FORM FOR READING

Teacher .... School .... Grade ....

Group	Basic Text	Level	Page	No. in Group
High	....	....	....	....
High Average	....	....	....	....
Average	....	....	....	....
Low Average	....	....	....	....
Low	....	....	....	....

In analyzing the information collected by grouping information forms, the following questions are appropriate:

1. Is the teacher truly providing for different levels? In an average classroom, the range will require a minimum of three reading levels.
2. Are the children clustered too closely? Are there too many children in one group?
3. Are high achievers progressing rapidly or being held back?
4. Are low achievers being pushed sufficiently and are they receiving adequate supplementary instruction?

This form can be adapted to fit other school organization plans, such as cross-grade grouping, team teaching, and totally individualized reading programs. Later, the administrator can plot his entire school reading status on a large chart. Semimonthly reports from teachers, using the same form, provide the principal with information about the progress of each group or individual.

Use of Informal Tests. Such tests, when properly used, help teacher and administrators identify specific needs. These should only be used if, after analysis, specific materials and a teaching program aimed at overcoming these weaknesses are to be utilized.

Reading Readiness and Maintenance Tests. Preventing reading failure early in grade 1 is not only highly desirable, but attainable as well. It is possible to identify potential high, average, and low achievers during the first week of first grade. No longer can communities afford the luxury of delaying formal instruction until late October or early November. These delays, sometimes labeled "getting to know my children time," result in June achievement scores at least two months below national norms. Readiness tests should be administered and analyzed at the beginning of the school year. Instructional groups should be organized and instruction begun as soon as possible. Teachers will learn more about the reading ability of children by directly teaching them than they will ever learn by observing them in informal situations.

One program which attempts to accomplish the above goal is in wide use in Northern California. The McHugh-McParland Reading Readiness Test[28] is administered early in grade 1. Children are grouped for instruction according to test scores and regrouped as necessary after instruction begins. In December the children are given the McHugh First Grade Maintenance Test.[29] From Readiness Test scores and an expectancy table, teachers and administrators can determine how well the children should be doing. Those children not performing according to expectancy can be easily identified and remedial instruction can be initiated in early January. No longer must a first-grader continue to fail until almost June before he receives specific, individualized help. It is through this type of analysis that failure in first-grade reading may now be prevented.

Planning In-Service Professional Staff Development Programs

When reading goals and needs are firmly established and total staff involvement and commitment have been achieved, improved quality programs of reading instruction can be initiated. One of the administrator's first tasks is to determine the direction such an endeavor will take, but the options may be so numerous that he may have difficulty in determining which way to go. Therefore, several strategies are offered below which may help the administrator. The strategy selected will depend upon his unique situation.

[28] Walter J. McHugh and Myrtle McParland, *McHugh-McParland Reading Readiness Test* (Hayward, Calif.: Cal-State Book Store, 1966).
[29] Walter J. McHugh and Carolyn Dashiell, *First Grade Level Maintenance Test* (mimeographed), California State College at Hayward, 1971.

DETERRENTS TO IMPROVED SCHOOL
READING PROGRAMS

A cautionary note is in order at this stage of planning. Some avenues taken by school faculties have not proven to be better programs at all, but merely different programs presenting new designs. Improved practice has not been achieved to any substantial degree by any of the following approaches initiated by concerned faculties and administrators.

Adopting a Totally New Reading Program. Publishers and their representatives are in the business of making money; they produce materials that they believe will sell well. They do this with the hope that their programs are superior to other programs. Rarely, if ever, can publishers produce any solid research to prove that their program is superior in any way to any other program, but they will all claim that their program is based on research. It is almost impossible to find reports of these new programs in reading research journals. Oh yes, publishers will direct your attention to the teacher in Hazardville, Kentucky, who not only raves about the program, but who can show results on 30 children. Such information should be taken lightly.

Also, beware of certain school districts that pride themselves on implementing new reading programs with a pilot group of selected teachers. For purposes of their study, they choose either teachers enthusiastic about that particular program, or very good teachers who could make almost any reading program work well. Never, to my knowledge, have studies by publishers been reported that demonstrate that students of average, mediocre, or even poor teachers show improved progress in reading as a result of a particular program. Extreme caution should be exercised before wholehearted adoption of any new program for a school or district, without precise bona fide research that it is clearly superior to the school's existing program.

Switching Instructional Grouping Patterns. This procedure appears to be the most current popular attempt to improve instructional practice. Attempts to reorganize the school reading program for team teaching, cooperative teaching, nongradedness, pod teaching, individually prescribed instruction, the use of hardware, massive teacher aide assistance, cross-grade tutoring, reading kits, and a varied assortment of similar and so-called unique designs, have failed to produce marked improvement in reading. Other efforts which have had limited success include systems of performance contracts, state and federally funded programs and systems, and both parent and volunteer involvement programs, as well as the slowly developing Right to Read programs.

It may be appropriate here to caution the administrator who is devising an in-service professional staff development program to include principles and practices that are clearly established and well documented in reading research literature; there are certain factors which have proved to have little influence or effect on reading programs:

> 1. No one organizational plan or pattern of grouping pupils has been so clearly superior to another design that it should be widely adopted or practiced.
>
> 2. There is a greater variety among ways in which individual teachers treat an organizational pattern than in the pattern itself.
>
> 3. The initial high teacher-principal-pupil interest in a new method of school or class grouping is short lived. Usually, after a three-year period, interest is low and initial promising results diminish. The search and interest for a different program to better meet pupil learning needs is instigated.
>
> 4. The need and demand for specialized teaching mushrooms as attempts at individualizing instruction are initiated. The more the grouping pattern highlights individual needs, the greater the challenge to the teacher's inventiveness and competency.
>
> 5. Each grouping pattern envisaged has one or more distinct advantages over other groupings. Conversely, each plan has its distinct shortcomings.[30]

It may be concluded from the above that:

> It may well be that we have placed entirely too much emphasis on the method of grouping and far too little on the method of teaching.
>
> Regardless of the grouping pattern, there is a vast difference in the instructional needs of children of similar reading achievement.
>
> The learning needs of children of similar reading achievement cannot be met by uniform instruction.
>
> Children within any reading group will progress at vastly different rates, even when the instruction is uniform.
>
> The learning problems of the bottom third of any group of children are vastly different and oftentimes complex and compounded.
>
> The intensity of needed instruction varies from group to group and from child to child.
>
> The enrichment of reading instruction is needed by all children, regardless of level, weakness, or rate of progress.[31]

Therefore, the administrator should be most concerned with a program of in-service education that will sharpen teacher competency in dealing with the children, in working with the materials available, plus, purchasing or building additional material to accommodate for individual differences of children enrolled in the classroom. The following five major learning needs of children—regardless of the program they are currently pursuing—should be met:

[30] Walter J. McHugh, "Factors Affecting the Organization of Elementary School Reading Programs," *Organization for Reading in the Elementary School* (Newark, Del.: International Reading Association, 1967), pp. 15–18.

[31] Ibid., pp. 16–17.

1. Provision for different levels of ability;
2. Provision for different rates of progress with mastery;
3. Provision for special weaknesses;
4. Provision for self-direction; and
5. Provision for enrichment

Determining a Format for In-Service Professional Staff Development

Three major facets of a good in-service program must be decided upon: (1) content and scope of the program; (2) leadership personnel to participate; and (3) activities of the in-service program. Topics for major study may be included from the following list which is often requested by teachers:

1. Methods of grouping children.
2. Classroom analysis of reading needs.
3. Methods of introducing and maintaining a sight vocabulary.
4. Methods of improving comprehension and recall.
5. Methods of teaching word analysis skills.
6. Supplementary reading aids, games, devices, independent reading-related activities.
7. Teaching reading in the content areas.
8. Teaching study and research skills.
9. Integrating reading with other language arts.
10. Teaching reading as a thinking process.
11. Linguistics for the classroom teacher's use.
12. Methods of teaching the bottom third in reading.
13. Methods of individualizing reading instruction.
14. Planning a balanced reading program.

To this list could be added special school or district problems or teacher recommendations for topics.

USE OF IN-DISTRICT READING SPECIALISTS

Personnel who are to take a leadership role should be carefully selected for competency in a particular area and, perhaps more importantly, for special ability to relate and communicate with teachers and to give specific, realistic examples which teachers can put into practice. Most likely, the principal is not able to do this and will seek outside help. As one of the most economical ways to staff an in-service program, he may turn to in-district personnel. Such district personnel should not only be able to give lectures, but they should be qualified to give genuine, on-the-site demonstrations with children. Crucial, too, is their subsequent availability. They must return to the school, visit teachers' classrooms, discuss problems with them, suggest alternate strategies, and be available to the school as needed. One of the major restrictions on the use of in-district curriculum specialists or reading coordinators, is that they must visit so many schools that their impact within any one school is often minimal. The more schools and teachers a reading consultant must serve, the less effective he becomes. An alternative is the building reading specialist. The "house specialist" often is the most familiar with teachers and the local program's strengths and weaknesses. Continuing contact with building personnel can be very effective in upgrading reading instruction if the specialist is acceptable to the other teachers. If the building specialist has the necessary competencies, he may well be the better choice.

USE OF OUTSIDE READING CONSULTANTS

The administrator has another option for improving the reading program; he may seek help from an outside reading specialist. Employing a consultant has both advantages and disadvantages and school and district needs must be examined before a decision is reached. Among the advantages of such consultants are:

1. They can bring to the district the latest information on programs, materials, techniques, and research that have proved effective in other school settings.
2. They can often circumvent local biases and pressures and so serve district goals in a productive and positive way.
3. As consultants, they usually have had wide experience in meeting with teacher groups and possess abilities proven effective in inservice programs in other locales.
4. They may have the ability to quickly grasp, analyze, and make recommendations to the local unit to improve reading instruction.

Before employing an outside consultant, the administrator should establish criteria for selection. The following list is presented in an attempt to aid the administration in selecting a highly competent outside consultant. A good out-of-district reading consultant should:

1. Spend time regularly in the public schools and be aware of typical school and teacher problems.
2. Work with teachers effectively.
3. Be able to efficiently and effectively analyze school or district needs.
4. Be highly flexible in working with diverse types of teachers and programs.
5. Be able to suggest several alternate plans, programs, types of materials, etc.
6. Be competent in working with low achieving groups and children of different backgrounds.

7. Visit classrooms, point out good and poor instructional practices, and give concrete suggestions for upgrading the teacher's program.
8. Have a clinical background in reading enabling him to analyze reading difficulties and offer corrective procedures and programs.
9. Have the ability to conduct demonstration lessons with children in front of an audience of teachers. Literally, he should be a master teacher.
10. Have the time and be willing to return to the district and *follow through*—to evaluate, analyze, and modify recommendations and methods suggested in in-service work.

All administrators should evaluate outside consultants in terms of their competency to serve the school or district goals and needs. Administrators also need to be aware of the limited competencies and breadth of some specialists in the field of reading.

Every field of human endeavor has personnel who are knowledgeable and enthusiastic, but who have limited areas of responsibility, interest, and expertise. The field of reading is no exception. Administrators should be keenly aware of the abilities of consultants in terms of total school or district need and direction. There are reading personnel who have the capability to infuse administrators and faculty with enthusiasm and motivation, but their solutions are too simplified. To categorize such individuals is most difficult. Yet, to point out certain characteristic types of such individuals may be in order. Perhaps the labels used to describe such persons are too strong, but the writer wishes to emphasize the dangers inherent in utilizing their services:

The Curriculum Guide Writer. This type will assemble a reading guide loaded with objectives of little or no value to teachers in their day-to-day teaching program, and usually with minimal relevance to the materials or program in local use. Few, if any, practical or specific aids and directions for teachers are found in such a guide.

The One-Way, One-Method Expert. This expert will recommend turning the school around and upside down by advocating a particular method or set of materials, touted as the true message and method. No valid evidence is advanced to prove the method superior to any other, yet, one emotion-packed anecdote may be so powerfully delivered that available research is overlooked. Among this group may be proponents of any of the following methods: I. T. A., Individualized Reading, the Language Experience Approach, Phonics Supplements, Programmed Learning/Linguistic methods, Reading by Color Clue programs and on and on.

The Share-the-Ignorance Type. Representatives of this type of outside consultants put teachers in small groups to discuss their special or peculiar success with different types of methods or materials, then ask them to report their results to the larger group. Such consultants bring nothing to share. They do capitalize on the innocent teacher's practices—which may be good or bad —which are shared with the whole group without critical analysis and evaluation. This is the same type who usually faces teachers and asks, "What do you want?" and then makes them find it, with no direction or input from the consultant.

The Excuse-Seeker Type. This type can solve all reading problems by blaming parents and others for the state of their children. Typical labels are "lacks love," "is immature," and on and on.

The Inspirers Type. "Give the children love and they will automatically get interested in reading." This group is more to be pitied than censured. Their understanding of what reading is all about is often shallow. Most children receive a great deal of love in their home and yet some fail to learn to read. Certainly for these children, love is just not enough.

The Anything-Goes Type. Everybody should do their own thing in this setting —a Summerhill-with-clothes-on approach. Play, draw, paint, whatever you like. Even read. Readiness will come. Just wait. (A friend has been waiting for clarinet readiness for 23 years! When will it come?)

ACTIVITIES OF IN-SERVICE PROGRAMS

The various choices of format should be mutually agreed upon by administrative leadership and teaching personnel according to need, available facilities, and the desired type of in-service program. It is not necessary that only one format be established for all staff development meetings. Any one or combination of the following formats may serve to assist the administrator in organizing such a program:

1. Lecture
2. Demonstration
3. Lecture/Demonstration
4. Open-end questioning sessions
5. Special interest groups
6. Grade-level groups
7. Cross-grade groups (i.e., primary, intermediate, secondary)
8. Subject-area groups
9. Teachers using same basic reading program
10. Team teaching, cross-grade groups, IPI groups, nongraded, pod groups, etc.
11. Open-end rap sessions or discussion groups
12. One-to-one consultant/teacher or teacher/administrator or consultant/administrator encounter sessions

This is but a beginning list of possibilities. Teacher and administrator will desire other formats that are conducive to maximum participation and results according to particular needs, desires, and aims.

Some Additional Recommendations

In the past fifteen years, this writer has served as consultant to many school districts. Although each district and its needs are different, there appear to be some common operational strands that lend to more effective staff development programs.

1. An on-going staff development program spread over a school year appears to be much more effective than an intensive, five-day in-service program. It is recommended that a meeting be scheduled each month throughout the school year, with regular visitations to teachers and administrators to determine teacher concerns, problems and progress.

2. One-day consultants or workshops are of little or no permanent value. Too often, such meetings are arranged simply to expend state or federal monies allocated to a district.

3. The utilization of many different consultants with opposing philosophical positions over a year's period to upgrade reading instruction produces more chaos and teacher insecurity than the use of a consultant who will stay with the district over an extended period and initiate and follow through on a planned, sequential program of staff development.

4. Textbook publishers' representatives can assist administrators and teachers in the proper use of their program and materials. However, they are usually not trained or effective in analyzing pupil learning problems, organizing a balanced reading program, or in establishing reading programs to teach the slow achievers or bottom third of a class. Therefore, although it can be very valuable, their usefulness is limited.

5. At in-service sessions, attendance of principals as well as teachers should be required. Desired change takes place more readily when both administrative and teaching forces are working toward the same goal. The administrator serves as catalyst to change, giving both impetus and enthusiasm to improved service. Teachers feel much more secure about launching new programs when they know that they have the encouragement, support, and understanding of the administration.

6. In-service credit for teacher participation in staff development programs (offered by the district or a neighboring college) adds additional enthusiasm and thrust to the improvement of pupil learning. Such an arrangement also allows a consultant (particularly a college professor) to expect greater impact and improvement than if teachers attend only a required in-district meeting that has no greater obligation than simply sitting and listening, without any commitment to improve practice.

7. Released time for in-service education is far superior to late-afternoon sessions. Teacher morale, acceptance of new approaches, and enthusiasm are enhanced when in-service training is considered on-the-job professional improvement.

8. Tuesday and Wednesday sessions have much greater appeal to teachers than those on any other days of the week.

9. The more personalized the consultant's role in staff development, the greater the impact seems to be. Large numbers of people assembled for in-service sessions do not allow for give-and-take, question-and-answer periods or discussion of teachers' particular problems. The fewer teachers involved in such an in-service program, the more personalized the session can be. Perhaps the very best of in-service endeavors is on a one-to-one basis, expensive and as time consuming as it may initially appear.

Conclusion

The main emphasis in this chapter has been on the building administrator's role in staff development. Yet, many school districts design in-service programs district-wide, usually at the district office administrative level. There are many advantages to such a procedure. However, although the typical building administrator does not hire his staff, he is usually the key person to evaluate his teachers. If the building administrator is to assume the responsibility of instructional leadership in his school, perhaps it is time we assist him in achieving this often stated, yet seldom fulfilled role. Hopefully, some of the suggestions for staff development mentioned in this chapter, carefully chosen according to particular needs and goals of individual schools, will help the administrator achieve the goal he has so long and so conscientiously desired to accomplish—helping every teacher and every child reach his full potential in reading.

BIBLIOGRAPHY

Austin, Mary, et al., *The Torch Lighters: Tomorrow's Teachers of Reading* (Cambridge, Mass.: Harvard University Press, 1961).

de Carlo, Mary Rossini, and Donald L. Cleland, "A Reading In-Service Education Program for Teachers," *The Reading Teacher*, vol. 22, no. 2 (November 1968).

Dinkel, Virginia G., "An In-Service Program: All Vocabularies," in H. Alan Robinson, ed., *Reading and the Language Arts*, vol. 25, no. 93 (Chicago: University of Chicago Press, December, 1963).

Durkin, Dolores, "In-Service Education That Makes a Difference," in J. Allen Figurel, ed., *Forging Ahead in Reading*, vol. 12, Part 1 (Newark, Del.: International Reading Association, 1968).

Durrell, Donald D., "Challenge and Experiment in Teaching Reading," *Challenge and Experiment in Reading,* vol. 7 (Newark, Del.: International Reading Association Conference Proceedings, 1962).

————, and Walter J. McHugh, "Analysis of Reading Services in Intermediate Grades," *The Reading Teacher* (September 1960).

Gray, Mary Jane, "Why Not a Pre-In-Service Reading Program?" *Journal of Reading,* vol. 10, no. 1 (October 1966).

Hahn, Harry T., "What is Needed in an In-Service Education?" in Paul C. Berg and John E. George, eds., *Highlights of the 1967 Pre-Convention Institutes* (Newark, Del.: International Reading Association, 1967).

Janes, Edith, "An In-Service Program Directed Toward Helping Teachers Motivate Reluctant Readers," in H. Alan Robinson, ed., *Reading: Seventy-Five Years of Progress,* vol. 28, no. 96 (Chicago: University of Chicago Press, December 1966).

Lloyd, Helene M., "The Big City In-Service Story," *Reading and Inquiry,* vol. 10 (Newark, Del.: International Reading Association, 1965).

Morrison, Coleman, "Can Administrators and Teachers Plan the Reading Program Together?" in J. Allen Figurel, ed., *Forging Ahead in Reading,* vol. 12, Part 1 (Newark, Del.: International Reading Association, 1968).

McHugh, Walter J., "A Promising In-Service Reading Program for a Small School District," *In-Service Reading Programs for Elementary and Secondary Schools* (Newark, Del.: International Reading Association, 1966).

————, "Factors Affecting the Organization of Elementary School Reading Programs," *Organization for Reading in the Elementary School* (Newark, Del.: International Reading Association, 1967).

————, "Successful Practices in In-Service Training for the Administrator and the Reading Teacher," *Current Administrative Problems in Reading* (Newark, Del.: International Reading Association, 1967).

————, and Walter F. Hauss, *The Teacher's Reading Program* (*Newhall Reading Guide,* rev. ed. Hayward, Calif.: JS2, Inc., Publishers, 1971).

Robinson, H. Alan, and Sidney J. Rauch, *Guiding the Reading Program* (Chicago: Science Research Associates, Inc., 1965).

Scribner, Harvey B., "Differentiated Instruction in the Dedham Schools," *Journal of Education,* vol. 142, no. 2 (December 1959).

Winkly, Carol K., "An In-Service Program Focused on Motivating Students to Read," In H. Alan Robinson, ed., *Meeting Individualized Differences in Reading,* vol. 26, no. 94 (Chicago: University of Chicago Press, December 1964).

9

Making Special Provisions for Disabled Readers

William Kottmeyer

Incidence of Disabled Readers

Administrators must proceed on the sound premise that reading disability, like the poor, will, in substantial measure, ever be with us in American schools. As the linguists repetitively and patiently assure us, language is oral and is continuously changing, while our English writing system, because of the vested interest of the printing industry and the petrified spellings of the dictionary, remains relatively unchanged. Unfortunately many words are not sounded to correspond with their spellings, and it is inevitable that some children will have difficulty in recognizing the words they see. With fixed sets of graphemes designed to represent the phonemes of Latin, the analyst of written language observes with foreboding how some 44 English phonemes are represented by only 26 capricious graphemes in the alphabet.

We can well expect some human beings to be handicapped in memorizing and attempting to use the varying graphemic patterns; that is, a considerable incidence of reading disability is to be expected, and administrators must expect to find a certain percentage of reading problems among the pupil population.

Reading Disability: Its Various Meanings

Although the term reading disability is bandied about freely by both professional educators and laymen, its meaning is fuzzy and it is used to identify loosely a variety of situations. It commonly occurs in the context of silent reading test score medians of one or more groups of pupils in graded schools.

When there is a considerable negative difference between the grade placement of pupils and their median achievement-test scores, "disability" is alleged. An index of reading disability may, of course, also be the number of pupils in one or more groups whose test scores are more or less lower than their grade placement. The degree of disparity is also more or less alarming, depending on the grade placement of the pupil: a deficiency of six months is more menacing in the second grade than in the ninth.

TYPES OF READING TESTS

The interpretation of reading test scores varies according to the nature of the test. Most silent reading tests designed for use in the first three grades are simply measures of the pupils' retention of sight vocabulary, largely as isolated word patterns, sometimes contained in narrative sentences, sometimes ap pearing in several sequential sentences which are generously labeled as para graphs.

Silent reading tests designed for use in higher grades fall into two general categories. One kind is loosely referred to as a *general comprehension test* It usually consists of a vocabulary test section of multiple choice test items in order of descending frequency of use. A second section, with or without time limits, usually consists of paragraphs of expository reading material in order of ascending length and complexity about which pupils make responses to questions of fact. A third section, designed to measure silent reading rate, is sometimes included. These subtest scores are commonly lumped into a composite score. Not highly diagnostic, and therefore not designed to indicate the nature of the pupil's deficiencies, this kind of test is primarily useful in determining whether the pupil is able to read with tolerable understanding the textbooks used in the graded classroom to which he is assigned.

Another type of silent reading test is broken down into various subtests and is therefore more highly diagnostic. Attempts are made to measure skills such as those involved in identifying central thought, recalling details, predicting outcomes, following directions, using reference works, and comprehending typical social studies or science content. As a rule, these subtest scores are illogically obscured by summarizing them into a composite score. The primary purpose of this kind of diagnostic silent reading test is to identify the specific reading skills that need attention in the instructional program.

INTERPRETATION AND USE
OF READING TEST SCORES

Thus, administrators who are impelled to give attention to the problems of reading disability ought to have a lucid notion of what they mean by "reading disability." Administrators should realize that the dimensions of reading disability will be determined by one of several kinds of measuring devices, that these measuring devices have various purposes and therefore provide various kinds of information about various kinds of disabilities.

Administrators can profitably be reminded of the traditional methods of constructing standardized tests, with particular reference to the establishment of norms. After administering tentative test forms to a representative sample of the total national school enrollment, the test mechanic constructs a table of raw score and grade level or percentile equivalencies. Thus, it becomes possible to assert that any pupil with a given raw score "reads" at a given grade level in terms of years and months, give or take the standard range of error for that particular test. However, although the sample may be accurately representative of the total population, the "grade level" does not represent any stable or identifiable degree of reading competence. The grade level score is merely a median or average of the scores of children who varied from low to high. That is, in the standardization population, one-half of the pupils were at or below the median, and the other half at or above the median. A spread of scores in the norming population is normal. A spread of scores is also to be expected in any group of pupils subsequently tested with the standardized instrument. All pupils in a grade cannot be expected to achieve the norm value for the grade. The achievement of any group will probably spread in more or less the same fashion as the norming population.

Practice has never been consistent in the use of silent reading tests to identify the disabled readers for whom special provisions are to be made. When these special provisions consist of remedial classes, they are often delayed until the seventh or ninth grades. Retardation of one, two, or more years as shown by the tests is commonly used as a criterion of eligibility for the remedial classes. Some administrators prefer to measure reading retardation by the difference between a pupil's mental age and his reading age. A simple and more realistic criterion is whether the pupil is able to participate profitably in learning activities involving the textbooks used in his classroom. A competent teacher can support his judgment with silent reading test results.

Reducing the Overhead

Special provisions for disabled readers cost more than the regular classroom programs, so any sensible administrator will concern himself with keeping at a minimum the number of pupils who will need special help. Certain aspects of typical classroom reading programs may therefore be relevantly reviewed.

The three years of instruction preceding grade 4 are traditionally devoted to the mastery of a sequence of reading skills that culminate in the ability to deal independently with the vocabulary and content of the fourth grade textbooks. Unless pupils are equipped with those fundamental skills when they must deal with a vocabulary which in large measure has not been repetitively exposed in the primary readers and with material which is predominantly exposition instead of narrative, they are disabled readers. If these deficiencies are not given prompt attention at this most critical stage, the gap between the pupil's skills and the relentlessly increasing difficulty of learning materials from grade to grade continues to widen. The textbooks of the fifth, sixth, and seventh grades are not designed to develop the rudimentary reading skills, and it is highly unlikely that pupils who are deficient in these skills will materially increase their competence by staring at the lines in their overly difficult textbooks.

Thus it would seem to be evident that the primary school must be defined in terms of sequential skills and not in the periods of time we call "grades," nor in the terms of materials which we call preprimers, primers, first, second, and third "readers." The objective of such a primary school must be to develop in pupils the basic reading skills in orderly sequence, moving from one level to the next only when pupils demonstrate control of the featured skills—not when a book is completed or a school year ends. Thus pupils should emerge from the primary school when the skills are mastered, whether that be in two, three, or four years—or any fractional part thereof.

Some years ago "ungraded primary" schools became moderately fashionable, and curricula to implement them appeared in some school systems with suspicious rapidity. "Grades" were abolished in June to be replaced by "levels" in September. All too frequently the "levels" were defined in terms of the books to which the pupils were to be exposed and rarely in terms of the skills to be mastered. The ungraded primary school organization, when it is clearly defined, understood, and practiced by classroom teachers has the potential of focusing the efforts of teachers on skills and of reducing considerably the number of disabled readers normally sent into the fourth grade.

Administrators, then, in preparing to deal intelligently and efficiently with the problem of reading disability, should do so in the broader context of the primary reading program. Obviously, the greater the attention that can be centered upon the systematic development of basic skills at this critical level, the less prevalent and the more manageable will be the remedial problem at later levels.

Administrators who are probing the virtues of reorganizing and housing pupils in groupings other than the traditional 8-4 and 6-3-3 patterns may profitably reflect upon those accruing to eight-room primary school structures. In the Saint Louis Public Schools these small primary schools, housing pupils in the kindergarten and the first three years of the ungraded primary, have been found to provide superior facilities, both educationally and economically. These schools are administered by Supervising Teachers, experienced and competent primary teachers who are able to devote most of their time to classroom supervision, to synchronizing and unifying the teaching efforts of the staff. Sites are cheaper and easier to acquire, the provisions for physical activities, lunchroom facilities, and other special facilities, are relatively inexpensive, the travel distance for small children is much shorter, the discipline problems are minimized, and the achievement is noticeably better. Twenty-one such structures are now in operation, and there are plans to increase that number.

Special Provisions for Disabled Readers

ROOMS OF TWENTY

As primary school pupils move from one level of skill to another at varying rates, a group of pupils, varying in numbers from community to community, identifies itself, after at least two years of effort, by making such conspicuously slow progress that the deliberate pacing of the skills program may well be abandoned in favor of more concentrated effort. Such an effort normally dictates reduction in class size. In Saint Louis it has proven necessary to sustain an elementary school pupil-teacher ratio of about 35 for many years, so the re-grouping of these pupils into classes of 20 for this purpose has been a substantial alleviation.

Clinic-trained teachers, thoroughly practiced in diagnostic and remedial procedures, are assigned to these classes. The regular classroom learning materials are replaced by more Spartan remedial reading materials. Teachers are emancipated from the restrictions of the regular curriculum, and spend the major part of their time stressing fundamental skills in reading, spelling, language, and arithmetic. The general objective is to turn out pupils who can function independently with fourth grade textbooks. For over a decade these Rooms of Twenty classrooms with such teachers have produced results which were curiously consistent. With a mean I.Q. in the low nineties, and no pupils with Binet I.Q.'s below 80, the teachers have been able to produce a year's progress in one semester in these four skill areas, as measured by standardized achievement tests. With similar consistency, about ten of the 20 pupils make enough progress to warrant assignment to regular fourth-grade classrooms after one semester of intense effort. The other ten need a full year of such instruction. The number of such rooms varies from year to year, depending upon the needs, the availability of qualified teachers, and classroom space. As many as 60 Rooms of Twenty have been in operation under these conditions for an eight-grade elementary school enrollment of about 120,000.

The compelling virtue of this kind of provision is that it is made before pupils without independent word perception skills are enrolled in regular fourth-grade classrooms. When remedial efforts for groups of pupils are postponed until after the pupils have struggled for several years with textbooks that are demoralizingly formidable, those efforts must be correspondingly more stimulating and skillful to elicit a satisfactory response from apathetic and discouraged youngsters. Administrators should also be reminded that the competence of a remedial teacher is of paramount importance.

READING CLINICS

The standard agency to deal with truly severe problems of reading disability is a reading clinic. A reading clinic staff normally performs two basic functions: Diagnosis of disability cases with which the classroom teacher cannot deal effectively, and intensive individual or very small-group remedial teaching which a classroom teacher cannot normally provide. Generally, clinic service should be available for pupils placed in grades four through six or eight, the terminal grade depending upon the prevailing kind of local school organization. There is no ready formula to determine how large a school district enrollment such an agency can serve. That depends upon the effectiveness of the regular classroom reading program, the size of the clinic staff, accessibility and travel distance for pupils, and similar factors. Reading clinics have been in existence in the Saint Louis Public Schools since 1943, and, although the needs in other or smaller communities may differ, a brief summary of practice in Saint Louis may be useful to administrators who have seen the reading disability problems multiply in recent years.

The Saint Louis clinics have grown through the years to become integral parts of decentralized administrative and supervisory services provided for each of the six city school districts, into which some 160 elementary and secondary schools are divided geographically. These districts are administered by a district superintendent, a staff including the elementary school supervisors, and the reading clinic staff, all housed under the same roof. Superintendents will be well advised not to isolate such a clinic service administratively from the regular school program.

Diagnostic Services. Local principals may request diagnostic service for pupils in their schools by scheduling appointments at the district clinic. The parent is directed to appear at the clinic with the child for diagnosis of disability, which normally requires a half day. Diagnoses are scheduled only through the school principal, never at the direct request of a parent. The report on findings and suggestions for remedial teaching are sent only to the principal of the sending school. All clinics use the same diagnostic measures and have a uniform formula for reporting to principals. The six local clinics make some 1250 diagnostic reports annually.

A brief form summarizing the pupil's school record should be transmitted by the principal to the clinic staff before the pupil is examined. Standard forms should be devised for the parent to fill in pertinent information about the child's background. Another standard report form to be filled in by the physician will help make the physical examinations thorough, uniform, and intelligible to the clinic staff members. Visual screening is necessary, and can be done on one of the several devices available for the purpose by a school nurse or by clinic staff members, who should be competent in the use of the instrument and in the interpretation of the findings. Similar procedure is desirable in assessing hearing handicaps by means of an audiometer.

Diagnosis includes a mental performance test, visual screening, an audiometer test, a general physical examination, silent and oral reading tests, a spelling test, a detailed analysis of word perception skills, and, in the most difficult cases, a diagnosis of emotional and psychological difficulties.

A complete report of the findings is mailed to the sending principal within one day after the pupil has been examined. If such a service is to be useful to principals and classroom teachers, the information should be clear and concise, devoid of the customary jargon, and based upon a fairly thorough diagnostic routine. The clinic director should be sure that the district principals are thoroughly familiar with the diagnostic procedures and can interpret the clinic reports properly.

Most administrators will not have the time to concern themselves with the multitudinous details of diagnostic procedures in reading clinics. They may, however, desirably be aware of some of the elements of orthodox practice. Administrators should know what *not* to do, as well as what should be done. It is not customary, for example, to assign mentally retarded pupils to the reading clinics, as other instructional programs will presumably be provided for them. Group intelligence tests which involve reading are of little use with handicapped pupils. Mental performance tests which do not require reading are more reliable measures of capacity and should be used. All clinic teachers should be trained in the administration and interpretation of these performance tests.

Relatively little use is made of oral reading tests in most classrooms although they are among the most helpful of diagnostic services. The few oral reading tests that are still being published are standardized and yield grade scores. In use, they are most helpful in giving a trained and perceptive observer opportunity to note precisely the pupil's control of word perception and other basic skills in dealing with segments of reading matter of graduated levels of difficulty. Such analysis can indicate rather quickly the deficiencies in the pupil's previous training and the elements of the remedial instruction which are required. Clinic teachers should, of course, be able to make such perceptive observations skillfully.

In addition to the usual information provided by the standardized silent reading and spelling tests, informal tests designed to yield data about specific skills and individual idiosyncracies are important in diagnosis. Such tests reveal the pupil's familiarity with the phoneme-grapheme relationships, ability to use context clues, methods in attacking unfamiliar words, reversal tendencies and other undesirable habits, familiarity with common prefixes and suffixes, syllabication skills, and other requisite skills.

Administrators will, of course, be aware that the creation of an independent agency to perform the function of diagnosis of reading disability will not, in itself, reduce the number of disabled readers. If the principals and teachers in the schools cannot effectively interpret the analyses made, if the recommendations are unrealistic for a classroom teacher to follow, or if there is no systematic provision for effective remediation, an elaborate and impressive diagnostic agency can waste a good deal of money before the next tax election fails.

Remedial Teaching. It really does not make much sense for a public school system to provide reading clinic service unless a substantial remedial teaching load can be assumed by an agency with a steady source of teacher supply. Practice in Saint Louis is to assign a supervising teacher permanently to direct the program in each of the six district clinics. The work in the clinics and the general administrative chores are coordinated by an administrator in charge of a larger division of Special Education, of which the Reading Clinics are a part. Teachers who have completed three years of probationary service in the regular classroom are eligible for clinic appointment, and are selected by the district superintendent for one school year of clinic service. Three such teachers are assigned to each of the six clinics at regular teaching salaries.

An intensive two-week in-service program is conducted for the 18 trainees by the supervising teachers. The teachers are given some preliminary instruction in the theory and practice of diagnostic and remedial techniques and are familiarized with the diagnostic instruments, testing procedures, remedial materials, and clinic routines. The teachers then begin their diagnostic and remedial work at the clinics under the close supervision and guidance of the supervising teachers. For the year of training the clinic teachers may earn from the local teachers college ten semester hours of college credit in the courses required by the State Department of Education for certification as remedial reading teachers.[1] After the year of clinic service, the teachers are assigned back to the schools, usually as teachers of Rooms of Twenty, special remedial reading teachers in large schools, or regular classroom teachers.

Principals in the school districts may request remedial teaching for their pupils above the primary grades and, when the diagnosis warrants, the pupils are enrolled in the clinics. The supervising teacher determines the number of pupils to be taken from each school in the district, so that all schools will get some service. Pupils continue to attend the sending schools while they are assigned to the clinic. Beginning clinic pupils are usually assigned three 45-minute periods a week of intensive individualized instruction. When they have developed independence in the basic word perception skills, they work in homogeneous groups of three and are given two weekly 60- to 75-minute instructional periods. Pupils provide their own transportation, are required to attend regularly, and are retained for instruction until they are able to participate profitably in classroom activities requiring the use of textbooks. The six clinics provide remedial teaching for about 750 pupils a year.

Principals are regularly reminded to be on the alert for disability symptoms, especially among the fourth graders, in order to get help for them before several years of classroom frustration make the remedial efforts more difficult.

[1] In Missouri, the requirements are as follows: Methods of Teaching Remedial Reading (2), Individual Intelligence Testing (2), Practicum in Diagnosis of Reading Problems (3), Practicum in Remedial Reading (3).

The clinic teachers issue regular reports of pupil progress both to the class-room teacher and to the home, transmit relevant information to the home school for incorporation into the pupil's permanent record, and periodically disturb the principal's peace by persistent demands to secure attention to any physical or sensory deficiencies which have been identified in the diagnosis. Following the pupils' release from the clinic, they are required, after ten weeks and again after 30 weeks, to report for re-examinations, in order to determine whether the gains made in reading skills are holding up and whether continued progress is being achieved in the classroom.

Reading clinics can, of course, be more or less generously staffed and equipped, so firm cost estimates are difficult to make. Clinics can be housed in existing school buildings wherever enough space is available. The location should be chosen with an eye on travel distance and convenience for the pupils. A fairly large open floor area that can accommodate a small library of recreational reading materials and a number of teaching cubicles is necessary. The cubicles should have superior illumination, chalkboards, a table and chairs for a teacher and three pupils. Clinic teachers should have individual desks and typewriters, storage space, and files for records and materials. Office space will be needed for the supervising teacher and the school nurse, as well as for the physical and sensory examinations. A soundproof cubicle for audiometer testing, adequate central storage space for tests, workbooks and supplies, and a room in which to store and use pacing and tachistoscopic devices and other diagnostic and teaching hardware should be provided.

In addition to the clinic teaching personnel, the services of a school nurse will be highly useful, and part-time medical and psychological service should be conveniently available. Clerical help is indispensable for maintaining a steady flow of communication with the district schools, for managing the appointment schedule, and for keeping a formidable bank of accurate pupil records.

A clinic ought to be supplied with a small library of recreational reading material, consisting largely of books that have content appeal for the older clinic pupils, written at lower levels of reading difficulty. A number of good bibliographies of such books are available to guide the initial selections.[2] The library book shelves should not be burdened uselessly with the usual sets of basal and supplementary readers. These textbooks are geared to the interests of young children and are unsuitable for remedial teaching.

The typical clinic hardware is fairly expensive and should be acquired gradually and cautiously. A visual screening device and a good individual audiometer are sure to be needed. There are a number of tachistoscopes, or rapid exposure devices on the market, as well as several kinds of variable speed film and filmstrip projectors and individual pacing instruments. Most of

---

[2] St. Louis Public Schools, *A Manual for Reading Clinic Teachers,* pp. 68–80. George Spache, *Good Reading for Poor Readers,* revised (Champaign, Ill.: Garrard Publishing Co., 1966).

them have some usefulness but they deal with only the increase in silent reading rate. They do not teach reading. In the course of remedial teaching, attention should be given to rate, but there are usually more pressing and critical problems that need to be dealt with first. Eye-movement cameras, which once played an important role in reading research, are also available, but have limited usefulness for diagnosis or as measures of progress.

Clinic teachers usually need a supply of consumable materials like tests and workbooks, and they should be able to supplement their stock of teaching aids from time to time. Thus, after the initial equipment and material purchases have been made, a modest supplementary fund for such purposes should be provided in the budget.

Precautions. There is no doubt that a substantial and efficient reading clinic service is the most effective means of dealing with the problems of reading disability. This kind of supportive service is relatively expensive, and administrators who are able to venture so much of an investment will do well to safeguard it by avoiding some common pitfalls.

The very nature of such an operation tends, in the course of time, to isolate it from the mainstream of school activities. If communication with the principals and classroom teachers weakens, the total effort to improve instruction is affected. The zealous initial effort to familiarize the principals and teachers with the diagnostic and remedial procedures has to be periodically repeated as new personnel replace the old. The clinic personnel ought, conversely, to maintain familiarity with the changing instructional materials and programs in the schools, or the communication will be impaired.

An administrator may well hesitate about inaugurating such a project unless realistic and continuing prospects of securing a competent clinic staff exist. It therefore seems that some form of training program such as that described must be incorporated into the service. Employing personnel trained in this field at various institutions with varying philosophies and curricula can result in assembling a staff with no common objectives or methodology. The consequent confusion and squabbling can readily impair the usefulness of the service.

If such a program is launched in a school system, it ought to be substantial enough to give promise of having a noticeable effect on the problem of reading disability. A service which is destined to be limited and available to only a handful of pupils is hardly worth the effort and cost. In the larger school systems the number of severely handicapped pupils is now so large that a formidable—and expensive—program appears to be necessary.

REMEDIAL CLASSES

Probably the most common means of dealing with reading disability problems is to organize remedial classes in the junior or senior high school and assign them to the most docile or the most recently acquired member of the English teaching staff. It is possible to effect some gains for some pupils with such programs when the instructor has a real interest in the problem and is competent in the field. But even when some spectacular individual gains in silent reading test scores are made, the fact is that the lost years of reading experience both in and out of school usually cannot be recovered. It should be obvious that aggressive remedial effort can most profitably be concentrated at the end of the primary program and at the beginning of the middle grades, before the invidious effects of several years of depressing classroom experience with unintelligible textbooks take their toll.

In large school systems with large elementary school enrollments, well-trained remedial reading teachers can perform a useful service, especially if there is no clinic program or if the numbers of disabled readers overflow the clinic facilities and the primary Rooms of Twenty. This kind of service should modestly attempt to provide locally the kind of treatment that clinic service does more thoroughly and elaborately. The advantages of coordinating these various services into a comprehensive reading program for the entire school system are evident.

Word Perception and Vocabulary Problems

Whatever else the primary-grade program is to accomplish, one of its basic objectives is to equip the pupils with the word perception skills which will enable them to deal independently with the burgeoning vocabulary of the middle-grade textbooks. In the middle grades the nature of the learning materials changes abruptly. Although the reading textbooks continue with narrative content, a controlled vocabulary and a systematic introduction of new vocabulary, the textbooks in science, health, social studies, arithmetic, etc., are largely expositional and the vocabulary, although it is more consciously restricted than it formerly was, must inexorably expand in each subject area and it has no relationship to the vocabulary of the reading textbooks. Much of this content vocabular*y* is not only a new challenge for the application of the pupil's word perception skills, it begins to present meaning difficulties. The tightly controlled nontechnical vocabulary of the primary reading textbooks consists of the most frequently used words in English, and, at this level, the reading textbook vocabulary rarely creates meaning problems, even for the inner-city pupils whose oral language growth may have been stunted by a restrictive slum environment. Thus, many pupils, laboriously extracting vague, or partial, or confused meanings from the middle-grade content textbooks, begin to develop the protective insulation of indifference and apathy which culminates in dropping out of school as soon as possible.

As the vocabulary load relentlessly mounts year by year, this factor, because of its delayed effect, has generally gone unrecognized as one of the significant causes of reading disability. Nor do the typical remedial reading materials seriously attempt to repair this accumulated deficiency. A foggy assumption has long prevailed that the traditional use of the content textbooks and extensive silent reading will present new vocabulary so frequently in contextual settings that adequate growth in word meaning will be an automatic by-product of textbook learning. Another invalid presumption is that middle-grade teachers are generally acutely sensitive to gradations of difficulty of textbook vocabulary and that they teach meanings of the content textbook vocabulary conscientiously and systematically.

The research which inquires into the effect upon reading comprehension of direct attempts to enlarge learners' knowledge of word meanings is generally skimpy. It is so simply because there are so many words and the researchers have apparently not had enough time to teach a large number of words over a necessarily lengthy learning period. The measurable effect upon reading comprehension of the learning of a hundred or several hundred words, or of becoming familiar with certain common prefixes or Latin roots, is apparently negligible for most pupils.

Another deterrent to developing a massive program of systematic teaching of word meanings to reduce reading disability has been the wide range of differences among pupils by the time they get into the fourth grade. With such a range of differences, it is physically impossible for a classroom teacher to individualize instruction and to keep accurate records of progress for 20 to 35 pupils. Even if it were, the logical extension of such a program from grade 4 through grade 12 would indeed be unrealistic. The objection to individualizing vocabulary growth, which would be quite practicable with computerized instruction, is that it denies the benefits of group teaching and learning and the continued application that ought to be made by the teacher during group use of the textbooks in which the same vocabulary will appear. The pupils, despite their differences, generally use the same content textbooks and are therefore confronted with the same vocabulary.

Another bland assumption with respect to this problem of contriving consistent growth in word meanings is that pupils are being effectively taught the use of the dictionary, usually in grade 4, and that they are being trained to become habitual users of that potentially useful learning tool. Indeed, the publishers have made such substantial improvements in school dictionaries during the past decade that administrators who have had time to examine them may understandably feel reassured that all is well. The proliferating use of picture dictionaries, pictionaries, and now of a third-fourth grade thesaurus supports such an impression. But the inclusion of a section of teaching routines in beginning dictionaries is no guarantee that teachers can or are universally making effective use of the materials. As the successful learning of dictionary spelling depends in large measure on the mastery of the sound-symbol relationships taught as word perception skills in the primary years, many pupils who have been exposed to the formal teaching of dictionary skills never learn to read pronunciations. Although publishers of school dictionaries have evidently worked at simplifying the definitions, many middle-grade pupils find the expositional prose of the dictionary definitions as unrewarding as that of their content textbooks. If many pupils cannot decode the pronunciations and cannot read the definitions with reasonable comprehension, the school dictionaries do little to curtail the reading disability that can become endemic in the middle grades.

School administrators who are persuaded that the textbook vocabulary may be at the root of some of our middle-grade reading disabilities may find it profitable to do some local experimenting in that direction. The Saint Louis schools are currently engaged in such an effort, which may be of interest to school administrators.

An experienced remedial reading teacher made a careful inspection of the first 10,000 words in the Thorndike-Longe lists, identifying in each thousand, the words that might cause an average fourth grade pupil meaning difficulty. Multiple choice vocabulary tests consisting of 20 words per test were then constructed for the first 1800 selected words. The word order was scrambled for each 20-word test in order to provide both a pretest and a retest for each group of 20 words. A mastery test of 100 items was then assembled for use after every nine pre- and retests, which had a total of 180 test words. The test forms were printed and packed into compartmentalized cardboard boxes, each set of tests being designated as one of a series of vocabulary levels. Thus, the Level A box contained 40 copies each of Pretests 1 through 9, with Retests 1 through 9 on the reverse side, and 40 copies of the Level A mastery test. Nine additional boxes for Levels B through K were prepared. Digetek answer sheets were supplied for the pretests, retests and mastery test of each level.

Six fourth-, six fifth-, and six sixth-grade classes were randomly selected in six elementary schools for a pilot program. The pupils were tested initially on standardized silent reading, spelling, and group intelligence tests. The program was begun by giving all pupils Level A Pretest 1 on the same day. On the following day all 18 groups listened to a 30-minute program on the school system's educational radio station. There are four such radio programs per week, Monday through Thursday. On Friday the Digetek answer sheets are picked up at the schools and are delivered to the computer center, where they are mechanically corrected by the test scanner. By the end of the next week the computer regurgitates, for each classroom teacher a class list, the number correct for each pupil on each of the four pretests and retests, and, at the completion of the level, the mastery test score for each pupil.

Myths, which are one or two double-spaced pages in length, are reproduced in quantities of one copy per pupil, and are sent to the schools for use as classroom reading material. After the vocabulary of the early levels has been presented, it has been possible to incorporate, in addition to the 20 test words for the day, between 100 and 200 test words from earlier tests. Thus, the test words, which presumably are blocking comprehension, reappear frequently in various narrative contexts. These test words, by virtue of their source, appear repeatedly in the middle-grade content textbooks. As the teachers in this program are directly involved in presenting the words and in listening to the radio discussions, they are alert to review the meanings as the words are encountered in the regular learning activities.

It is too early to report results of this effort as three more months will be needed from the time of this writing to complete the teaching of the 1800 test words. The considerable differences observed to date between the pretest and retest scores and the reports of the classroom teachers that they are able to make more effective use of the content textbooks encourage cautious optimism about the terminal testing results. It is evident that the pace of 80 words a week is somewhat rapid for fourth graders, although some of the words are familiar to most of them. It has also become apparent that fourth graders need more slowly paced drills in detecting phonemes, in relating them to the dictionary symbols, and in reading dictionary pronunciations accurately. Fifteen-minute programs and 40 words a week will probably be a more comfortable load for the fourth graders. Similar programs at the more advanced grade levels are being planned. They could, of course, usefully be extended through grade 12.

Administrators might profitably reflect upon the possibilities of a cooperative effort whereby any number of school systems could share professionally prepared learning materials of this kind. We all do use the same words and the same textbooks.

Conclusion

Disabled readers are those with a wide negative disparity between their level of reading achievement and their grade level. Not included are children who are seriously mentally retarded.

Administrators should aim at school programs where primary children acquire the sequential reading skills demanded in their use of textbooks and informational books in fourth grade and above. Some children may require more than three years of primary education if such skills are to be mastered. Here properly run ungraded classrooms serve well. Then each child can master the skills in his individually optimum time.

Special, relatively expensive programs are needed for disabled readers. Those discussed in this chapter are (1) Rooms of Twenty where specially trained teachers handle groups of no more than 20, (2) organized diagnostic clinics, and (3) related remedial teaching to remove deficiencies revealed by clinical diagnosis.

Administrators must be certain that their school systems can provide such expert attention on a continuous basis. Financial support and a program for preparing teachers to work with disabled readers are perennially essential.

Administrators need to cooperate in an exchange of successful ideas and procedures used in meeting the needs of disabled readers. Such exchanges ideally should include any local development of learning materials.

Knowledgeable administrative leadership is vital to meeting the needs of disabled readers.

10

Meeting the Needs of Other Divergent Learners

Muriel Crosby

Administrative Responsibility for Divergent Learners[1]

The increasing numbers of divergent learners in the public schools of the nation (particularly in urban schools) are compounding public school problems. Administrators are faced with demands that they create a battery of strategies designed to assure effective education for these students, who are rapidly becoming the majority among youngsters enrolled in the schools.

The education of divergent learners has reached a crisis status; it demands the most perceptive educational leadership by administrators. But principals and superintendents and their top administrative staffs are faced with other demands which drain time, energies, and talents from the primary leadership task of administration. Administration must restore proper priorities to developing curriculum, educational planning, and implementation of professional growth programs for the staff.

[1] For the purposes of this chapter, "divergent learners" are defined as those children and youth who are economically deprived. It is simply another label for those learners more commonly classified as "disadvantaged" or "deprived." They are often the victims of prejudice on the basis of race or national origin, as well as their poverty. The writer wishes to emphasize that the subject treated in this chapter refers to the "poverty-bound," our nation's largest minority.

For more descriptive definitions from the fields of sociology and psychology, see Helen E. Rees, *Deprivation and Compensatory Education* (Boston: Houghton Mifflin, 1968), pp. 9–14, and Robert J. Havighurst, A. Harry Passow et al., "The Nature and Needs of the Disadvantaged," in Paul A. Witty, ed., *The Sixty-sixth Yearbook of the National Society for the Study of Education: The Educationally Retarded and Disadvantaged* (Chicago: University of Chicago Press, 1967), pp. 13–20.

As we ponder the lessons learned during the 1960's, administrators facing the job of creating good schools for the 1970's know that much of their time will be spent on

1. working with community pressure groups who are demanding more involvement in the education of their children. The demands range from the inclusion of Black History in the curriculum, with the community given a voice in how it is taught, to the actual administration of a school, including the firing or removal of professional staff and central boards of education.
2. obtaining adequate financing for needed educational programs from the local and state governments at a time when removal of property from the tax list to be used for construction of public housing, highway development, and other measures designed to revitalize our cities is whittling down the tax base for support of education.
3. developing proficiency in dealing with the federal government to gain financial support for special projects for divergent learners, under what could be called the "here today, gone tomorrow" policies of a government increasingly involved in the education of its citizens.

In addition, the school administrator is beset by a house divided. Because of the rising militancy of teachers and the struggle for power by both major teacher organizations, the NEA and AFT, the interests of children and youth often seem to be last in the list of priorities.

With a public generally disenchanted with its schools, with an "inner family" power struggle in full bloom, with problems of financing public education a top priority, an overriding problem of school administrators of the seventies will continue to be that of identifying the educational needs of divergent learners. Administrators must then delegate to selected staff members the responsibility for continuing efforts in upgrading education for the total school population. Educational leadership remains the prime function of school superintendents, but he must delegate implementation to those who are professionally prepared to educate children and youth.

This chapter is designed to assist school administrators, as educational leaders, in planning programs to meet some of the problems encountered in helping divergent learners become readers. The minority groups in America are bound together by a common need, that of becoming educated. A pivotal requisite is growth in command of the English language, with particular reference to its written symbol system and the meanings associated with it. The ability to read is of critical importance because it is related not only to academic success but is also closely associated with personal development and economic independence. Both of these factors are critical issues in the current social revolution.

Major Blocks to Learning[2]

Divergent learners are not different in kind from their more fortunate peers. They have all of the problems faced by all youngsters maturing in a complicated social matrix. Added to these problems, however, is their own unique problem "package." It is in the uniqueness of divergent learners that administrators will find their greatest bafflement and their greatest challenge.

1. Those divergent learners who are victims of economic deprivation may be permanently crippled early in life, figuratively and sometimes literally, by the circumstances which shape their lives.
2. Divergent learners often suffer emotional blight which warps personality development and renders them incapable and ineffective both in and out of school.
3. Divergent learners often come from home and community environments which are sterile in their learning potential and almost void of experiences which foster command of standard English.
4. Divergent learners are frequently retarded in oral language development, without which it is highly unlikely that they will become readers.

UNFORTUNATE SOCIAL CONDITIONS

Long before the current social revolution, the schools recognized the fact that the hungry child, the sick child, the neglected child were likely to be poor academic achievers. Now the problem of educating these children has become a monumental task. Realization of the increasing numbers of the economically deprived, generally concentrated in the inner city of urbania, has focused attention on the physical needs of divergent learners as a top educational priority.

The task of learning to read is much more difficult than most adults remember. It requires strong motivation, concentration, and energy. These requirements are missing among vast numbers of divergent learners. A look at the typical economically deprived family unveils the reasons.[3]

---

[2] Major blocks to learning were discovered by the writer during an experimental study in the Wilmington, Delaware, public schools. These findings were later supported by research studies, for example, Muriel Crosby, *An Adventure in Human Relations: A Three-Year Study of Schools in Changing Neighborhoods,* sponsored by The National Conference of Christians and Jews (Chicago: Follett, 1965), pp. 8–10; Charles Galloway, "Promises and Puzzles: The Plight of the Inner City," *Educational Leadership, Journal of the Association for Supervision and Curriculum Development,* vol. 25, no. 1 (October 1967), pp. 17–18; The University of the State of New York, The State Education Department, Division of Research, *The Education of Disadvantaged Children: A Survey of the Literature* (Albany, 1967), pp. 11–12.

[3] The circumstances of life in the slums of the city are documented by children, school

The economically deprived family in the inner city usually consists of a mother, grandmother, or foster mother, and a large number of children. Seldom is there a permanent adult male in the family. If the father is present, he is often out of work and the mother or a mother substitute is the chief source of income, possibly through meager earnings from menial work or more probably welfare. Often this financially precarious state has existed for several generations.

The family frequently lives in substandard housing, often one of many families occupying a former one-family house and sharing common bath and kitchen facilities. There is general lack of privacy, faulty plumbing, broken windows and doors, defective roofs. This environment may also be infested with rats and vermin.

There is little furniture and often only one bed serves many adults, sometimes in shifts. Cramped, uncomfortable quarters result in a home which children would rather avoid than live in.

Meals of a family together are frequently an unknown experience and there are few socializing experiences.

If the mother works outside the home, the children receive little adult supervision. Most of the daylight hours of the older children must be spent in looking after younger ones.

An increasing number of deprived families are found in low-cost, subsidized public housing. Although public housing provides improved shelter, heat and light, many of the residents resent the controlled space requirements and sanitary regulations. All too often such families have no sense of home or community. In fact, in one public housing community where the total school enrollment of 1000 lives in subsidized housing, with 80 percent receiving welfare aid, no one speaks of his living quarters as home. In inviting someone to visit, no mother ever says, "Come over to my house or apartment." "Come over to my unit" is the accepted form of invitation.

Even under the more favorable shelter conditions, however, these families of poverty suffer the same dietary and medical needs as the families in private, dilapidated housing. The migrant child is, perhaps, the greatest sufferer. He experiences all of the physical needs of his city-bound peers, but lacks opportunity to put down roots. Too often, because of his transiency he cannot secure aid from those who could help.

How the Schools Can Meet the Problem. Administrators must exercise leader-

staffs, the black press, and formal studies in the following sampling of references: Crosby, op. cit., pp. 28–29; 114–115; 232–240; Rees, op. cit., pp. 44–48; Abraham J. Tannenbaum, "Social and Psychological Considerations in the Study of the Socially Disadvantaged," *The Sixty-sixth Yearbook of the National Society for the Study of Education* (Chicago: University of Chicago Press, 1967), pp. 51–57; Morrison T. Warren, "How Parents View Urban Education," *Educational Leadership,* vol. 25, no. 1 (October 1967), p. 30; "Wilmington Finds an Answer," *Ebony,* vol. XX, no. 9 (July 1965), pp. 57–64.

ship in many ways in order to meet the needs of divergent learners. A number of areas for leadership are indicated below.

1. School budgets must be increased to provide a full-time nurse in every school, regardless of size. The nurse must be able to establish rapport with families, know their health needs, and assist in arrangements with clinics and other service agencies to improve their health. This often means taking a mother and child, timid about strange experiences, to the clinic rather than simply scheduling appointments. The nurse will implement preventive and corrective programs and assist in educational programs in health. She will be especially helpful in detecting speech, hearing, and vision problems.
2. A coordination of school health services with those provided by other agencies is essential, for one nurse cannot carry out major preventive programs alone. Health agency staffs must be brought into the schools for vaccination programs; orthopedic detection clinics, diabetes detection programs, and other major health measures must be provided in the schools if they are to be available to needy families.
3. Free breakfast and lunch programs must be provided for it is in school that many youngsters have their only complete meals and often their major food intake for the day.

Many more illustrations can be given, but those above illustrate why new health services must be built into every public school budget if divergent learners are to be educated and if eager readers are to be developed.

The American people can be highly concerned and stirred to action, for example, by reports of the pitiable plight of the Biafrans. Yet, the principal of every inner-city school in America can identify children who have never had a full stomach. Although this is true, citizens of wealth remain either ignorant of or unconcerned about the hungry children growing up in their midst.

While the health needs of the deprived must become the concern and the focus of programs initiated under the direction of central administration, each principal must be the effective agent. It is he who must bring aid and personal concern to the job of providing for families of each school neighborhood. In one urban area, each elementary principal of an inner city school has a teammate principal in an affluent school neighborhood. Contributions of food, clothing and other aid are arranged on an emergency basis so that no child suffers. Some principals have arrangements with community fraternal organizations, churches, or temples. For example, one church or women's club "adopts" a school and gears its efforts to the welfare needs of that particular school. It is the personalizing of a service that brings satisfaction in giving and receiving. The usual concept of impersonal financial help can be a cold and blighting experience for those in need and harms the giver as well as the recipient.

EMOTIONAL BLIGHT AND ITS ALLEVIATION

Children of minority groups constitute the largest percentage of the educationally retarded.[4] They seldom stay in school long enough to graduate from high school and when they do, graduation is often based upon years served rather than achievement. In reading achievement they become only semiliterate, being among those youth and adults who cannot read on a fifth-grade level. A common practice of the school is to blame the child for lack of motivation and effort. However, observation of the divergent learner in a minority group reveals that the blame rests with the community and school, rather than inside the child or within his family.

The minority child, often born into a family affected by generations of poverty, discovers early in life that he is looked down upon, and is considered of little value as a human being. Having parents with little or no education, his expectation for becoming educated is severely limited. Parents who have become aware of the power of education to change life for the better and want it for their children are often unaware of what to do to achieve it. They frequently see no relationship between education and regular school attendance or getting to school on time. Thus, the family expectation of an education (characteristic of many middle-income families regardless of race or origin of nationality) is missing.

By the age of five, many minority children have already experienced rejection because of race or origin of nationality. By 16, such children have learned the futility of aspiring for something better and have found school unbearable. As one youngster explained to a substitute teacher, "We are the rejects."

The black boy is particularly vulnerable.[5] With no male figure in the household, or one that is ineffectual, the boy has little to emulate in shaping his sex role. The impoverished black family is usually a matriarchy with the mother holding the family together and supporting it. The black mother who works hard for her family and believes in education usually tries to keep one child in school for high school graduation. This child is usually a girl who has had the mother as the image of aspiration before her, and who tends to conform

[4] Daniel Schreiber, "The School Dropout," *The Sixty-sixth Yearbook of the National Society for the Study of Education* (Chicago: University of Chicago Press, 1967), pp. 217–236.

[5] The matriarchal system and the poor self-image of black boys from the slums are of concern to teachers and sociologists, as the sampling of references suggested document: *Ebony*, vol. XX, no. 9 (July 1965), p. 62; Rees, op. cit., pp. 42–48; Mary A. Sarvis, "Reactions of Children from Crowded Areas," *Childhood Education, Journal of the Association for Childhood Education International*, vol. 39, no. 9 (May 1963), pp. 413–14.

in school. Thus, the matriarchy is continued. The self-image of the boy plummets.

As early as kindergarten, children of poverty often reveal an acceptance of the reality of their world and know that life holds nothing for them. One five year old, in defining a "wish," explained, "It's something you want very bad and know you'll never get."

Psychologists have long known that "feelings are facts";[6] that if you are rejected for reasons beyond your control, you tend either to withdraw, or to become overly aggressive. If you feel unloved, you cannot love; if you feel unworthy and unable, you cannot achieve.

Despite the availability of this psychological information, schools often have failed to act upon it and create a climate of warmth and support, develop curriculum appropriate to the learner, and set realistic standards. One of the most common complaints of teachers whose middle-income school neighborhoods have changed to poverty neighborhoods has been that "these children have changed our schools." It should be the teachers and the schools that have changed constructively in order to meet the needs and develop the potentials of the divergent learners.

How the Schools Can Meet the Problem. When the superintendent and the principal hear this teacher complaint, they are in trouble. They have a staff re-education problem of mammoth proportions. For children whose life out of school only serves to continue the vicious circle of poverty, there is only one hope, that of finding a school life which will help them develop new attitudes, new aspirations. The children must find in school adults who believe in them, who identify with them, who hold realistic standards of achievement for them, and who are skilled in creating conditions for teaching and learning which provide "success experiences."

Administrative leadership in providing professional growth programs is essential, for the single most important factor in the education of the divergent learner is the attitude of the school staff. The administration must institute and encourage a professional in-service program geared to helping the staff change attitudes and, at the same time, develop teaching strategies that are effective in reaching the deprived. This means putting more money into professional growth activities.

---

[6] This psychological principle is of such significance in effective education for divergent learners that the reader is urged to study the following references: Anna Freud, "Emotional and Social Development of Young Children," *Feelings and Learning* (Washington, D.C.: Association for Childhood Education International, 1965), pp. 41–47. Dorothy E. M. Gardner, "Emotions: A Basis for Learning," *Feelings and Learning* (Washington, D.C.: Association for Childhood Education International, 1965), pp. 34–40. Lois Barclay Murphy, "Feelings and Learning," *Feelings and Learning* (Washington, D.C.: Association for Childhood Education International, 1965), pp. 26–33. "My Teacher Doesn't Like Me," *Transaction: Social Science and Modern Society*, vol. 7, no. 920 (August 1970), pp. 10–13 [a review of research conducted by Walter H. Yee from *The Journal of Educational Psychology*, vol. 59, no. 4 (1968)].

Most staff members of inner city schools do not live in their school neighborhoods. Therefore, administrators must be prepared to provide learning experiences for the staff which help all adults working in the school to understand the life circumstances of the children and their families. The following paragraphs illustrate some constructive practices that have been developed.

One superintendent arranged for shortened school days and released time for teachers at the beginning of the school year so that they could visit every child's home (where parents were receptive to such a visit). This was a time for getting acquainted before problems had developed and was a pleasant experience for both teachers and parents. It paid real dividends later in the school year when problems appeared.

One principal built into his before-school staff workshop a walking tour of the school neighborhood. The staff saw things never visible in their drive to school each day. Evident were the efforts at creating beauty, the rose in a bottle on the windowsill, the patch of flowers being tended carefully in an otherwise trash-laden yard, the healthy fat baby arriving at the well-baby clinic. Many were the signs of caring by those who live in the midst of decay. They saw, too, the garage on a side street which was home to the dispossessed "weinsteins," human derelicts who precede the trash collectors and collect junk to be sold for enough to purchase a bottle of cheap wine for a few hours of respite from the world of reality. The staff saw for the first time what their pupils lived with each day, the good and the bad.

One administrator launched a staff program designed to develop a knowledge of the human skills, sensitivities, knowledge, and information needed in understanding youngsters living in poverty. The staff learned and used the sociometric techniques and instruments available to help them understand the children's concepts of themselves and their world. Then they planned curriculum around their findings. One teacher found that most of his sixth-graders handled the family food budget and were responsible for food shopping while a mother worked. He used this as the take-off-point for a study in economic education. The problem he assigned required the planning of a supper menu representing a balanced meal, the parallel setting up of a shopping list from the food advertisements for the weekend, and the determination of costs consistent with the amount of money each child had to spend at the store. The children attacked this problem avidly as they used reading, arithmetic, and other skills for a real purpose that had meaning to them.

One principal, finding that most of her youngsters came from fatherless homes, instituted a weekly "Men's Day" for older elementary boys. On "Men's Day," the older boys had the cafeteria to themselves after the children had finished lunch. Seated at tables for eight, each group of boys had a male visitor who was a volunteer from the businesses located near the school. Here, boys who had little contact with men could talk "men's talk," as the visitor talked about his hobbies, his work, or his activities in the community. Seldom was an older boy absent on "Men's Day."

To develop readers among divergent learners, we must help the children acquire a self-awareness that tells them that they *can* learn, they *can* read, they *can* achieve. Some youngsters who are having success in school express this conviction with relish in their own words, "We can *be somebody*."

THE LANGUAGE BARRIER

The physical and emotional needs of divergent learners are a critical factor in any successful reading program. An equally critical factor is their lack of command of informal standard English. Divergent learners usually speak a nonstandard dialect. Often their families are fluent in their familiar dialect, and it is the instrument for verbal communication within the family and among the families in the neighborhood. Some families, however, might be classified as nonverbal, that is, they rarely engage in family conversations, news discussions, storytelling, or reading of newspapers. Grunts and occasional part-sentences constitute their use of language.

Children of poverty bring to school the only language they know, their non-standard dialects. To such children, the informal standard English of the teacher is as strange as their dialects are to the teacher. When the children sense rejection of their language, they tend to withdraw, to remain quiet, and are often labeled "nonverbal" when, in fact, they can and should be highly verbal in their own dialects.

The only way to grow in language power is to *use* language. We learn by using language; we learn language by using it. A child cut off from the only language he knows because the teacher considers it incorrect or too earthy or vulgar, has, in an important sense, been cut off from becoming proficient in informal standard English.

Linguistic studies[7] are reinforcing some of the practices that were found to be sucessful in the schools. Through trial and error, certain teachers have opened avenues in language growth for divergent learners. The following are principles that underlie constructive procedures.

1. Nonstandard dialects are "respectable." They have all of the components of the informal standard dialects, i.e., their own grammar, form, structures, style, and vocabulary.
2. Nonstandard dialects have deep-rooted emotional ties for the child. Language, in any form, is a powerful component in personality development.
3. Most educated people command several dialects, those of the work world, of the family, of various social, professional, and religious groups.
4. The child of poverty needs his nonstandard dialect to communicate with the people he loves. He needs to develop a standard dialect to become educated and economically self-sufficient.

[7] A. L. Davis, ed., *On the Dialects of Children* (Champaign, Ill.: National Council of Teachers of English, 1968).

5. A practice that is becoming more prevalent in schools is to foster the child's nonstandard dialect while also providing situations demanding the use of informal standard English. Thus, the emphasis is upon helping the child determine the dialect appropriate to the situation.

How the Schools Can Meet the Problem. Many teachers are fearful of arousing public ire if they encourage the use of nonstandard dialects in such oral language situations as the informal conversations, storytelling, and discussions that prepare the child for reading. To have to learn to read (a difficult process in itself) through the use of materials written in a dialect as foreign to many children as another language is an almost impossible task. Here are some suggested practices.

1. The administration should become a source of support to the teacher by promoting a many-faceted professional growth program to help teachers learn more about the English language and its varying dialects, both standard and nonstandard. A certain respect for the child's nonstandard language should be cultivated.
2. Most teachers, even traditionally prepared English majors, have had few, if any, courses devoted to the study of language and do not know the science of language. Most elementary teachers are woefully ignorant of this subject. For the entire staff in inner-city schools, study of language and its dialects is a "must." This is especially important for school principals because they are responsible for leadership in staff development and have important roles in public relations in their school neighborhoods or communities.
3. Superintendents and their central office staffs will find it necessary to work closely with teacher education institutions. Professional education must introduce the study of languages to all education majors in all academic fields. Every prospective teacher will be a teacher of language, whatever the subjects to be taught.
4. Similarly, top administrative staff must work with state certification officers to require language study as a prerequisite for those entering teaching. Although all teachers need this knowledge, those who work with divergent learners who speak a nonstandard dialect or who must learn English as a second language will find it the deciding factor in the success or failure of their youngsters.

One school system faced a traumatic change in racial and economic ratios. From middle-income, largely white children, the school population shifted to underprivileged, black youngsters in the matter of a few years. The administration launched a staff program of language study, with particular emphasis on dialects used in the schools. In one school, every staff member accepted the responsibility for reinforcing vocabulary and stimulating interest in reading.

The physical education teacher, working with the school librarian, created bulletin board displays in the gym; book jackets and interesting captions were displayed whenever a new game was introduced. In the same school, the school nurse accepted the responsibility for building vocabulary appropriate to describe the human body and its functions. The school doctor had introduced this need by discussing the reluctance of older children to describe physical conditions during examinations, because they lacked the appropriate vocabulary.

WHEN READING BECOMES FOOD FOR THE SPIRIT

For many years it has been known that reading cannot be removed from its total language context. Language and thinking are one, and language, thinking, and personality are inextricably interwoven. It took the crisis of a social revolution and a tidal wave of economically deprived, educationally retarded children and youth converging on the nation's inner cities to alert the schools to the dangers of continuing to meet the reading problems of its youngsters through emphasis upon more of the same methods and materials which had not worked up to that time. Fortunately, the mistakes made in the hundreds of reading projects funded through federal government support in the earlier years of "poverty" legislation are being corrected as administrators develop a full awareness of what reading and becoming a reader are all about.

Although the peddlers of "hardware" and "packaged learning programs" are still going strong, and while there is a place for technical and mechanical products in any eclectic reading program, school administrators are reaching an understanding of the fact that the uniqueness of teaching and learning resides in the teacher and the learner, and not in a machine.

School administrators are slowly realizing that there is no one method of teaching reading superior to all others and adequate for all purposes or for all learners.

How the School Can Meet the Problem. School administrators must recognize professional teachers as their peers, with the right to develop their own unique methods. Teachers should select those processes and materials which work for them, then tailor them to the needs of the learner or the situation. Reading will then be more effectively taught to all children, not only the divergent. When this happens, school administrators will:

1. Establish the right and responsibility of teachers, under reasonable controls, to select their own teaching and learning materials.
2. Establish the right and responsibility of individual and school principals and their staffs, rather than central office staff, to administer budgets allocated to them. Budget allocations should be flexible enough to meet the needs of particular schools.
3. Eliminate unduly binding restrictions on expendable materials and

encourage the spending of book allocations for paperbacks, news-papers, periodicals, as well as for text and trade books.

4. Establish, in every school, libraries staffed by professional school librarians, either as an important part of a materials center or separately.
5. Provide leadership in development among staff of a new apprecia-tion of literature and its potential for developing human person-ality, for feeding the spirit and for contributing to the educated man. This will call for a critical look at the curriculum and a new conception of priorities related to content and balance.

Literature is more than books. It is a builder of language, character, self-insight, and self-respect. The dominant thrust of all elementary schools is the language development of children. Literature must play its part. More than ever is the command of language vital for economic survival and social accep-tance for millions of America's children.

For those teachers schooled only in the traditional methodology, learning to read is the single target. For those teachers whose knowledge of total lan-guage development is broad, the oral aspects of language have taken on greater significance. It is recognized that the oral and written aspects of language are closely enmeshed and that emphasis on one reinforces the other.

The process of learning to read provides a potent context for developing competencies in all aspects of language. Just as the oral aspects of language provide the base for attaining success in learning to read, so a growing com-mand of the printed symbols of language makes it possible for the child to grow in interest and sensitivity to the many facets of language. And as the child grows in command of the totality of language, literature provides the experiences which serve as a basis for deeper concepts of man and his achieve-ments, his aspirations and goals.

Books themselves offer the creative teacher an opportunity to enrich all aspects of language development. For this reason alone, it is important for teachers to have a broad knowledge and a genuine appreciation of children's literature.

Children's literature is more than books. It provides a context in which children growing toward maturity: face their problems with new courage be-cause other children in books, with the same problems, find solutions that work for them; discover that language is more than communication, that it is a means of self-fulfillment through books; realize that there is a beauty and power in words which makes it possible to live in the world of the imagination as well as the world of reality and find that both are good.

Capitalizing on the interrelationships of reading and the other language arts enables the good teacher to develop children who can listen, speak, read, and write skillfully. More than this, she is making it possible for children to grow toward maturity with confidence in a world demanding increasing competence in their native language.

Appreciation of the beauty and power of the English language, the ability to make words, both written and spoken, bend to their will is the right of every child.

Conclusion

I know of no school administrator who is not concerned about the quality of reading instruction. I know of no community which fails, more or less, to be critical of the schools' achievement in reading. I know of no minority group representing divergent learners which does not place improved education for its people as a top priority in its list of grievances.

When school administration comprehends and implements reading programs which differentiate between children who *can* read and children who *do* read as an end goal, helping divergent learners become readers will be achieved because they attend a school in which:

1. The staff not only accepts, but identifies with them and their customary language.
2. The staff believes that making a reader means building a human being.
3. The staff looks beyond stereotypes of "divergent learners," recognizes untapped potential in each child, and accepts him as a worthwhile individual.
4. The staff feels, knows, and acts like professionals with the right and responsibility for using their unique talents and methods in helping youngsters learn more about their language and become fluent readers.
5. The staff has access to and a determining voice in the selection of materials and library services.
6. The staff believes that it must build a curriculum that is not limited to the "academic hobbies" of a superintendent or a principal, and accepts the goal of placing as top priority those subjects, such as literature, which help create the humane, educated man. Such a staff knows that reading is not an end goal, but the means to an end, that of helping youngsters discover the excitement in learning.

The school administrator who creates such conditions with his staff, as have been described above, will find not only more readers in his schools, but more satisfied, creative teachers, more community support, and a lower "mortality rate" for school superintendents.

Appendix 10.1

SELECTED BIBLIOGRAPHY OF CHILDREN'S LITERATURE

Books can provide the stimulus needed to create an interest in language. The titles listed in this section have been selected as examples of the types of books which will capture a child's imagination.

What child fails to respond to the delightful poems of Dorothy Aldis' collection, *Hello Day* (Putnam, 1959)? Here are the many "firsts" so familiar to the very young, the birthday party, the new baby brother, squirrels and butterflies, picnics, and dolls.

When a child sees with broader and deeper vision what has been commonplace, he is on the way to becoming a richer individual. It has been said that children are the only true poets. Long ago, Elizabeth Barrett Browning told us that, "The poet hath the child's sight in his breast and sees all new. What oftenest he has viewed he views with the first glory."

A skillfully developed language arts program is rich in experiences with poetry. The lilt and rhythm of poetry, its uniqueness in pattern and pace, its creative use of words, will influence speech, stimulate the imagination, and create an interest in language. These are qualities that the good reader prizes.

Books provide the opportunity to sensitize children to contrasting moods and to the value of using the voice to create the effect of moods. The manuscript of Margaret Wise Brown's delightful book, *A Child's Good Night Book* (William R. Scott, 1950), was read to a group of four year olds. When all the birds in the book tucked their heads under their wings all the children tucked *their* heads under *their* "wings." Such was the effect the teacher was able to convey as she read to the children in the slow rhythm of a sleepy world.

Quite different is the effect of *Curious George* (by Hans Augusto Rey, Houghton Mifflin, 1941) whose misadventures create some rollicking moments as children listen to this all-time favorite. Opportunities to embellish and enlarge on the theme are seldom missed by the children. The child who becomes adept in all phases of language development is a master at embellishment.

Books demonstrate the joys of sharing ideas that stretch the imagination—an experience all good readers need. Such books stimulate discussion. What group of any age fails to respond to the hilarious situations created by Leonore Klein in *What Would You Do If?* (W. R. Scott, 1956). Klein has the knack of selecting highly improbable situations that tickle the fancy and spur youngsters on to creating more improbable situations. Out of these creative efforts in storytelling have come some delightful children's original stories which are read and reread with relish.

For unbelieving adults who think that such "improbabilities" as Klein reports cannot happen, remember that *Nobody Listens to Andrew* (Elizabeth Guilfoile, Follett, 1957) is a true story. And only a year ago *The New York Times* reported that "2 Young Swiss Meet Hippo Out for a Stroll" and in the same edition, "Coast Man Discovers Elephant in His Carport."

Books stimulate a keen interest in language and in words. Margaret Wise Brown is the master of creating books which capitalize on the child's keen enthusiasm for words. *Four Fur Feet* (W. R. Scott, 1961) has the detail children crave, the repetition they demand, the story element that creates a spirit of adventure. Leonore Klein accomplishes the same objectives in *Mud, Mud, Mud* (Knopf, 1962), a book especially designed for mud-lovers of all ages. The author's light and whimsical touch sparks the humor of the very young. For the older child, the same subtle humor is found in Oliver Selfridge's *Sticks* (Houghton Mifflin, 1967).

At the other end of the scale of human emotions, we find in fine literature for children such books as Margaret Wise Brown's *The Dead Bird* (W. R. Scott, 1958), for the very young, and Pearl Buck's *The Big Wave* (Scholastic Book Services, 1960), for older boys and girls. Both books deal with the concept of death.

These few brief illustrations of books that are more than books demonstrate the value in children's literature for kindling an interest in both oral and written language that reinforces learning in all of the language arts. In addition, children learn to value literature for itself, for the pleasure it brings.

BIBLIOGRAPHY

Association for Supervision and Curriculum Development, *Curriculum Decisions and Social Realities* (Washington, D.C.: ASCD, 1968).

Board of Education of the City of New York, *Nonstandard Dialects* (Champaign, Ill.: National Council of Teachers of English, 1967).

Corbin, Richard, and Muriel Crosby, eds., *Language Programs for the Disadvantaged* (Champaign, Ill.: National Council of Teachers of English, 1965).

Davis, A. L., ed., *On the Dialects of Children* (Champaign, Ill.: National Council of Teachers of English, 1968).

de Hirsch, Kabrina, Jeannette J. Jansky, and William S. Langford, *Predicting Reading Failure* (New York: Harper and Row, 1968).

Henry, Mabel Wright, ed., *Creative Experiences in Oral Language* (Champaign, Ill.: National Council of Teachers of English, 1967).

Petty, Walter, *Research in Oral Language* (Champaign, Ill.: National Council of Teachers of English, 1967).

Rees, Helen E., *Deprivation and Compensatory Education* (Boston: Houghton Mifflin, 1968).

Rollins, Charlemae, *We Build Together* (Champaign, Ill.: National Council of Teachers of English, 1967).

Shuy, Roger, *Discovering American Dialects* (Champaign, Ill.: National Council of Teachers of English, 1967).

Shuy, Roger, ed., *Social Dialects and Language Learning* (Champaign, Ill.: National Council of Teachers of English, 1964).

Stauffer, Russell, ed., *Language and the Higher Thought Processes,* National Conference on Research in English (Champaign, Ill.: National Council of Teachers of English, 1965).

Vygotsky, Lev S., *Thought and Language* (Cambridge, Mass.: M.I.T. Press, 1962).

III
Innovative Practices

11

New Patterns in Early Childhood Reading

Elaine Vilscek Wolfe

The momentum of haphazard, often misdirected, whirlwind change in early childhood reading appears at last to be dissipating. The past decade in early childhood reading has been characterized by a search for innovative practice and often by a hysteria for acceptance of innovation for innovation's sake. To be innovative is desirable. But innovation as a label is regrettable when the specifics of teacher-pupil-supervisor-administrator behaviors to be elicited and evaluated are either inappropriate, confused, garbled, or unidentified.

Now at the crossroads of the seventies, those concerned with pre-primary and primary reading instruction are beginning to clear away the debris of panaceatic ensurances of success for all children. More realistic consideration is being given to various teaching approaches and techniques, the instructional staff, instructional hardware and software, research focused on the individual child, and funds available for reading programs in our diversified and rapidly changing society.

It is the author's purpose to highlight and evaluate emerging trends and patterns in early childhood reading and to propose questions on some of the trends and patterns that appear to merit further research. More specifically, the three topics listed below will be considered in this chapter.

1. The relationship of early childhood reading to other aspects of early childhood communication processes.
2. The primary pupil as an individual learner.
3. Varied teaching approaches, techniques, materials, technological media, and different administrative organizations that affect learning-teaching.

The Relationship of Reading to Other Communication Processes

All educators today would agree that learning to communicate is one of the most important goals that pupils pursue. Power in communication is a vehicle for socializing, for expressing needs and feelings, for acquiring information, and for storing perceptions that have been categorized and labeled through language. Each child uses language as he experiences and explores in the realms of the social sciences, mathematics, natural sciences, recreation, and the arts.

From infancy, children exhibit a desire to participate in processes of communication. They begin to perceive the external environment, to discriminate between sounds, to comprehend what is heard, and also to employ nonvocal signals in communicating. They express themselves vocally, and later will dictate orally for the sake of observing their personal speech being graphically recorded. Subsequently, expression takes the form of independent writing with the realization that dictated-recorded or independently written expression may be reread personally and by others.

As further emphasized by Strickland:

> Every child who has learned to talk has learned to concentrate on what he has heard. He has learned to give attention to patterns, to schemes of operation, and apply them in his own way. He has learned the basic phonology of a language and also its basic syntax. In doing all this, he has learned to give his attention to sound and schemes of operation. He is deeply interested in language and recognizes its worth in his daily living. Certainly all of this activity is of value in learning to read.[1]

Each of the processes of communication may be of equal importance to the child in the primary grades. Each process may contribute to facility in another. It is a sound trend in early childhood education to consider reading as just one of the processes of communication. Perceptual, aural, oral, and nonvocal communication processes are the firm foundations of language experiences that ensure success in early childhood reading.

Unknown as yet, however, are the critical and optimal ages for individual children to be systematically exposed to procedures that will encourage interest in and facility with language. Deutsch[2] maintains that individual learners reach the optimal or critical levels of greatest learning plasticity at different times for each of the processes of communication. Though research related to optimal learning periods for preschoolers is now in exploratory stages, Scott[3] and

---

[1] Ruth Strickland, "Building on What We Know," in J. Allen Figurel, ed., *Reading and Realism*, vol. 13, Part I (Newark, Del.: International Reading Association, 1969), p. 59.

[2] Martin Deutsch, "Facilitating Development in the Pre-School Child: Social and Psychological Perspectives," *Merrill-Palmer Quarterly*, vol. 10, no. 3 (July 1964), pp. 249–63.

[3] J. P. Scott, "Critical Periods in Behavioral Development," *Science*, no. 138 (1962), pp. 949–55.

others have speculated that the critical or optimal periods for learning to communicate occur at the time a child initially attempts to socialize or has a desire to do so, generally at the ages of two to four years. But greater definitive research in this area is warranted.

We have, nevertheless, observed that when children enter kindergarten and first-grade classrooms, their language patterns are well established. The divergent language patterns of disadvantaged children became a major reason for Head Start Programs for two to five year olds, financed by the Economic Opportunity Act of 1964.[4] The impact, quality, and general success of these programs as well as the follow-up offered to children in first-grade programs have been widely criticized.

Perhaps the most appropriate question about Head Start Programs is whether or not these experiences should have been provided for those at all levels of our national economy who might have benefited. If in fact individual children do reach optimal periods for learning at different times and these periods occur in the prekindergarten years, opportunities for a systematized "head start" ought to be described and perhaps subsidized for all children within our nation's diversified economic strata.

Parents of preschoolers are concerned with whether to provide their children with an early start in reading at home or through a private agency. Several books and magazines have featured programs for teaching infants to read. It is the responsibility of public educators to at least explore the advantages and disadvantages of both procedures for assessing and prescribing preschool learning experiences and environments that are relevant to the physical, social, intellectual, and emotional needs of prekindergarten children.

The Primary Pupil As an Individual Learner

There are many psychological, sociological, economic, national, and international influences that affect a child's learning to read. Attention to some of these influences is basic to an individualized learning design for each child.

Among the factors affecting a child's initial reading successes are psychological theories that set an instructional mode for initial learning to read. For example, the "stimulus-response-associationist" would support a reading curricular design in which learning is a nonpurposive, habit forming process set by conditioning. The Gestaltist would theorize that beginning learning is most efficiently accomplished through pupil discovery techniques. And the perceptual theorist believes that learning to read successfully is based on the child's field of perception at the time of his behaving, his personal self-concept, and his feeling of a need for reading as a tool of communication.[5] Each of

---

[4] Julius Richmond, "Communities in Action: A Report on Project Head Start," *Reading Teacher,* vol. 19, no. 5 (February 1966), pp. 323–31.

[5] J. Gwynn and John Chase, *Curriculum Principles and Social Trends* (New York: Macmillan Co., 1969), Part II.

these psychological theorists is concerned about the impact of pupil motivation, interests, readiness, reward or satisfaction, physiology, and total growth patterns on learning.

Several sociological, economic, and educational agencies affect early childhood successes in reading. The child's family size, stability, mobility, and cultural heritage should be known. The interest-shifting mechanisms within his peer or play group at times may help in engendering cooperative activity in learning. Noncommercial community agencies such as book clubs or Cub Scouts can generate interests. Leisure time agencies such as the TV, radio, and camping activities contribute to the development of the experiential base that is so essential to comprehension. Federal school and social legislation, economic, scientific—technological—developments, and proposals to improve pre-service and in-service teacher education are all promising contributors to an individualized and more appropriate learning design for beginning readers.[6]

Individualization of instruction is an attempt to list behaviorally some sequenced outcomes of instruction that are desirable and measurable within the structures of the discipline. Pupils are diagnostically placed at some points along a reading-learning continuum in skills, abilities, habits, attitudes, and appreciations, or in specified knowledges. These learning continuums may be precisely stated in a simplified system of classification or in a classification system such as that by Bloom, Krathwohl, and others,[7,8] that reflects complexities. Pupils may progress along such a continuum at variable rates; their progress can be either self-paced, or directed and paced by a teacher's instructional prescription.

Reading behaviors to be developed may be charted on a grid labeled "the reading instructional continuum." Standardized reading readiness tests, reading survey tests, diagnostic reading tests, tests of reading potential, and some measures of pupils' intelligence are administered. Informal evaluative procedures, such as learning demonstration tasks, observations, and anecdotal records are examined. Published tests of a variety of types, including those accompanying published reading series and perhaps a computerized criterion test for a learning program, are also analyzed.[9]

On the basis of formal and informal evaluations, pupils' needs, levels, and potentials are plotted on the reading instructional continuum grid. Goals for all pupils on the reading continuum are those that should be met by all, but usually even for such goals there are some provisions for individualized pacing. In this context, individualized instruction means that teachers develop instruc-

---

[6] J. Gwynn and John Chase, op. cit., Part III.

[7] Benjamin Bloom, ed., *Taxonomy of Education Objectives: Handbook I: Cognitive Domain* (New York: David McKay Co., 1956).

[8] David Krathwohl, Benjamin Bloom, and Bertram Masia, *Taxonomy of Education Objectives: Handbook II: Affective Domain* (New York: David McKay Co., 1964).

[9] Elaine Vilscek, "Individualizing Instruction," in Wallace Ramsey, ed., *Perspectives in Reading,* No. 9 (Newark, Del.: International Reading Association, 1967), pp. 47–68.

tional prescriptions that allow pupils to accomplish similar goals at different rates, but also provide necessary variations in the ceilings of attainment for each child.

Improvements in technology and the scientific measurement of a child's needs, attainments, and potential in reading and the other language arts, could, in the 1970's, result in the development of a different definition of the term "individualized." It may be possible then for appropriate individualized learning behaviors to be determined and charted for each child. Classroom computerized data processing would hasten and facilitate the initial designing of individualized learning grids and efficiently supply teachers with a daily reanalysis of pupil progress and needs. Teachers could then create more appropriate learning environments and employ prescriptive instructional procedures that would be most appropriate to each learner's individual reading-learning mode.

FACTORS AFFECTING LEARNING-TEACHING

There has been great controversy surrounding primary reading programs of the sixties. Many questions were posed; many answers can be found in the literature. A few of the questions follow.

1. What constitutes a pre-first grade reading readiness and subsequent reading follow-up program? Should programs prior to Grade 1 be incidental or highly structured?
2. Which instructional approaches and techniques will best ensure pupils' successes in beginning reading? Shall I teach less or more phonics?
3. What kinds of published and audiovisual materials are commercially available that would make individualized reading instruction possible? What kits and mechanical aids are needed that would assist individualization?
4. How many pupils should primary grade reading classes contain? What should be done about instructional grouping? What kind of building best facilitates individualization of reading instruction?
5. What types of administrative organization facilitate individualization of instruction? Will team teaching, nongrading, self-contained classroom structuring, departmentalizing, unitizing the school system, or a dual progressing plan result in the most efficient and effective individualized plan for reading instruction?

For each of these questions the answers suggested by "scientific researchers" of the sixties are in many instances in complete contrast to the answers of other researchers. Nevertheless, the following are attempts to highlight some of the answers found in related research and literature.

PRE-FIRST GRADE READING PROGRAMS
DURING THE SIXTIES

The programs established in the sixties represented a range in quality and type. Some were highly structured while others were primarily incidental. A number of school systems at kindergarten levels adopted and used commercial prereading and beginning reading programs. Examples included materials such as the kit of instructional devices, *Learning About Sounds and Letters,* published by Ginn, or the *Sounds of Language Readers* by Holt, Rinehart and Winston. Other prekindergarten and kindergarten reading-oriented programs were designed completely by creative teachers.

Several preparatory reading programs, initiated in Head Start classes, nursery schools, and public kindergartens, were publicized in the sixties. Included among them were the Montessori approach, Responsive Environment, and the Denver Program. Though each had unique features, in all programs some focus was placed upon language readiness as a basic foundation. Each highlighted the importance of extending children's experiences in concept building. The prereading skills, such as auditory discrimination and perception, eye-hand coordination, and left-to-right directional orientation, were also emphasized. Researchers of each program reported the successes of pupils involved.

The Montessori Approach. A unique feature of the Montessori approach is its emphasis on sensory training and concept formation. First initiated in Italy in 1894 by Maria Montessori, balanced attention is given to a child's biological, psychological, and educational development. As children explore in a structured Montessori school environment, they are directed toward seeking learning circumstances that match their developmental levels and interests. Opportunities to distinguish between various shaped objects; to shake, listen, and auditorily match similar sounding cylinders; to lace shoes, to count colored beads in a left-to-right progression are typical in Montessori schools.[10] These are kinds of reading readiness skill training exercises also common to many other types of programs.

The Responsive Environment Approach. O. K. Moore devised a pre-primary program entitled a "Responsive Environment Approach." Within a "Responsive Environment Classroom," pupils are given numerous opportunities to experiment with language in a rather unstructured fashion. Classrooms contain hidden tape recorders that pick up fragmentary oral language patterns of individual or groups of pre-school pupils. The tapes are transcribed into printed materials then serve as reading readiness or reading material in a modified "language experience approach." To facilitate the independent acquisition of visual discriminatory skills, visual-auditory associational skills,

[10] E. M. Standing, *Maria Montessori—Her Life and Work* (New York: New American Library Inc., 1962).

directional orientation skills, and eye-hand coordination abilities, modified computerized and programmed media and materials are employed. For example, pre-schoolers play with language vocally and observe it being recorded and repeated orally through the use of a talking typewriter. Or they may practice discriminating between objects visually, using a computerized device that presents stimuli, elicits a pupil response, and reinforces the correct answer. Admittedly, these devices are unique but do encourage learning through an extrinsic form of motivation and reward.[11]

The Denver Program. In the sixties, McKee and Harrison wrote a guide for parents called, *Preparing Your Child for Reading.* The guide contains lesson plans for parents to use in developing the preschoolers' listening and speaking abilities as well as their ability to discriminate between sounds and to associate visual and auditory symbols. The guide was published by Houghton Mifflin Company and has been used experimentally with thousands of children in the Denver Public Schools. Sixteen in-service training sessions for parents were provided through the medium of television.[12]

Typically, pre-first grade reading readiness and subsequent follow-up programs in the sixties

1. included an emphasis on extending pupils' sensory experiences and eliciting language experimentation.
2. encouraged individual and group dictation of stories, poems, and labels written by teachers while observed by a child or children dictating.
3. emphasized patterning of oral language through materials such as the "Kinder-Owl" book, *Brown Bear, Brown Bear, What Do You See?* by Holt, Rinehart and Winston.
4. provided some systematized instruction in auditory discrimination and perception of graphemes, visual auditory association of phonemes and their graphemic representation, left-to-right directional orientation, and eye-hand coordination.
5. sought to develop pupils' interests in hearing literature and language, in speaking, in experimenting with graphics or art to express ideas, and in reading pictures or print in books.

Durkin concluded that some children were successful at very early ages in learning about language and learning to read. But in her research findings she specified that the successes of individual children were directly proportional to their readiness, maturation, and general interest in language and books.[13]

[11] O. K. Moore, "The Responsive Environment Project," *The Learning Research and Development Center* (Pittsburgh: University of Pittsburgh Press, 1966), pp. 12–13.

[12] Joseph Brzeinski, "Beginning Reading in Denver," *Reading Teacher,* vol. 18, no. 1 (October 1964), pp. 16–21.

[13] Dolores Durkin, *Children Who Read Early* (New York: Teachers College Press 1966).

Studies in child development provide evidence that children are physiologically, socially, emotionally, and intellectually ready for reading at different periods between the ages of two and seven years of age. To subscribe to a particular program policy in pre-first grade reading seems absurd.

Furthermore, the literature and research of the sixties do not clearly indicate what the long-term advantages are for the child who is ready for an early pre-first grade start in reading. Nor do we know what type of program focus might be best, nor how highly structured or intentionally incidental a pre-first grade reading program ought to be. The research of the seventies should be concerned with some obviously pertinent questions.

EXPERIMENTATION IN THE SIXTIES

In the 1960's those concerned with change in early reading instruction experimented with one or a number of the ways that children could be taught to read. Varied instructional approaches to beginning reading were studied; such as, basal reading, phonics, linguistics, individualized reading, and language experience. For each of these approaches, varied definitions and conceptions developed.

A set of philosophical tenets was undoubtedly basic to each approach. But, as each subscriber to an approach to teaching reading attempted to make it operational, much diversity occurred. Within any one of the five approaches differences could be observed in expected learning outcomes, in instructional techniques and materials, in the degree of program structure versus incidental learning, in the roles of teachers, and in the degree of individualization of instruction that resulted.

The chart on page 218 includes a listing and description of the approaches and some representative programs reflecting the underlying basic philosophy.

Some supporters of each approach felt that a highly structured curricular guide for teachers was essential. In any approach there is disagreement as to the priority or importance to be attached to various reading skills. To some, recognition of phonemic-graphemic regularity was considered more important than comprehension ability. For others, an interest and desire to select and read materials was far more essential than facility in reading that which was selected. The teacher's role within each approach varied from that of a prescriber of goals, initiator of learning, and pacer of instruction to that of merely providing the environment in which the child selected his reading goals, sought them independently, and paced his learning. As much diversity existed within an approach as between approaches in the matter of priority or importance of specific goals.

Another innovation that was examined was the use of a simplified coding system in the introduction of reading. The initial teaching alphabet (I.T.A.) of 44 characters, introduced by Downing and Pitman of Great Britain, posed the question of whether or not children could more easily learn to read with this innovative orthographic medium. Another orthography, Unifon, was

APPROACHES TO BEGINNING READING

I. *Basal Reading Approaches*
   A. *Description:* Bound, graded series of stories for pupils with a vocabulary that is controlled in introduction and repetition; teacher's manuals that describe a sequential introduction of reading skills; pupils' workbooks for teaching, reinforcing, or testing pupils' skills competencies.
   B. *Published Programs: The Ginn 100 Series* by Ginn and Company; *The Multi-Ethnic Coordinated Basal Reading Program* by Scott Foresman and Company.
II. *Phonetic Reading Approaches*
   A. *Description:* Teacher's guides that suggest an initially heavy and completely sequenced introduction of phonics in beginning reading; workbooks for pupil practice, some packaged paperbound or hardbound books that pupils may read for reinforcing phonetic generalizations.
   B. *Published Programs: Phono-Visual Approach* by Phono-Visual Inc.; *Phonetic Keys to Reading* by Economy Press, Inc.
III. *Phonemic-Linguistic Reading Approaches*
   A. *Description:* Bound, graded series of stories or selections for pupils that contain vocabulary selected on the basis of phonemic-graphemic regularities; teacher's manuals that emphasize the teaching of reading as a phonemic-graphemic decoding process; little or no emphasis on comprehension of symbols initially; pictures in pupils' stories eliminated or kept to a minimum because of their distracting qualities.
   B. *Published Programs: Programmed Reading* by Sullivan Associates, McGraw-Hill Company; *Linguistic Science Readers* by Harper & Row; *Merrill Linguistic Readers* by Charles E. Merrill Company.
IV. *Individualized Reading Approaches*
   A. *Description:* Based on the learning theory involving pupil self-selection, self-seeking, and self-pacing; no published guide for teachers; much emphasis on teaching reading skills as pupils encounter the need of a skill while reading in trade books; a ratio of five to eight trade books per child at a time; many individual pupil-teacher conferences.
   B. *Published Programs:* None except professional resources for teachers such as: *Educator's Guide to Personalized Reading Instruction* by Walter Barbe, Prentice-Hall Inc.; *Individualizing Your Reading Program* by Jeannette Veatch, G. P. Putnam's Sons.
V. *Language Experience Approaches*
   A. *Description:* Pupils' oral language is recorded by teachers on charts; reading readiness and reading skills are taught using pupils' dictated and independently written materials; published guides are available

to teachers; pupils make the transition from learning to read their own dictations to reading in trade books; much emphasis is placed on learning other communication skills (listening, speaking, perceiving, nonvocal signaling, writing) as well as reading.

B. *Published Programs: Language Experiences in Reading,* Teacher's Resource Books by Roach Van and Claryce Allen, Encyclopedia Britannica Corp.; *An Integrated Experienced Approach to Communication,* Teacher's Guides by Elaine Vilscek and Lorraine Morgan, U.S.O.E. publication.

---

introduced. Both Unifon and I.T.A. could be employed with any one or a combination of instructional approaches. Hopefully, the beginnings of learning to read with a different orthography would reduce and simplify problems some beginning readers have in visual discrimination of letters. After an initial introduction to reading with I.T.A. or Unifon, using one or more highly individualized instructional approaches, pupils are required to make a transition to regular English orthography.

During the sixties many research studies examined varied approaches and orthographies. "The Coordinated Research in Beginning Reading Instruction," a major national effort begun in 1964, involved 27 centers in research on pupil successes in the various reading approaches. The findings of these individual studies were reported in 1966 and 1967 in the May and October issues, respectively, of *The Reading Teacher.* Of the original 27 centers, 14 conducted a follow-up study of pupils in their second year in an approach. About five centers were subsidized for a third year in order to continue to observe the progress of pupils.

As might have been expected, the studies revealed a multitude of differences between pupils, teachers, schools, communities, and approaches. The University of Minnesota was selected as the coordinating center for all the research projects. Despite the difficulties of controlling statistically the different inter- and intra-project center variables, processing of data was completed and reported by Bond and Dykstra. Their most significant concluding remarks were:

1. Teacher variables had a greater impact on pupil progress than did the variables of method.
2. Pupils in any approach who were exposed to systematic programs of phonics or linguistics exhibited a greater amount of decoding power.[14]

Unfortunately, the degree of individualization of instruction within ap-

---

[14] Guy Bond and Robert Dykstra, "Interpreting First Grade Reading Studies," in Russell Stauffer, ed., *First Grade Reading Studies* (Newark, Del.: International Reading Association, 1967), pp. 1–9.

proaches or among teachers was not considered. Data was accumulated primarily through group measurement techniques. Research findings, too, reflected comparisons of groups rather than individual pupils. The most important questions related to method or approach that remain to be answered in the 1970's are:

1. Which approach or approaches are most effective in developing reading behaviors?
2. Which approach or approaches most successfully facilitate individualized instruction?
3. In view of the problems some pupils experience in making the transition from I.T.A. to a regular orthography,[15] how can those pupils who might benefit from an I.T.A. beginning in reading be initially identified?

PUBLICATIONS AND TECHNOLOGICAL DEVICES OF THE SIXTIES

To list all of the latest educational developments that focus on individualized reading instruction would be difficult. Some selected examples of such materials will be described.

Trade books as well as basal reading books received a new look in the 1960's. Informational books truly contained information. Various artistic media and techniques were employed by book illustrators. Attention was being directed to reading materials for children of different economic and ethnic backgrounds, different geographic environments, and of both sexes. Some books contained no pictures or illustrations of any kind. Type setting developed a new look as well. Both print script as well as cursive type script appeared in trade books for primary pupils. Different styles of writing were introduced to primary readers as well as various other literary qualities. These trends and new looks in books were evident in the *Owl Series* of collected trade books published by Holt, Rinehart and Winston and are continued as a new look in 1970 basal reading series such as the *Ginn 360 Basic Reading Series* by Ginn and Company. Many more materials are being published for the older primary child with a reading problem—books of high interest, but low vocabulary and readability load.

Audiovisual devices, too, were of a variety of types and could be used in a number of ways to facilitate individualization of instruction. Most popular were the Controlled Readers and accompanying filmstrips produced by Education Development Laboratories. Teachers who had separate viewing facilities for pupils could use these audiovisual novelties to provide reinforcement of comprehension skills in primary grades. The Language Master by

---

[15] John Downing, "Nature and Functions of I.T.A. in Beginning Reading," in Elaine Vilscek, ed., *A Decade of Innovations: Approaches to Beginning Reading*, vol. 12, Part 3 (Newark, Del.: International Reading Association, 1968), pp. 149–61.

Appleton-Century-Crofts and the MTA Scholar by Modern Teaching Associates are additional examples of audiovisual devices that can contribute to instructional differentiation, particularly in furthering differentiated reading vocabulary skills.

Most teachers in the sixties had access to at least one or more kits that included exercises in reading comprehension or word recognition, coded by difficulty levels for any given interest-age level for the primary pupil. Examples include the SRA Reading Labs, the Lyons and Carnahan phonics games boxes or spelling games boxes, and the Webster Classroom Reading Clinic. These materials were means by which a teacher could provide individual pupils with self-directive and corrective learning while she devoted her attention to other pupils.

Programmed reading materials were available at all grade levels. Two rather widely used programs were the *Programmed Linguistic Reading Series* by Sullivan Associates and the *Programmed Primer* by Teaching Machines, Inc. Their lockstep progression with little or no branching provisions for remediation or reinforcement of a principle to be acquired was, for both pupils and teachers, a major problem.

With an emphasis on creativity of response in the sixties, workbooks shed to a degree their stereotype as dull drill experiences. Those by Roach Van and Claryce Allen that accompany the *Language Experiences in Reading* program published by Encyclopedia Britannica Press and *Invitations to Creative Thinking* by Paul Torrance published by Ginn and Company are refreshing. The 1970's promise more of these kinds of workbook materials. Teachers will appropriately select those pages in the workbooks that will be of value to individual pupils rather than insisting that each child have and complete an identical workbook for the mere sake of keeping him occupied.

In the sixties computerized instruction evolved and was in its infancy. These computers were used for three kinds of learning systems: a drill and practice system for learning reinforcement, a tutorial system to replace the teacher in introducing a new skill, and a dialogue system to allow the pupil to question as he faced computerized program problems. Since 1966, Atkinson and Hansen have been conducting research on computer-assisted instruction in initial reading.[16] Thus far, their research reports are primarily descriptive and incomplete. There is no doubt that computer-assisted instruction will be improved during the seventies. It may be an effective medium, highly motivating, and capable of implementing more individualized instruction than is presently practical.

Teachers, supervisors, and administrators must tell publishers and distributors of materials the kinds of materials they find most useful in the process of differentiating instruction. Materials of the 1970's ought to more consistently reflect what teachers and school personnel need rather than what publishing companies *think* they need.

[16] Richard Atkinson and Duncan Hansen, "Computer-Assisted Instruction in Initial Reading: The Stanford Project," *Reading Research Quarterly* (1966), pp. 5–26.

How much material of one type or another is needed to ensure instructional diversification in the early reading years is a moot question. Funds, diversity of pupils' reading needs, and the degree to which a teacher can become acquainted with and organize or supervise pupil use of multiple materials are guidelines to be considered in the process of selection.

INDIVIDUALIZATION OF INSTRUCTION AND INDIVIDUAL PUPIL TUTORING

If used synonymously, the terms individualization of instruction and individual pupil tutoring may represent an inappropriate means of instructional diversification. Obviously, smaller class enrollments result in a greater probability of knowing and meeting the needs of individual learners. There is a trend, therefore, to reduce the numbers of pupils in a unit of instruction at early instructional levels.

In-class grouping in early reading instruction can be managed in a number of ways, regardless of the instructional approach being employed. Pupils may be grouped for basal reading or reading in trade books according to their general reading level. They may be regrouped as needed for instruction in various skills and subskills. It is not unlikely to find pupils at any level of readability who may be below that level in a skill or subskill. Grouping for special interests is also important. Children enjoy reading together and talking about selections that are of common interest to them. Finally, social grouping in reading is particularly appealing to the early reader who enjoys reading with or to a special friend.

A modern classroom or school building is not necessary in order to individualize instruction. It helps, however, to have furniture that is movable and to have at least an anteroom in which small groups of pupils may work without distraction. To facilitate reading interests, each primary reading classroom ought to have an adequate number of books which pupils may browse through or read, an instructional materials center that encourages children to enter, a comfortable place for sitting or lying on a rug while reading, and, most important, a teacher who reflects her own appreciations of children's books and reading.

NONGRADED CLASSES

The relationships of various administrative systems to individualization of instruction have been studied, among them are nongrading, self-contained structuring; departmentalizing; unitizing the responsibilities of teachers, supervisors, and administrators in instruction, and dual progression with its two-track system of pupil mastery of cultural imperatives, including reading, and election of other academic areas such as mathematics and science. Advantages and disadvantages of these systems of administrative organizations have been cited many times in the literature.[17]

Nongrading at primary levels seems to be the most predominant of current organizational plans and the most likely to continue to receive attention in the seventies. Therefore, nongrading in reading at primary levels will be discussed in some detail.

Although there is wide diversity among nongraded schools, there are basic principles characteristic of all. In the *Dictionary of Education* the ungraded primary school is defined as one containing flexible pupil grouping regardless of pupils' ages without finely drawn grade level distinctions.[18]

According to Dufay, it is "a philosophy of education that includes the notion of continuous pupil progress, which promotes flexibility in grouping by the device of removing grade labels, which is designed to facilitate the teacher's role in providing for pupils' individual differences, and which is intended to eliminate or lessen the problems of retention and acceleration."[19]

Consequently, the nongraded school, unlike the six-grade elementary organization, permits a pupil to work to a level of accomplishment in each subject at a pace commensurate with his potential for progress. This situation exists in all areas of his educational curriculum. More clearly Dufay states:

> There is a single basic difference between the graded and the ungraded schools. In the truly graded schools, the program is first established—according to grades—and the children are expected to adapt to that existing program. That one program is geared to that mythical 'average' child.
>
> In the truly ungraded school, the ultimate objective is the tailoring of programs to the individual child, with adjustments made in the program.
>
> Replacing upward movement on a grade basis, the notion of continuous progress permits upward movement according to the real abilities of students. This movement is not dictated by previously set time sections, but by actual growth, whatever the pupil rate of learning.[20]

This philosophy, as expressed, would necessitate the ungrading of areas such as reading, physical education, and art even though they might be taught by a specialist.

Tewksbury[21] maintains that in current public educational plans few if any schools are completely nongraded. The three basic types of nongrading defined by Tewksbury include:

    1. multileveled instruction in self-contained heterogeneous classes;

[17] William Ragan, *Modern Elementary Curriculum,* 3rd ed. (New York: Holt Rinehart & Winston, 1966), Chapter 7.

[18] Carter V. Good, *Dictionary of Education* (New York: Brown and Sons, 1957).

[19] Frank Dufay, *Ungrading the Elementary School* (New York: Parker Publishing Co., 1966), p. 24.

[20] Frank Dufay, op. cit., pp. 25–28.

[21] John Tewksbury, *Nongrading in the Elementary School* (Columbus, Ohio: Charles E. Merrill Books, Inc., 1967), pp. 5–9.

2. self-contained classes with pupils assigned according to performance levels with provisions for instruction suited to each level of difficulty; and
3. large aggregations of children regrouped during the day or week to form clusters or classes in each curriculum area, working on different levels under the direction of different teachers.

It is apparent that nongrading is an attempt to achieve the best relationship between pupil assignment or grouping and the structure of a flexible yet organized curriculum. In any one of the three plans described by Tewksbury, pupils may represent a single common chronological age level or may be within mixed or multi-age level instructional groupings. Selecting a basic plan from the above three or from a modification of these will certainly affect curricular organization for reading instruction. Decisions about the basic plan of organizational procedures must precede all other curricular planning in specific areas of instruction.

Reading instruction in a nongraded plan will undoubtedly affect pupils, teachers, staff personnel, and supervisors, as well as school plant planning, and providing for storage of instructional materials. Establishing an effective environment for learning is no small task. As the basic educational consumer in a nongraded reading instructional environment, each pupil will be given an opportunity to begin work at his level of readiness. Failures would occur less often and successes should lead to more favorable pupil attitudes toward reading, reading teachers, and the school itself. Better accommodations can be made for the slow learner, the gifted child, and the child who needs corrective reading instruction.

It should be reasonable, too, for pupils who are absent for long periods to resume their reading programs at the points they had reached before the absence. Failure at any grade level should literally vanish since pupils will follow their planned learning continuums in early reading. Pupils' performance levels in reading might be different from their levels of performance in other instructional areas. If a child is to begin his reading program at a determined level of performance, teachers must play a key role in assessment and decision making related to assessment.

Perhaps, the key to some teacher-personnel problems may be a completely unique redefinition of the teacher's role in reading instruction. Specialization of teachers, the employment of various types of semiprofessional teacher aides, the computer, and mechanical and electronic devices will undoubtedly be involved in the redefinition.

Ensuring continuity for each child's reading instruction may become one of the major responsibilities of the reading supervisor assisted by the building principal. If reading instructional improvements can be defined as observable changes in a pupil's behavior, then, supervisors must be qualified to initiate in-service experiences that lead teachers to explore and chart desirable outcomes of a reading program along a defined continuum of progress for each pupil. Subsequently, materials, experiences, and learning environments which contribute to pupil progress will need to be selected and provided.

Some modifications of current school buildings, constructed as graded structures, will need to be made in order to provide for flexible instruction. New buildings can be planned so as to accommodate a unique curricular plan of organization in reading and other subject areas. Physical provision will undoubtedly have to be made for computer-assisted and media-oriented instruction of pupils and for in-service training of teachers of reading just as surely as more adequate provision must be made for necessary "software," such as books.[22]

Nongrading in primary reading requires that teachers have many kinds of materials available in a central location thus providing for their nongraded distribution. Some of these materials may be media-oriented while others may be more conventional in type. Nevertheless, a qualified staff member plus several nonprofessional aides may be needed for the efficient placement and dissemination of such materials.

Time for planning, selecting, and purchasing materials, and the in-service orientation of teachers in a nongraded plan are indispensable. School systems will need to modify many current premises and procedures of operation.

Although modified nongraded organizational plans existed in Athens, Georgia, and Youngstown, Ohio, as early as 1938, it was not until the postwar period that an appreciable number of schools adopted the plans. Even then, adoption was not widespread. In fact, prior to 1959 districts attempting such organizational changes were small in number.

Since 1959, many more plans have been implemented and some attempts have been made to research the effectiveness of nongrading. As one surveys and reviews current nongraded schools, it is obvious that the label, nongraded, has been applied to diverse organization structures.

Brown[23] describes nongrading at both primary and intermediate grade levels in Melbourne, Florida. At primary levels, children are assigned to self-contained, mixed-age classrooms. Interclassroom achievement grouping is based entirely upon reading achievement. In contrast, at intermediate grade levels, nongrading is accomplished through mixed-age departmentalized classes organized according to achievement levels.

Dufay[24] details how he and his staff have nongraded the elementary school in Plainview, Long Island, where he is principal. A Kindergarten Check-Sheet for Reading Readiness is employed to rank pupils at one of four levels of readiness. The sheet, designed by teachers, contains the following categories: Auditory rhyming, auditory beginning sounds, visual-gross shapes, visual-

---

[22] Patrick Suppes, "Plug-In Instruction," *Saturday Review* (July 1966), pp. 25–30.

[23] Frank Brown, *The Appropriate Placement School: A Sophisticated Non-Graded Curriculum* (New York: Parker Publishing Co., 1965).

[24] Frank Dufay, op. cit., pp. 35–95.

matching words and letters, letter names, speaking vocabulary, listening vocabulary, following directions, attention span, retention, eye-hand coordination, and interest in learning to read. At other age levels, a pupil's instructional
level for reading is based on an informal reading inventory. At both kindergarten and upper levels, the total pupil population at a level is ranked in thirds
according to achievement. Pupils are then placed homogeneously (in terms
of achievement) in self-contained classes. Multiple-basal instruction is employed by all teachers. The reading consultant acts as the remedial reading
teacher.

In viewing Dufay's proposal for nongrading in reading, many inflexibilities
are visible. Within an achievement level, youngsters may vary considerably in
special skills. Multiple-basal materials and procedures are by no means the
only tool that should be used in meeting individual pupil's needs. No single
set or system of techniques or approaches can be completely accepted as the
tool to remedy all reading needs and ills.

Goodlad[25] describes another variation of nongrading in the reading program at the University Elementary School, University of California. Goodlad's
recommendations include thorough pupil assessment, multi-age grouping in
areas of diagnosed needs and strengths, and implementation of the instructional program through the individualized reading approach.

An emphasis on independent study and learning to read through self-
directive, corrective materials in a suburban St. Louis elementary school is
presented by Black.[26] He suggests that pupils spend increasing amounts of
time in independent learning tasks. The school's centrally located learning
materials center is designed to encourage much instructional flexibility. The
building also provides instructional areas with movable partitions to accommodate varied sized groups.

Martin[27] describes a continuous progress program in reading in Corpus
Christi, Texas. Eight reading levels are substituted for the three grades of the
primary school. The eight levels correspond to the usual basal textbook organization from readiness to the 3^2 reader. Readiness tests and teachers' judgments
are used as placement criteria at the primary level. Although the school ex-
pects every student to complete every basal reader, workbook, and supplementary book, the students are given different amounts of time to do so.
Varieties of library books and other multileveled materials are used as supplements. This plan seems to be a very narrow conceptualization of nongraded
individualization of instruction in that every child must read all materials at
each level, whether appropriate or not.

25 John Goodlad, "Meeting Children Where They Are," *Saturday Review* (February
1963), pp. 274–77.

26 Hillel Black, "A School Where Children Teach Themselves," *Saturday Evening Post*
CCXXXVIII (June 1965), pp. 80–85.

27 Marjorie Martin, "Organizing Instruction in Ungraded Primary Schools," in J. Allen
Figurel, ed., *Vistas in Reading* (Newark, Del.: International Reading Association, 1966),
pp. 136–40.

Multi-age grouping is featured in a nongraded program in San Diego county as described by Ross.[28] All kindergarten, first-, second-, and third-grade pupils are assigned at random to primary teachers. Thus, a nongraded unit of pupils will include equal numbers of five, six, seven, and eight year olds. As pupils progress through the primary unit, they may, in two or more years, move into the intermediate grade unit. Team teaching, pupil-teaming for learning from one another, and prescriptive teaching are featured. Individualized checklists are employed by teachers for pupil placement and recording progress. Both the language experience and the individualized reading approaches are being utilized in teaching reading. Ross' description is certainly an oversimplification of a complex system that deserves careful planning and implementation.

This review of current programs is by no means exhaustive. It is intended merely to illustrate the contrasts in reading instruction as defined and labeled under administrative plans in nongraded organizational structures of the sixties.

Systems or approaches to teaching reading within any type of administrative organizational structure can and should be varied to meet the pupils' observable needs. On the reading scene today, the many widely recognized major categories of instructional approaches such as the basal reader approach, the linguistic approach, phonics, language experience, individualized reading, or combinations of these can aid in the differentiation of instruction.

Each of these instructional approaches could be used within the nongraded school. With in-service experiences to support them, teachers could advantageously use certain approaches with selected children. In schools employing nongraded plans, a number of these approaches could be used.

Using Varied Approaches Within a Multileveled Instructional Plan

IN SELF-CONTAINED HETEROGENEOUS CLASSES

A multileveled instructional plan in a self-contained classroom can be defined as one by which the teacher meets the reading needs of 30 to 35 pupils of like or varied ages through many types of grouping procedures.[29] Reading instruction is differentiated for groups that have similar skills deficits, groups that exhibit similar levels of achievements, and on occasion groups that have similar interests.

Once a pupil's instructional reading level, independent reading level, potential reading level, reading skill deficiencies, and specialized interests have been defined, any one of the five major instructional approaches may be em-

---

[28] Ramon Ross, "Reading Instruction in the Ungraded Primary," in J. Allen Figurel, ed., *Reading and Inquiry* (Newark, Del.: International Reading Association, 1965), pp. 128–29.

[29] John Tewksbury, op. cit., pp. 6–9.

ployed. Teachers must select an approach or approaches that are in keeping with the continuing school instructional philosophies and programs. Yet, each teacher must also attempt to surmise which approach will be most effective and will best serve the needs of groups of youngsters.

More specifically, one group of youngsters may learn most effectively through the basal reader approach. Another group may respond better to combined language experience and individualized reading procedures. A third group of children who are confused by the irregularities of sound-symbol sets may, on the other hand, achieve best through a linguistic orientation.

Within each group approach, the teacher should use varied levels of materials to accommodate pupil differences. For example, youngsters in a basal reading group may be using different levels of the basal reader. Silent guided reading can be effectively directed by the teacher with each child or several children reading from different basal books. Vocabulary practice becomes an individualized matter but oral reading is maintained both as an avenue for sharing ideas about what one has read and as a means of diagnosis. Pupils in this group may be regrouped with those taught through language experience, phonetic, individualized, or linguistic approaches for specialized instruction in skill areas as needed.

Occasionally, pupils of various ages, achievement levels, and skills needs may be assembled for the purpose of sharing common reading interests. Reporting on supplementary or library reading is one means of purposeful interest groupings.

Multileveled instruction within self-contained classrooms is perhaps the most manageable and valuable pattern of nongraded structuring. A well-organized, well-prepared teacher can achieve maximum flexibility within this plan.

IN SELF-CONTAINED HOMOGENEOUS CLASSES

A majority of well-designed studies dealing with the effectiveness of homogeneous grouping clearly indicate that homogeneity is possible in only one area of a child's reading patterns. One of the most representative and carefully executed studies was by Balow and Curtin.[30] They were able to conclude that when pupils were grouped homogeneously by reading comprehension scores, their subscores on the Iowa Every Pupil Test of Basic Skills represented a heterogeneous array.

In view of such findings one can assume that as much variability might exist within these classes as within those classes grouped on other bases. The same principles of selecting and implementing approaches with varied in-class groupings would be desirable. Since homogeneity on subskills cannot be established, grouping children on the basis of comprehension scores is unworkable.

[30] B. Balow and J. Curtin, "Reading Comprehension Score As a Means of Establishing Homogeneous Classes," *The Reading Teacher*, no. 19 (1965), pp. 169–73.

IN LARGE AGGREGATIONS OF CHILDREN

Team teaching in reading can be an effective procedure in a nongraded administrative plan. Teachers, in such a program, share their strengths by using preferred instructional approaches with the pupils assigned to them. Much flexibility can be ensured if teachers and pupils are regrouped for needed skills instruction. Team teaching assumes that teachers are different and their best competencies should be used in the best interests of children.

With larger numbers of pupil contacts, teachers need more time for sharing information about pupils' needs. Planning for the various types of grouping is time consuming and should be done during periods set aside for that purpose. At times, it may even be appropriate for one teacher to work with a group of 100 to 150 pupils.

Much more research on the effects of nongrading plans or other kinds of administrative organizational plan is needed in the seventies. Administrative organizational plans are worthwhile only to the degree that they allow individualization of instruction.

Conclusion

In this chapter an attempt has been made to survey the relationship of early childhood reading to other communication processes. The primary child has been viewed as an individual learner, and varied teaching approaches, techniques, materials, technological media, and administrative organizations have been considered.

Learning to read is a multifaceted process clearly associated with other communication arts as well as the creative arts. Successes of the learner in other communication and creative arts are elicitors for successes in reading. Each child, too, is distinctively different in patterns of development and reactions to learning through specific ways, with specific materials, and within particular kinds of organizational environments.

Administrators need to keep the individual learner and his differences in mind when selecting teachers, providing teachers with in-service programs and other aids, and in making varied materials available to teaching personnel. Pilot programs that are innovative and lend clues to the probable future successes of readers should be established. Teachers need to be given time for planning their work with children and for learning about new modes and means of reading instruction. Consequently, the seventies should reflect significant improvements in early primary reading as compared to the sixties.

BIBLIOGRAPHY

Atkinson, Richard, and Duncan Hansen, "Computer-Assisted Instruction in Initial Reading: The Stanford Project," *Reading Research Quarterly* (1966).

Balow, B., and J. Curtin, "Reading Comprehension Score As a Means of Establishing Homogeneous Classes," *The Reading Teacher*, no. 19 (1965).

Black, Hillel, "A School Where Children Teach Themselves," *Saturday Evening Post*, CCXXXVIII (June 1965).

Bloom, Benjamin, ed., *Taxonomy of Education Objectives: Handbook I:* Cognitive Domain (New York: David McKay Co., 1956).

Bond, Guy, and Robert Dykstra, "Interpreting First Grade Reading Studies," in Russel Stauffer, ed., *First Grade Reading Studies* (Newark, Del.: International Reading Association, 1967).

Brown, Frank, *The Appropriate Placement School: A Sophisticated Non-Graded Curriculum* (New York: Parker Publishing Co., 1965).

Brzeinski, Joseph, "Beginning Reading in Denver," *Reading Teacher*, vol. 18, no. 1 (October 1964).

Deutsch, Martin, "Facilitating Development in the Pre-School Child: Social and Psychological Perspectives," *Merrill-Palmer Quarterly*, vol. 10, no. 3 (July 1964).

Downing, John, "Nature and Functions of I. T. A. in Beginning Reading," in Elaine Vilscek, ed., *A Decade of Innovations: Approaches to Beginning Reading*, vol. 12, Part 3 (Newark, Del.: International Reading Association, 1968).

Dufay, Frank, *Ungrading the Elementary School* (New York: Parker Publishing Co., 1966).

Durkin, Dolores, *Children Who Read Early* (New York: Teachers College Press, 1966).

Good, Carter V., *Dictionary of Education* (New York: Brown and Sons, 1957).

Goodlad, John, "Meeting Children Where They Are," *Saturday Review* (February 1963).

Gwynn, J., and John Chase, *Curriculum Principles and Social Trends* (New York: Macmillan Co., 1969).

Krathwohl, David, Benjamin Bloom, and Bertram Masia, *Taxonomy of Education Objectives: Handbook II: Affective Domain* (New York: David McKay Co., 1964).

Martin, Marjorie, "Organizing Instruction in Ungraded Primary Schools," in J. Allen Figurel, ed., *Vistas in Reading* (Newark, Del.: International Reading Association, 1966).

Moore, O. K., "The Responsive Environment Project," *The Learning Research and Development Center* (Pittsburgh: University of Pittsburgh Press, 1966).

Ragan, William, *Modern Elementary Curriculum* (New York: Holt, Rinehart & Winston, 1966).

Richmond, Julius, "Communities in Action: A Report on Project Head Start," *Reading Teacher*, vol. 19, no. 5 February 1966).

Scott, J. P., "Critical Periods in Behavioral Development," *Science*, no. 138 (1962).

Standing, E. M., *Maria Montessori—Her Life and Work* (New York: New American Library Inc., 1962).

Strickland, Ruth, "Building on What We Know," in J. Allen Figurel, ed., *Reading and Realism,* vol. 13, Part I (Newark, Del.: International Reading Association, 1969).

Suppes, Patrick, "Plug-In Instruction," *Saturday Review* (July 1966).

Tewksbury, John, *Nongrading in the Elementary School* (Columbus, Ohio: Charles E. Merrill Books, Inc., 1967).

Vilscek, Elaine, "Individualizing Instruction," in Wallace Ramsey, ed., *Perspectives in Reading,* no. 9 (Newark, Del.: International Reading Association, 1967).

12

Current Patterns in Middle Childhood Reading

Ellsworth S. Woestehoff

Introduction

Middle-grade reading is the *Stiefkind* of American reading instruction. While there is agreement concerning the need for continuous attention to the development of reading skills and abilities at all grade levels, practice more commonly reflects a "yes, but" attitude. For example, the evidence clearly shows that individual differences in reading achievement increase at an accelerating rate as children move through the grades. Yet, the instructional adjustments so common in the primary grades generally do not exist at the intermediate-grade levels.

A substantial part of this situation can, of course, be attributed to an ever-expanding curriculum and a consequent decrease in both the absolute and relative amounts of time available for direct instruction in reading. A significant portion may likewise be related to the generally held assumption that at grade 4, the emphasis must necessarily shift from "learning to read" to "reading to learn." Ideally these factors should be integrated; a reaction which merely accepts the first of these premises as reality and rejects the latter for any of a number of reasons would resolve nothing.

Within the body of this chapter, an attempt will be made to consider middle-grade reading as a facet of a total educational program. In this process attention will be directed to conditions which are common to reading instruction at all levels as well as those which appear to have unique application to the middle grades. While it is unlikely that general principles associated with school administration are subject to variation solely on account of grade levels, there can be no question that unique characteristics of children, particularly in terms of their learning needs, will demand special attention.

There is a strong belief that the nature of reading instruction must be determined primarily by the characteristics of learners. This chapter will, therefore, attempt to consider current patterns of reading for the middle grades from that point of view.

Such a procedure will require substantial reference to the characteristics of children at the middle-grade ages as well as to the processes and functions of reading. Although such statements may represent common knowledge, their inclusion here is necessary to the discussion to follow.

The Middle-Grade Child

For purposes of convenience, children in this group may be considered to be between nine and twelve years of age, having from three to five years of prior reading instruction.

From a personal standpoint, it is important to bear in mind that children of these ages grow in a variety of ways. Physical growth, for example, which may occur in rapid spurts, can have a profound effect upon the amount of energy available for mental as well as physical tasks. Since reading is by nature a sedentary type of activity, the need for physical movement may at times not allow for the type of concentration required for reading. The physical needs of these children must be given the same recognition as are the needs of the primary-grade child.

Perhaps a more direct impact upon learning comes from other more personal kinds of growth. For example, there begins to develop an increasing level of social sophistication which carries children's interests far beyond their immediate environment. As a result of greater mobility and expanding communications, they are able to view the world and even the universe in a more realistic manner. Peer relationships likewise extend beyond primary social and play activities to wide-ranging matters of personal behavior.

The availability of seemingly limitless experiences can drastically modify the child's interests. For example, the reading of an account of man's first walk on the moon cannot possibly provide the emotional impact of viewing it by means of direct television transmission. In a society which places such a premium on human endeavor, this kind of extension can only serve to make the instructional task more difficult. The school must learn to compete with the excitement of the out-of-school experiences so readily available. Quite obviously, this has serious implications for the content of children's reading material, particularly when the motivation which comes from learning a new skill—in this case, reading—is no longer available.

Related to the matter of personal interests is the somewhat more discernible variability in reading achievement. Bond and Tinker[1] have pointed out that, in unselected groups of children, it would not be unusual to find a five-year range in reading achievement at grade 4 and a seven-year range at grade 6.

[1] Guy L. Bond and Miles A. Tinker, *Reading Difficulties: Their Diagnosis and Treatment,* 2nd ed. (New York: Appleton-Century-Crofts, 1967), p. 47.

Of even greater interest is the fact that, when such a class is divided into groups of equal size, the range of achievement in the upper and lower thirds of the total group is likely to be twice as great as the range in the middle third. The existence of such conditions has extremely important implications for both instructional and organizational procedures in the middle grades.

Middle-Grade Reading

Because formal education must respond to the needs of a society as well as to those of individual children, it is necessary to take into account the general goals of reading instruction in the middle-childhood grades. These goals must be reflected in the elements of instructional programs.

Most authorities would agree that the instructional program in reading should provide four basic types of experiences. The first and primary responsibility is for fundamental skill development which generally takes place within a relatively structured setting. The second includes those activities which allow the child to make functional use of his reading skills in a wide range of learning experiences. The third is perhaps most intimately associated with the growth of each individual, and comprises reading related to areas of personal interest. Looked upon by the school, it is essentially a leisure-time activity. Finally, there is that element of the instructional program which provides for the remediation of learning which in some respect has been either incomplete or ineffective. For obvious reasons, the concern here is for the first two of these.

A decrease in emphasis upon direct reading instruction in the middle grades was earlier attributed to seemingly necessary priority assignment of time. This may be justifiable in the sense that it is related to the expansion of children's interests and learning needs. It does, however, require that the most effective use is made of the time that is available. Since learning needs tend to become more individual, for example, it stands to reason that instruction must become more specific and individualized. The transition which appears in terms of stronger emphasis upon the utilization of reading skills and abilities for learning in the content or substantive aspects of the curriculum also has implications for reading instruction. Here it might well be argued that skill instruction in each subject area should be provided when necessary. While this may well be an acceptable means of meeting immediate needs, it is of questionable value for generalized learnings which are perhaps the more significant goals. In addition, experience has shown that when the choice is between content and the reading skill necessary to deal with the content, skill instruction is rarely given priority.

When reading skills are at a relatively immature level, it is particularly difficult to develop clear knowledge and understanding of conditions which are remote in terms of time and space. This is especially true in the social sciences where there is often great difficulty in closing the gap between children's life experiences and the realities which they may be expected to understand.

The disparity is somewhat less serious in the natural sciences where many conditions can be replicated in the laboratory and the experiment or its written description may clarify hazy concepts.

The fact remains, however, that each subject area does make unique reading demands on children, and the requisite knowledge and skills are not likely to develop without direct instructional intervention. There is sufficient commonality in skill development to warrant a generalized instructional program. One condition which appears to be an important feature of the instructional organization at this level is the development of increasing independence on the part of the learner. This is particularly true in terms of locating sources of information and dealing independently with these sources.

Throughout much of the primary-grade period, the content of the basic instructional program tends to represent the most difficult reading the child is expected to do. Since this is essentially directed reading activity, with the direction being supplied by the teacher, growth in independence on the part of the pupil will generally emphasize the development of skills. In short, the instruction is directed toward the learning elements necessary for the development of independence.

In the intermediate years, the extension of reading into diverse fields, into materials which lack tight control of vocabulary and concepts, requires the pupil to make increasingly wider use of his reading independence. If the reading skills required for independent learning are not well developed, serious problems may result. In such instances, the argument for continuous reading instruction gains in strength.

Developing Goals for Reading Instruction

For many teachers, formal consideration of instructional objectives recalls academic exercises of questionable merit, performed outside the context of a real teaching situation. Yet, unless such goals are set, it is highly unlikely that effective teaching leading to meaningful learning will occur.

Planning for teaching and learning must, of necessity, include provision for identifying general and specific as well as immediate and long-range goals. It must likewise take into account forces which give rise to such objectives. While it may be unnecessary or even inappropriate to consider this matter at length here, there should be recognition that learning goals may find their origin in society in its broadest sense or in any element within that society, including especially teachers and pupils. Any instructional program must, therefore, give careful attention to both the source and nature of possible goals of learning.

The specification of goals for the instructional program in reading, as in other areas, serves a two-fold purpose. First, it provides direction and suggests content for the program, and secondly, it functions as a basis for the evaluation of pupil progress. Such instructional objectives may be stated in a number of ways. At the present time, the statement of objectives in behavioral terms has found much favor among educators.

As a process, this has considerable merit, since it reduces learning outcomes to conditions which can be observed. Specifying the nature of outcomes and ways in which they might be manifested not only gives direction and purpose to the learning but provides the framework for evaluation as well.

The specificity of such learning outcomes in terms of observable behavior is a source of both strength and weakness. The strength, as indicated above, lies primarily in facilitating the process of evaluation. The weakness lies in the danger of fragmentation which makes the development of interrelationships among learnings difficult if not impossible.

One of the dangers which may accompany concern for considering instructional outcomes within a logical framework is the possibility that they may assume discrete and rigid identities. A crucial element, then, is the development of an operational scheme which provides for instructional flexibility based upon known needs of individual learners.

Organization for Instruction

The economics of education, at least at the present time, dictate that a single teacher must be associated with a number of pupils. This fact, coupled with the variability in rate and extent of learning, requires organization for instruction. A substantial amount of that organization must be dedicated to an accounting of the differences which occur in learning.

INDIVIDUALIZED VERSUS GROUP INSTRUCTION

There are three relatively distinct tendencies among the instructional patterns currently utilized in the intermediate grades. First, while the evidence is not clearly available, it is likely that middle-grade classrooms do not maintain the kind of differentiation provided through grouping practices commonly found in the primary grades. Much of this change may be related to the time problems discussed earlier in this chapter.

In cases where variable patterns do exist, two divergent trends may be found. The first is that of maintaining the group concept while accounting for variability through the multilevel structuring of materials. Such approaches are designed to take advantage of the values of group participation while adjusting skill instruction and skill demands to a greater extent than is possible within uni-level materials.

The second approach to the use of the multilevel concept combines such materials with individual study, usually employing some means of self-correction. Programmed texts and unbound reading kits most commonly represent this type of material.

In attempting to determine the relative merit of these two approaches, little guidance can be obtained from the findings of research. As is so frequently the case, the results of related research are equivocal. The alternative, then, would appear to consider the nature of the possible learnings each might produce and the particular demands which may be made upon teachers and students.

For example, a specific learning task may be secured most effectively with the aid of clarification which group discussion affords. On the other hand, group-oriented instruction can never be truly personalized, and the learning is generally geared to an average or less than average rate. The problem here is particularly acute in the areas of specific reading skill development which tends to be relatively restricted in range compared with the great latitude generally available when dealing with comprehension abilities.

Differences may also exist in terms of motivation. In the group setting, this can be controlled by the skill of the teacher, but in individual work it must be generated by the task and maintained by the pupil. Obviously, the extent to which a given pupil has developed the ability to work without direct and continuous teacher supervision will be a crucial factor in deciding which approach to utilize.

CROSS-CLASS GROUPING

A common plan for organizing reading instruction is the so-called Joplin Plan of inter-class scheduling. Under this plan, children are assigned to instructional groups on the basis of a general estimate of reading ability tempered by teacher evaluation and judgment. The specific group assignment may or may not take into account the grade placement of the pupils.

The advantages of such a plan obviously include the reduction of the range of differences within an instructional group. Even when the selection is based upon the best available evidence, substantial variation in reading subskill development will exist and, therefore, careful attention to individual learning needs is required. Skill grouping will still be necessary, and the plight of the teacher may only be eased. In addition, significant opportunities for additional instruction may be lost because an individual child's reading teacher may not be his teacher in other areas where related learning needs might occur. This type of departmentalization, then, calls for careful and continuous communication among teachers.

FUNCTIONAL SKILL DEVELOPMENT

It would be inappropriate to leave the matter of organizational patterns without attention to the type of individualized approach which gives primary attention to relatively immediate learning needs. Individualized reading which focuses on the seeking, self-selecting, pacing concepts of human behavior has been discussed at some length within other portions of this book and will not be considered here. Quite obviously, the individualized approach does seriously consider the matter of individual growth rates and leans heavily upon the motivation which develops out of personal interest.

The problem of time allotment referred to earlier in this chapter is important to instructional organization. On this basis alone, some would argue that middle-grade reading instruction should be limited to taking care of the immediate reading needs found within subject-matter materials.

While this may be termed opportunistic, a case could be made for shifting instructional attention from an organized, structured program to the materials which the pupils actually read. The organized program may then be used selectively as a source of instruction rather than its determinant.

In an operational sense, the teacher would need first to analyze the functional reading material in terms of the demands it makes upon readers. Next, he would make judgments concerning the extent to which his pupils possess learnings sufficient for these reading tasks. Finally, he would provide direct instruction for specific pupils in their areas of deficiency.

COMPUTER-ASSISTED INSTRUCTION

With every great technological advance in the field of communication, the decline of reading as a means of learning has been predicted. To the present time, this has not come to pass. The early claims relative to computer technology have suggested that the replacement is more likely to involve the means of instruction than the reading itself. While some limited attempts have been made to provide instruction in early reading skills via computer, the present indication is that reading skill development may not become an important computer function.

It is somewhat more likely that the rapid analysis which the computer can provide will be more helpful in diagnosing difficulties and prescribing instruction as an aid to the teacher than it would be in dealing with the actual instruction.

Other Functions of Reading Instruction

Up to this point, the discussion of current patterns in middle-grade reading has focused primarily upon the processes of instruction. In general, they reflect concerns for learning without consideration of possible side-effects. Most of the questions dealing with how children learn have been answered by reference, either directly or indirectly, to learning psychology. Under pressure created by sociological concerns, attention is now being directed to the total relationship between instructional material and learner characteristics. The immediate effect has been the appearance of multi-ethnic readers.

Except for the exclusion of Negro characters, school readers have in fact been multi-ethnic for many years. The early inclusion of black minority groups was accomplished by modification of illustrations rather than content. However, the cosmetic effect of such modification is likely to be neither complete nor permanent. Far from it. Therefore, current textbook writers have found it desirable to modify the content as well in order to present a higher level of reality. Since most problems of social interrelationships are basically attitudinal, even the indirect effects of such changes may be considerable.

The social problems which reflect and are reflected by new materials are of concern to everyone, and therefore become attitudinal effects of learning to read. Perhaps equally important is the need to provide materials which deal with situations which are real to the reader. If comprehension in reading involves the restructuring of experience, then the instructional material must utilize situations which are familiar to the child who does the reading.

Inspection of reading materials reveals that, while the values represented may be commendable, they may not necessarily be realistic for all children. For example, most of the action in early readers took place in carefully manicured yards and involved well-groomed children. While few would argue that these conditions are not desirable, no one could reasonably conclude that they are typical.

As a result, most reading materials now give substantial emphasis to inner-urban settings and at least one reading series deals exclusively with urban backgrounds.

It would be folly, of course, to suggest that such changes will resolve all problems. The differences which exist within urban settings are just as extensive as those which occur between urban and suburban, or urban and rural. While there is the likelihood that the situations may more nearly approximate a reality which the child can understand, it will remain extremely important to ensure that appropriate backgrounds do exist. To assume that a child from the city will automatically be able to deal effectively with material which utilizes the city for its setting is to invite disaster.

The use of multi-ethnic or urban-oriented readers may have many positive effects on human behaviors, including reading. In some instances, the effect may be motivational and thus be immediately related to learning to read. In all likelihood, the effect may be somewhat more wide-ranging and more enduring. In this instance, it may well be related to learning to live.

The Role of the Administrator

Throughout this chapter, a conscious effort has been made to provide only limited reference to specific instructional procedures. This is a reflection of the belief that the administrative role is one dedicated to the broad spectrum of educational leadership. In this sense, his attitudes, understandings, and knowledge must necessarily operate over a somewhat wider range than that required of a teacher. By the same token, his skills must be directed primarily toward affecting the behavior of teachers rather than children. Thus, his greatest need is not necessarily for the possession of specific instructional skills related to teaching children to read.

What is required is sufficient knowledge and understanding of the entire field of reading to give aid and comfort to the teacher. This suggests the need for a thorough understanding not only of the process of reading but of the conditions necessary for learning to take place. Instructional skill develops only with increased knowledge and understanding. A primary administrative task, therefore, is to provide for teacher growth in these two areas.

It is the view here that improvement of instruction can be most effectively accomplished by careful consideration of instructional or learning goals. In order to translate proposed outcomes into reality, more definitive questions must be considered. These questions involve elements such as organizational patterns, instructional materials, and teaching strategies, to mention only three.

Having specified learner attitudes appropriate to the attainment of a generalized educational objective, for example, it is necessary to give serious thought to the identification of effective learning conditions. What organizational pattern will most effectively bring about these learnings? What specific instructional procedures would most efficiently and clearly provide for the learnings? What materials would provide for making the learning secure?

Questions like these must be raised regarding all aspects of learning outcomes. Most important, however, is the need to formulate the answers in terms of the characteristics of the children for whom the objectives are being established.

Working within an educational field that has, perhaps, been subjected to more research than any other, it would seem logical to expect these answers to be readily available. Unfortunately this is not the case, since most of the research directed toward the effectiveness of methods and materials of instruction has, by design, successfully controlled the two primary sources of variation. Ensuring that any study of methods and materials involves teachers and learners assigned to experimental and control groups having equal variability can only be expected to produce equivocal results. The moderate correlations found between intellectual ability and general reading achievement suggest that significant variation is attributable to elements which are usually lacking when experimental control is exercised.

A combination of fear and faith has often functioned to discourage attempts to deal with individual learning problems. The faith, frequently unwarranted, grows from the comfort derived from habituated teaching behavior. The fear, as is almost universally true, comes from the unknown. In this case, the unknown is intimately related to the characteristics of pupils which might very well identify appropriate conditions for learning. A further task of the administrator, then, is to encourage thoughtful experimentation on the part of his teachers with a view toward defining the most effective learning conditions for individuals. Only on this basis can questions concerning organization, learning materials, and instructional practices be resolved.

BIBLIOGRAPHY

Bond, G. L. and E. B. Wagner, *Teaching the Child to Read,* 4th ed. (New York: The Macmillan Company, 1966).

Bush, C. L. and M. H. Huebner, *Strategies for Reading in the Elementary School* (New York: The Macmillan Company, 1970).

Dechant, Emerald, *Improving the Teaching of Reading,* 2nd ed. (Englewood-Cliffs, N.J.: Prentice-Hall, Inc., 1970).

Gans, Roma, *Common Sense in Teaching Reading* (Indianapolis: Bobbs-Merrill and Co., 1963).

Harris, Albert J. and Edward R. Sipay, *Effective Teaching of Reading,* 2nd ed. (New York: David McKay Co., 1971).

Mager, Robert F., *Preparing Educational Objectives* (Palo Alto, Calif.: Fearon Publishers, 1962).

Shepherd, David L., ed. *Reading and the Elementary School Curriculum* (Newark, Del.: International Reading Association, 1969).

Smith, Frank, *Understanding Reading* (New York: Holt, Rinehart & Winston, 1971).

Stahl, Stanley S., *The Teaching of Reading in the Intermediate Grades* (Dubuque, Iowa: William C. Brown Co., 1965).

Stauffer, Russell G., *Directing Reading Maturity as a Cognitive Process* (New York: Harper and Row, Publishers, Inc., 1969).

13

New Patterns in the Secondary School

H. Alan Robinson

"We've got a reading program but I never get any help with my problem readers!" This statement was made by a ninth-grade general science teacher during the survey of a midwestern city's reading program. After a member of the survey team had observed a reading teacher working with 20 students who were receiving corrective help in reading (primarily a literature course), and having watched a remedial reading teacher in a "reading clinic" class prescribe a series of skill-building materials for nine individuals, the team member stepped across the hall to the general science classroom. Here was an eager young teacher struggling with a single textbook and 38 students, almost all of them unable to understand most of the textbook, and a number who could not begin to contend with it. This teacher's plea was not for the development or expansion of a reading program inserted into the schedule, but for active, concrete assistance in helping his students unlock ideas within his content area.

The Scope of Reading

The reading program in a secondary school ought to be considered ". . . a vast array of skills and attitudes forming an intertwined network throughout the disciplines represented in a curriculum. . . ." In terms of the learner, the program should ". . . be considered the complete set of reading skills and attitudes needed in order to contend with all of the materials to be read . . . during his school career."[1]

[1] H. Alan Robinson, "Reading in the Total School Curriculum," in J. Allen Figurel, ed., *Reading and Realism,* Proceedings of the Thirteenth Annual Convention (Newark, Del.: International Reading Association, 1969), p. 2.

A planned reading program in the secondary school is essential to meet the needs of students in a complex, demanding society. It is important that the secondary school place its emphasis on communication rather than on delivery of knowledge. No teacher can "teach" all of the ideas and information about any subject within a school year. Besides, many of those ideas may be ancient history by the time the student graduates. It would be much more beneficial to help students learn to unlock ideas on their own and to have teachers ready to discuss, evaluate, and utilize those ideas with them.

Integrating Reading with the School Program

A reading program inserted into the school schedule, designed so that students attend "reading" periods or "study" reading-skill development solely, makes little contact with the reality of the curriculum or of the contemporary problems facing youth. Here are examples of typical programs that are unlikely to be of real benefit: (1) Mrs. Jones is employed as a reading teacher. She teaches "reading" during the first, second, third, sixth, and eighth periods, is free during the fourth, eats lunch during the fifth, and has a study hall during seventh period. In some instances students are sent to her for either developmental or corrective reading; others may come on a voluntary basis. She customarily uses those materials particularly developed for the teaching of reading skills and does not introduce the types of materials used in content area classrooms. (2) Mr. Smith operates a reading laboratory equipped with myriad reading-skill materials purchased prior to (often without any) diagnosis of the specific reading strengths and weaknesses of the students who will be coming to the laboratory, other than the vague, general results reported on the usual standardized reading test. A few students are specifically scheduled for remedial work, others attend on a voluntary or semi-voluntary basis and come at random from study halls. Aside from teaching an English class, Mr. Smith mans the reading laboratory all day, directing students to materials, correcting their work, and providing whatever assistance he can within the framework of the situation. Both Mrs. Jones and Mr. Smith attempt to give informal assistance to classroom teachers when they have time.

A secondary school reading program may be self-defeating if it is not integrated into the total school curriculum. Faculty members faced with a reading program which is independent of the rest of the curriculum usually feel little relationship with it; and if they feel that it has a minimal effect on their disciplines, they tend to accept it as something that exists but remains in its own vacuum. A secondary school reading program, then, which is conceived of and executed as though it were a separate entity may be meaningless to everyone except the reading teachers and those few students who are gifted enough or highly motivated enough to transfer what they learn from the sterile reading-skills situation to the content-area classroom situations.

If we accept what we have learned from the studies of transfer of learning, we know that many learners do not automatically transfer what they learn from one situation to another. Yet we appear to have assumed that if reading skills are stressed in the elementary school, or in English class, or in a secondary school reading class or laboratory, students should be able to apply these skills in all their reading activities. We seem to have accepted the questionable generalization that reading is reading, regardless of content. Without specific guidance, most students have difficulty in grasping main ideas equally well in such diverse areas as mathematics, science, social studies, English, industrial arts, or homemaking.

Reading is a process, not a subject, and has no content of its own. It depends upon the total school curriculum to make it viable. Without assistance, it is impossible for most students to learn reading skills in one situation and make successful transfer to situations very different from the one in which the skills were learned. There is a great difference between the process of reading narrative materials and reading expository materials. There are differences in the patterns and styles of writing in the various content areas and from one piece of material to the next. Learners need guidance within the framework of each subject being taught.

The suggested steps and illustrations which comprise most of the rest of this chapter are not meant to be a blueprint for change. Certainly a number of the suggestions might need to be altered, interrelated, or omitted in specific situations. The order of presentation is simply a means of presenting ideas with some rough indication of sequence. Obviously the administrator and his staff will need to adapt the suggestions to the reality of their own environment.

Initial Steps

Some type of reading program exists in any school long before an administrator, reading specialist, or faculty committee thinks of developing one. It is there because reading materials are used for instruction. It is there because materials are accessible in the library. It is there because individual students show evidence of needing guidance in ferreting out the ideas from the written materials used in each discipline. It is there because numerous teachers make efforts to meet individual reading needs.

Many content area teachers incorporate reading and study aids in their daily teaching without conceiving of such activity as *reading*. These same teachers, if asked to teach the process of reading, would be insecure and probably would state openly their lack of knowledge and inability to proceed. Hence, if a well-designed, schoolwide reading program is to be developed, one cannot overlook what is already going on. Teachers need to be helped to identify what they already do well, what they can easily improve, and what more needs to be done in order to give needed assistance to their students.

CONDUCTING A READING SURVEY

A useful method of evaluating reading instruction is to organize a reading survey committee. This committee should have two main purposes: accumulating evidence about the strengths and weaknesses of current reading instruction, and making suitable recommendations for further action. The chairman of the committee should, of course, have an interest in the activity and possess positive leadership qualities. Members of the committee should, when possible, have an active interest in the project, and each department (academic and nonacademic) and each service area should be represented.

The following questions might serve as guidelines for conducting the survey:

1. Which content areas rely on reading as a tool for gaining information and ideas?
2. What are the types of materials students must read in each of these content areas (narrative versus expository, textbook and/or varied materials)?
3. How do these materials match the reading levels and experiential backgrounds of the students?
4. What techniques do teachers use which seem helpful in improving reading skills in each content area?
5. What techniques do teachers use, in each content area, to help in the development of lifetime reading habits? (This question also applies to those departments in which reading is sparingly used as a tool of learning.)
6. If a corrective and/or remedial reading program exists, what is its relationship to the total ongoing curriculum?
7. What role does the central library or materials center play in servicing teachers and students in the development of skills and lifetime reading habits?

The survey committee will undoubtedly spend a number of months planning the survey. Such planning must include a study of the nature of reading at the secondary level so that committee members become acquainted with skills and procedures. While the depth of the survey will depend in large measure upon the composition of the committee and its "reading sophistication," the information gained will be valuable in planning next steps. Obviously, observation schedules will need to be organized, for committee members must see teachers in action. The committee will also have to study test scores and other cumulative data.

In some schools, students, parents, and other lay people have been included in a survey committee. Such inclusion has merit. Much basic information, often unattainable elsewhere, can be supplied by parents and students. Others, particularly those who service the physical and mental health of the community, can offer valuable suggestions in regard to related aspects of reading problems. However, it is usually most economical of time and energy to have the staff members on the committee accumulate the data. Students, parents, and other lay people may then be used in an advisory capacity.

USING THE SURVEY

If an effective reading program is to be developed, results and recommendations must be shared with the total faculty. New programs and personnel that do not have faculty understanding and backing will not bring about the desired goal of intermeshing reading instruction with the total curriculum. Ample time should be devoted to department meetings, interdepartment meetings, and informal discussions so the faculty may fully understand their own and their students' strengths, weaknesses, and needs. The final recommendations for action should have the support of the bulk of the faculty.

After such careful thought and exploration, in most secondary school situations the staff will recommend the hiring of a qualified reading specialist if one is not already employed. If they are concerned with the total curriculum and the role reading plays in it, they will emphasize the need for someone who can help classroom teachers. According to Newton,

> A few years ago a school administrator often felt he had "solved" the reading problems in his school by the hiring of a remedial teacher. This teacher was expected to work almost entirely with all the problem readers leaving the other teachers to go about the business of teaching. This philosophy had the effect of placing reading instruction on a treadmill. The reading teacher had to work faster, with larger groups, as more and more boys and girls were found to be in need of help. Emphasis was on correction rather than prevention.
>
> Now schools are seeing that the professionally competent reading specialist is fully as important as are directors of curriculum and of instruction. The emphasis is shifting slowly but steadily from working with children to working with teachers—classroom teachers. Clinical work must be continued by highly trained technicians. However, the long-term view, most productive in improving learning situations and hence involving preventive work, is in this area of improving instruction in the classroom.[2]

In a very small school or in a school with very few disabled readers, it is possible for the reading specialist to service students and teachers adequately. However, once the specialist is scheduled to work with students more than two periods in a school day, his effectiveness in helping the total staff is lost. The best schedule for the reading specialist is a very flexible one which will allow him to service teachers, and students at times, on demand.

[2] J. Roy Newton, "The Rationale for a System-Wide Reading Committee," in J. Allen Figurel, ed., *Forging Ahead in Reading,* Proceedings of the Twelfth Annual Convention (Newark, Del.: International Reading Association, 1968), pp. 243–44.

The Reading Consultant

The International Reading Association, in a brochure[3] available on request, recognizes four types of reading specialists: special teachers of reading, reading clinicians, reading consultants, and reading supervisors. The job category of reading consultant best fits the needs of most secondary school reading programs. (Special teachers of reading and reading clinicians might also be employed in large secondary schools. A school system might employ a reading supervisor, coordinator, or director who provides systemwide leadership in all phases of the reading program.) The reading consultant's major role is to work with the school staff in improving the reading program.

DEFINING THE CONSULTANT'S ROLE

The role of reading consultant in a secondary school is complex. Even when a faculty has asked for him, he cannot walk into a particular classroom and *demonstrate* the teaching of reading. He must be invited. He must plan with the teacher. Because the reading process cannot be separated from the content to be read he must learn something about the given content area. After all, in each classroom, he faces specialists, largely untrained in reading, but trained in their disciplines. The consultant must walk a tightrope at least in the initial stages of a program.

Perhaps the problem—and its solution—can best be demonstrated by actual example. Below is an excerpt from a report by a former secondary school principal, Willard Congreve.

> The faculty of the University of Chicago Laboratory High School, a school with an enrollment of some 700 students, has, like other faculties, been bombarded with demands to adopt the various popular reading innovations. . . . The faculty knew, even though the students were bright and seemed to be doing exceptionally well, that more needed to be done in the area of reading. Yet no one was about to jump onto one or more of the current bandwagons. Therefore, after considerable discussion the faculty, along with a principal who was concerned and also not interested in being caught up with the current fad, decided that a specialist was needed to help the teachers study reading problems and to find ways of meeting student needs revealed by such inquiry.
>
> But what should this person be? Should a reading teacher be added who would work with a handful of students? Or should someone be found who could help all teachers become creative in improving reading instruction? For teachers who wanted help in learning how to improve reading rather

[3] Copies of this brochure, *Reading Specialists: Roles, Responsibilities, and Qualifications,* are available upon request by writing to: International Reading Association, Six Tyre Avenue, Newark, Delaware 19711.

than substitutes who would take over the responsibility, the latter alternative made the most sense. . . .

When the consultant arrived, she joined with colleagues who were well seasoned in determining the instructional programs for their particular disciplines. Therefore, she did not come to direct but, rather, to help. It was recognized from the onset that any attempt to establish for the consultant a role which might be viewed by the faculty as reducing their decision-making role with regard to the curriculum, would be met with resistance and perhaps doomed to failure. Upon arrival, therefore, the consultant, stocked with all sorts of helping materials, became available to serve on request.[4]

And now, here is the statement of that reading consultant, Ellen Thomas.

On the train . . . I made plans. There would be an "instant all-school drive" for better study; I had read about such drives in books. There would be "instant demonstrations" on reading in the content areas. Whole departments—the whole faculty—would attend.

My plans lasted exactly one day, and then I had a conference with the principal about my job. I was there to help teachers "if and when they asked" and not to "intrude" or "tell them what to do. . . ." . . . Weeks passed. I was in my office—not rushing in, available on request, burning candles at altars, praying to be consulted, longing for home.

. . . . Then one day a teacher sent Carole to me. "She studies night after night until midnight. Please help her study faster." Carole brought along her assignment, a book on Stone Age weapons so advanced and so technical that only a professional archeologist could read it. Girl and assignment were hopelessly apart. Soon other troubled readers came with Adam Smith's *Wealth of Nations,* having commentary intended for students at Yale.

Some teachers—especially new teachers—were thinking, "This is the Lab School. My students can all do college reading." Actually there was a full seven-year range at each grade level. Perhaps, after all, I had a reason for being. . . .[5]

Miss Thomas, the reading consultant at the University of Chicago Laboratory High School, has been busy ever since—not with individual students but with classroom teachers.

When feasible and in certain circumstances the "long wait" described by Miss Thomas can be shortened or eliminated. (1) If the faculty has planned well and over a period of time so they are eager to have the services of a con-

[4] Willard J. Congreve, "The Birth and Development of a Comprehensive Reading Program," in H. Alan Robinson and Ellen Lamar Thomas, eds., *Fusing Reading Skills and Content* (Newark, Del.: International Reading Association, 1969), pp. 38–39.

[5] Ellen Lamar Thomas, "The Role of the Reading Consultant," in H. Alan Robinson and Ellen Lamar Thomas, eds., *Fusing Reading Skills and Content* (Newark, Del.: International Reading Association, 1969), 47–48.

sultant, a few beginning tasks might be waiting for the consultant, growing out of the recommendations of the reading survey committee. (2) Or if the consultant has been hired during the spring preceding the first year of employment, he can meet with the staff from time to time during the spring and even during the summer (with suitable compensation for all involved) in order to plan a list of priorities. (3) Certainly in a school with a large number of new, beginning teachers, the consultant will usually be heartily welcomed as an aide. (4) In schools where reading problems are multitudinous, the consultant's role is essential—right from the first hour of the first day of school.

Once the reading consultant's job has been roughly defined by all concerned, he should be asked to provide specific goals and procedures for the areas discussed. It is usually most rewarding for the consultant, and most effective in terms of the job to be accomplished, if the goals, and the procedures for meeting those goals, are spelled out over at least a three-year period. If the consultant writes them down, realizing they are subject to change, and asks the administrator and his staff for their reactions, the resulting plan will give direction to the reading program.

RELATIONS WITH THE ADMINISTRATOR

Particularly in a secondary school, where each member of the staff is a specialist concerned with his own area, the type of reading program we are speaking of can easily fade into oblivion. Although the staff may have been involved in the planning, and even with the continuous striving of an excellent reading consultant, the program is doomed to failure without the strong and constant support of the school administrator. This support needs to be knowledgeable, pertinent, and specific, not vague and general.

> It is vital that the administrator view reading as an intrinsic part of the curriculum and that he be willing actively and publicly to support the activities of the reading consultant. In fact, as they both try to meet objectives, the consultant has the right to expect that the administrator be familiar with the objectives and practices of the reading program and with the behavior of his school population. . . . On his part, the reading consultant should be prepared to answer any questions that the administrator might ask about reading instruction and theory. . . .[6]

Since the reading program will hopefully permeate the total curriculum, it is much more difficult to implement than the program concerned only with the teaching of reading during several periods of the school day. The reading consultant requires time for planning and must have an opportunity to discuss his plans with the administrator. In some cases, the administrator's active, publically stated support will be necessary in order to ensure invitations to department meetings for the consultant. In other situations, the consultant will only

---

[6] H. Alan Robinson and Sidney J. Rauch, *Guiding the Reading Program: A Reading Consultant's Handbook* (Chicago: Science Research Association, 1965), p. 12.

want suggestions on how to proceed by himself. The administrator should anticipate speaking with the consultant, or the consultant and a reading committee, about such topics as line and staff responsibilities, scheduling problems, budget, plant facilities, policies and practices, and in-service programs.

The Reading Committee

In the discussion of initial steps, the reading survey committee was organized for the specific purpose of helping to define the job to be done. It is often very useful to retain this group as a reading committee or a reading improvement committee. Specific representation might change but the complexion of the group should remain the same. Such a committee gives power to the program and also serves as an in-service tool. In fact, in very small secondary schools or in schools where the budget cannot support a reading consultant, the reading committee plays a most significant role in trying to help solve problems, particularly by establishing sound in-service practices.

The major reasons for the existence of a reading committee are to evaluate the reading program and implement essential improvements when necessary or desirable. Dietrich, a systemwide director of reading, states that "the reading committee should be a policy-making body who develops a broad framework within which the consultant is able to function."[7] At times the problems that arise may cause new committee members to feel overwhelmed by their obligations, but they can take solace in the knowledge that a sound reading program is built over a period of years and instantaneous results cannot be expected.

If a reading committee is to render effective service, each staff member must be a part of the whole communication system. That is, each committee member must represent a definite, small group of staff members. He must act as a liaison between the committee and his group. Then, when decisions are made, the total faculty will have played a part in the planning. The committee member can reach his "group" by holding brief meetings occasionally, by speaking to members of his "group" individually, or by asking them to react to some information he has brought to their attention. Unless the total faculty is very small (35 or less), the procedure suggested above is more effective than total faculty meetings.

Dietrich points out that "a reading committee's success depends upon the sincerity of higher administrative officials who support it, of members of the committee who believe in its importance, of the reading consultants who work toward the building of a reading program which will make better readers of teachers who cooperate by complying with the decisions of the committee."[8]

---

[7] Dorothy M. Dietrich, "The Functioning of a Reading Committee," in J. Allen Figurel, ed., *Forging Ahead in Reading,* Proceedings of the Twelfth Annual Convention (Newark, Del.: International Reading Association, 1968), p. 245.

[8] Ibid., p. 247.

There is little question that the work of the reading committee tends to be ineffective without the confidence and support of the school's leadership. The supportive administrator can help such a committee engage in a vital role which is bound to affect curriculum development. Since reading is such an integral part of the total curriculum, the reading committee's work must soon become intertwined with other areas of the curriculum. The eventual outcome of the work of a reading committee may be changes not only in reading instruction but in many other areas of the curriculum.

An excellent description of the activities of a reading committee at Nicolet High School, Milwaukee, Wisconsin, is available in a book on secondary school reading published recently by the International Reading Association.[9]

In-Service Activities

A developmental reading program in the secondary school is essentially an in-service program. Since the major goal is to help students cope with the material they must read within and beyond the school curriculum, the emphasis must always be placed on assisting the classroom teachers meet the reading needs of their students. The kinds of help teachers need will differ from individual to individual, from classroom to classroom, from department to department, from school to school.

Broad, general in-service courses consisting mainly of lectures and discussions will reap few benefits. One can understand the desire of a school administrator, reading consultant, or reading committee to get at least one course going, to compensate in part for the lack of necessary training during the preservice program. But a general course in reading methods is not the answer. As one senior high school teacher speaking for others, Burr[10] states that the major criticism of such courses is that they *tell* teachers about reading rather than assist them to ". . . incorporate the developmental teaching of reading skills within their own subject areas. They want practical retooling for a sound reading program."

Practical courses for specific departments can be available, but probably the most *functional* value derives from activities directed toward day-to-day teaching, a type of individual and/or small group on-the-job training. The reading consultant and/or members of the reading committee can guide teachers toward the building of a reading program which will make better readers of

[9] Eileen E. Sargent, "Integrating Reading Skills in the Content Areas," in H. Alan Robinson and Ellen Lamar Thomas, eds., *Fusing Reading Skills and Content* (Newark, Del.: International Reading Association, 1969), pp. 19–23.

[10] Miriam Burr, "What the Classroom Teacher Looks For in Leadership—Secondary Level," in David L. Shepherd, ed., *Roles of the Administrator and Parent in the School Reading Program,* Proceedings of Hofstra University Reading Conference, I (Hempstead, N.Y.: Hofstra University, 1966), pp. 38–40.

good readers, adequate readers of fair readers, and provide some help for the problem reader. (Classroom teachers cannot take care of all the needs of severely retarded readers. Remedial reading is discussed in a subsequent section of this chapter.)

Several of the ensuing illustrations of in-service activities are from the program at the University of Chicago Laboratory High School. This school has been outstanding in its integration of the teaching of the reading skills with the content areas. A more complete account of their acivities may be found in Part I of *Fusing Reading Skills and Content.*[11]

UTILIZATION OF TEST RESULTS

Personalized score kits appear to be very effective with all teachers at the University of Chicago Laboratory High School. The consultant gives the teacher a kit of cards for each class—one card per student. Cards differ slightly depending upon the content area and contain test scores pertinent to reading strengths and weaknesses, made understandable for all teachers. The scores are only rough estimates at best, but they serve to demonstrate the range of reading ability in a class, encourage a teacher to look at individuals in that light, and serve as an entree for further work with the reading consultant or reading committee. Reading ranges for total classes (sophomores, juniors, seniors) may also be organized on posters and discussed at department or grade-level meetings. Individual sheets with such class ranges on them can also be reproduced and given to teachers as reminders of the spread of reading abilities.

The personalized score cards with additional information can be very useful to school librarians. Librarians can offer service appropriate to the reading ability of each student with just a glance at a score card—realizing that the information, though only approximate in accuracy, can be a wedge until they get to know the students better.

Jerome Flescher, reading consultant at Newfield High School in Selden, New York, takes a further step by presenting a written anaylsis and interpretation of standardized test scores of individual students to classroom teachers. Although he is aware of the inadequacies of any given test, he believes that such reports give content area teachers "hints" about the needs of their students.

Possibly the best types of reading tests for giving immediate help to content area teachers are informal inventories. Such inventories can be, and are, prepared by reading consultants and members of reading committees, usually with the assistance of content area teachers. An inventory is usually designed to test whether students have developed the skills needed for the effective

---

[11] H. Alan Robinson and Ellen Lamar Thomas, eds., *Fusing Reading Skills and Content* (Newark, Del.: International Reading Association, 1969), pp. 37–126.

reading of a given set of materials in a particular content area. Ruth Viox,[12] reading consultant for the Kenmore Public Schools, Kenmore, New York, has organized a booklet of such informal inventories specifically for content area teachers in the secondary school.

MATCHING READERS AND MATERIALS

Once teachers are convinced of the wide variation in reading levels within each of their classes, they begin to search for ways of matching students and materials. Coping with individual differences is not an easy task for these teachers. Certainly the reading committee and reading consultant should actively encourage and promote the introduction of multilevel and varied materials, but the insecurity of many teachers approaching a new procedure must be recognized.

The teacher who has used the single textbook approach for a long time should probably make changes gradually. The reading consultant and/or reading committee members in a particular department should help the teacher think through his course of study and find supplements to the text that will help to make the reading more meaningful for some of the students in the classroom. One step is to have both the content specialist and the reading specialist examine alternative textbooks available for a particular course. Books should then be ranked in order of difficulty so the teacher may choose one or two titles in addition to the regular textbook. Textbooks can then be better matched to the reading needs of the students.

Aside from informal judgments of teacher and consultant, the reading committee ought to agree upon a procedure for estimating readability. It is useful to make use of one or more readability formules. Although they will give rough and uneven estimates, they are probably most functional when used to rank similar materials from easiest to hardest—and this is usually the task at hand. At the secondary level, the Dale-Chall[13] formula gives adequate results if supplemented by the judgment of the content area specialist.

It is also wise to add the judgment of students to those of the formula, the reading specialist, and the content area specialist. A few students reading at varied but known levels should read several passages from the material being evaluated and answer questions about what they have read. Since readability levels, as well as students' reading levels, will often vary from one type of reading material to the next, such measurements should take place whenever the purchase of new materials is being contemplated.

The secondary school administrator should be aware that varied materials in place of the single text will be somewhat more costly. However, as depart-

[12] Ruth Viox, *Evaluating Reading and Study Skills in the Secondary Classroom,* Reading Aid No. 205 (Newark, Del.: International Reading Association, 1968).

[13] Edgar Dale and Jeanne Chall, "A Formula for Predicting Readability," *Educational Research Bulletin,* no. 27 (1948), pp. 11–20.

ments buy materials suitable for varying reading levels, they will be purchasing more titles but fewer copies of each. Hence, the increased cost is not as great as the variety in titles might indicate. Any increased cost is a small investment, however, in relation to the values that accrue from involvement of classroom teachers in the total school reading program. Positive changes will result in teaching behaviors, and essential revisions will be made in curricula.

TRAINING PROCEDURES

Traditionally, in-service education in reading at the secondary school level has been conducted through coursework lasting a semester or more. Faculty attendance has been voluntary. Usually some type of in-service or salary-scale credit has been given. Most frequently, the courses have been offered one afternoon or evening a week. Outside lecturers have, in the main, dealt with the topics set up by the consultant or reading committee. Sometimes the course has been sponsored by a university with university credit.

The "traditional" approach does not seem to pay significant dividends. There is no reason why members of a secondary school staff cannot profit from group enterprise, but activities are more useful when carried on within a department, or on occasion, at a grade level. It is also important to conduct group training during school hours if at all feasible even if the consultant has to repeat the process with several groups or individuals because of scheduling problems. Such in-service sequences should be brief and should focus on specific problems rather than a broad topic, such as "Improving Reading in the Content Areas." A group might need to consider "how to teach grasping main ideas in social studies textbooks," or "differentiating reading assignments in biology."

For example, at Bloom Township High School in Chicago Heights, Illinois, teachers of freshman English and reading teachers work together to uncover the skill weaknesses and strengths of the freshmen, and plan reading improvement programs. English teachers learn a diagnostic approach to reading problems and specific procedures for helping their students. Part of the work is done in the school's Developmental Reading Laboratory, and part is done in the English classroom. Reading lessons apply skills to the content ordinarily taught in the classroom.

In reporting on the project described above, Paulsen, Dorinson, and Fiedler state,

> We look upon this new plan as a vital part of an in-service training program which will enable teachers to become active partners in building curriculum. First, good instructional adaptations will be recorded and shared with other teachers who are teaching the same unit. Then these adaptations will be tried out by members of the group. Finally, those reading practices that have real worth will be taken by curriculum committees working during the summer and fused into content units.[14]

[14] Leitha Paulsen, Zena Dorinson, and Margaret Fiedler, "Building Reading into the

Ellen Thomas, at the University of Chicago Laboratory High School, uses a technique which has been most successful in helping groups of teachers work together to upgrade reading instruction. In informal discussions and at group meetings she has asked about the methods which teachers use in their class-rooms to meet the needs of their students in reading the content area materials. She adds her own ideas, compiles a list of methods, and returns them to the teachers who invariably come up with more. As a result, a number of articles coauthored by Ellen Thomas and groups of teachers have been pub-lished in national magazines. Teachers naturally grow through the writing of such an article, keep on the lookout for new ways of helping students, and continue to be interested in improving the teaching of reading.

Ellen Thomas has also created, with individual teachers and groups of teachers, some excellent material for instruction—tailored to the needs of the content area teachers concerned. For example, she and Mr. Tirro, music teacher, organized a self-help unit of study skills for the vocabulary of music theory. Mrs. Szymkowicz, home economics teacher, and the reading consultant prepared a set of guidelines for reading the directions on package mixes. Five geometry teachers and Miss Thomas worked out a unit to help improve the reading of the geometry textbook. The program even extends to the physical education department where Mr. Patlak actively encourages boys to read. He has just developed a booklist of sports stories representing a variety of read-ing levels.[15]

Many reading consultants do most of their work with individual teachers. They give demonstration lessons planned with the classroom teacher; they do team teaching; they help the teacher plan lessons to include or feature certain reading skills; and they write and produce lessons and other kinds of materials which will be of particular help to specific teachers. Miss Thomas occupies a classroom which is filled to overflowing with materials, mainly teacher and/or consultant-made. Other consultants collaborate with content area teachers in planning lessons which tackle pertinent problems within the classroom setting. They also use multi-media materials to capitalize on other learning modalities as they focus on a reading skill.

There are, of course, a multitude of additional in-service activities which, when summed up, essentially constitute the school's reading program. A dynamic and effective reading program in the secondary school should have as its goal the continuous process of upgrading reading instruction so the stu-dents in a particular school may reach, or come close to reaching, their potentials. Activities must be chosen that will move toward such a goal. The administrator with his reading committee and consultant, aware of teacher

High School Curriculum," in J. Allen Figurel, ed., *Forging Ahead in Reading,* Proceed-ings of the Twelfth Annual Convention (Newark, Del.: International Reading Associa-tion, 1968), pp. 207–8.

[15] Sanford Patlak, "Sandy's 99 Sports Books for Reluctant Readers," in H. Alan Robinson and Ellen Lamar Thomas, eds., *Fusing Reading Skills and Content* (Newark, Del.: International Reading Association, 1969), pp. 201–4.

and curriculum weaknesses, must constantly inspect and evaluate the program and search for additional means of improving the local reading program.

Reading Classes

The chapter up to this point has concentrated on the most vital part of a reading program in the secondary school—the reading activities going on within each classroom. It has been assumed that, with expert in-service activities, the reading program for good, average, and even weak readers may be conducted in the classrooms with some assistance from reading consultants and/or reading committee members. In the jargon of the reading specialist, the developmental and corrective aspects of the reading program may be handled through knowledgeable, individualized or small-group instruction within the content area classrooms.

REMEDIAL READING

A small proportion of the total student population in any school will need remedial help in reading. If the percentage needing remedial help rises much above ten percent, curricular changes are needed, since those students cannot be helped sufficiently in short periods of remedial instruction. They must have a total curriculum dedicated to their needs.

A reading clinic or laboratory should be available to service the needs of the severely retarded reader (reading a year or more below his capacity and two or more years below his grade level). The reading lab should be staffed by one or more special reading teachers trained in remedial reading. (In very small schools with limited budgets the reading consultant may need to do a limited amount of remedial work with students.) Special teachers of reading should work closely with the reading committee and the reading consultant. They should have enough leeway in their schedules, particularly at the beginning and end of each school year, to diagnose adequately those students who are candidates for remedial reading. Diagnosis at the secondary level is most effective at the end of the school year so students may be grouped on the basis of need and scheduled for such help before the master schedule for the following year is complete.

Special teachers of reading should have the equivalent of one day free to write reports, contact parents and referral agencies, and to visit classrooms in all content areas to which their retarded readers have been scheduled. It is most important for special teachers of reading to see their students in action in their regular classrooms if they are to be cognizant of problems and able to plan instruction to solve such problems. The special teachers of reading should have conferences with classroom teachers from time to time, offering suggestions about simple techniques that might be used with certain individuals. On the other hand, classroom teachers ought to be encouraged, and given time, to observe what goes on in the reading lab or clinic.

Students who have been frustrated readers for many years cannot make significant progress with a lab program isolated from the rest of the school curriculum. Students should be scheduled, as early in their secondary school lives as feasible, to a concentrated period of work on reading procedures which help them cope with the materials they will encounter in each content area classroom. Emphasis must be placed on helping them understand ideas expressed in the vocabulary and rhetoric peculiar to each subject. Lessons that only stress generalized skills such as finding main ideas or drawing conclusions may not help much. The problem is learning to understand the key concepts and generalizations in each content area. In all probability, the reading lab should house copies of all of the materials being used in each content area so that a part of the period of instruction will be devoted to reading skills demanded by those materials. If content area teachers object strongly to the use of their materials, similar materials may be utilized. It seems almost impossible to separate the reading process from the content and hence skills should be taught in direct relation to content. Certainly the severely retarded reader can use such double exposure.

As teachers in content area classrooms become more accustomed to meeting the reading demands of the individuals in their classes, they too will play a role in the remedial reading program. They will be giving retarded readers an opportunity to make use of the skills they acquire in the lab by providing them with materials they can read successfully and assignments they can master. The remedial reading program in most of our secondary schools has too often been unrelated to anything else going on in the school. If it is to succeed, it must be planned by the total staff (through the coordinating efforts of the reading committee); it must be understood by the staff; the staff should feel some responsibility for planning, and then actually work with the remedial program.

SPECIAL READING GROUPS

It may be possible for the special teacher of reading, and sometimes the reading consultant, to handle some corrective problems and developmental needs. Sometimes, as a result of reading committee or department meetings, one or more teachers will feel that their classes or groups of students seem to need help in specific areas such as "how to read for cause and effect relationships" or "how to survey a textbook." The reading teacher and/or the consultant should then try to plan a short-term schedule of work with these students. It might be worked out with the teacher during class time in a team teaching situation. Or a ten-session course might be planned for a three- to five-week period during study hall. The sessions would concentrate on the particular area which demands attention. In this way the special teacher of reading may be preventing the need for future remedial help.

It could be that during the junior year, for example, there were complaints from college-bound students about their inability to read fast enough for their purposes, or that they were not learning some of the study techniques they would need in college. The special teacher of reading could plan a certain number of sessions in the reading lab to work with those students during their senior year. This might be done on a voluntary basis, placing necessary limits on the number accepted.

THE ADMINISTRATOR'S ROLE

The attitude of the secondary school principal is a most important influence. If the principal shows that he is knowledgeable about the job of the special teacher of reading, and if he is openly and actively enthusiastic about it, the rest of the staff will tend to be supportive. Special teachers of reading are particularly sensitive to the barbs of staff members who claim reading teachers have "such easy jobs teaching small groups and have such flexible schedules." Administrators who understand the significance of small-group instruction and flexible scheduling are able to support the specialist and help classroom teachers understand the true situation.

Most importantly, the administrator must be sure that the personnel selected as special teachers of reading are well trained. As Burr says:

> Some teachers voice disappointment in the reading program in their high school because they believe that the appointed specialists are not really qualified experts in the reading field. . . . Classroom teachers suggest that those appointed to a specialist rank should meet specific requirements, such as special training in reading.[16]

The brochure on reading specialists (cited earlier in the chapter), published by the International Reading Association, provides help by outlining minimum standards for the special teacher of reading.

Lifetime Readers

Every member of the staff should aid the student in developing lifetime reading habits. Surely an enthusiastic physical education instructor can attract reluctant boys to reading good sports books more than the English teacher. Each staff member should have a commitment to this part of the reading program.

[16] Miriam Burr, "What the Classroom Teacher Looks For in Leadership—Secondary Level," in David L. Shepherd, ed., *Roles of the Administrator and Parent in the School Reading Program,* Proceedings of Hofstra University Reading Conference, Part I (Hempstead, N.Y.: Hofstra University, 1966), p. 39.

Teaching reading skills well serves little purpose if students do not voluntarily and freely turn to reading as recreation and a source of knowledge.

LIBRARIES

Reading is a habit, and habits grow out of repetitive activity. If students are to turn to reading, the materials must be accessible and pertinent to their interests and needs. Although the central school library is essential, books and other reading materials must be available throughout the building, including the classrooms in which students spend the bulk of their time. In some situations the classroom library may need to be under lock and key when a teacher is not present, in others teachers may move from room to room, consequently such libraries may not always be advisable. But whenever feasible, the classroom library is an important part of the total program. Students are prone to turn instantly to books at the very moment they feel a need or they have been stimulated to read by the teacher or a peer.

If the school library *is* to play an important role in developing lifetime reading habits, it cannot be constantly scheduled as a study hall or as a library skills training center. It must be accessible at any time to students who want to locate reading materials, and the librarian must be free to help students find suitable materials. The librarian should be a consultant to students and staff, not a custodian of books. A vital librarian can get students "hooked on books" by knowing the student and his background, and by knowing when and when not to give active service.

The librarian can also work with classes of students on projects that will help broaden their reading horizons. Such work is most meaningful when connected with a unit in the classroom where the librarian may team teach with the classroom teacher both in the library and in the classroom. From time to time the librarian can trundle new acquisitions to a classroom and "sell" them to the students.

STAFF INVOLVEMENT

Staff members need to be encouraged to read for recreation. It is difficult to develop a generation of readers if they have few models to emulate. Staff members should be seen carrying books they are reading and, on occasion, let students see them reading. Teachers may advisedly share their reactions about books, or read excerpts, so that students may observe an active and enthusiastic participant in reading.

A committee of staff members and students may be interested in serving as a book advertising group, or in putting up simple displays throughout the school building about new materials available in the library. Attractive displays of books or posters about books attract teenagers as long as the content of the books is related to their interests and needs. Displays need to be changed frequently if the students are not to lose interest and subconsciously realize that those who have set up the displays do not really have an active interest in promoting the reading of the latest acquisitions. A further discussion of specific techniques is available in an article in the *Journal of Reading*.[17]

All teachers should be prepared to talk about current books and magazines. They must show that they are aware of what is available and they should bring as much as possible of the wide world of reading into their teaching. In our complex, changing society it is essential for students to be directed to a host of contemporary materials since a given textbook cannot provide all the information they need on a topic. Actually skill development and motivation work hand in hand. If a teacher is teaching those skills a student needs in order to read the instructional materials, and if he is attempting to motivate the learner to read widely, he is setting up the environment for development of lifetime reading habits. The students who has achieved the skill to understand what he reads, and who is given the types of assignments which encourage broad reading, is likely to turn to reading for much of his information and enjoyment.

Evaluation

Evaluation of a reading program that permeates the curriculum is complex. Perhaps the best test is an investigation of student achievement through an examination of the results of both standardized and informal tests, teachers' evaluations of students' progress, and grades in the content areas. Although improved achievement on reading tests may give some indication of the value of the program, in the long run progress must be measured by improved achievement in all content areas. If the students do not show forward movement on formal and informal evaluations of their ability to cope with the materials of the various content areas, the reading program must be carefully re-examined.

Congreve, former principal of the University of Chicago Laboratory High School, states, "One can look at the cold hard facts of the reading scores. . . . But, in addition to improvement in the standardized reading score, U-High has three other broad objectives: wide involvement of teachers in every content area teaching reading, students who use reading effectively to gain information, and students who turn to reading for enjoyment. . . . three out of every four teachers at U-High who teach 'reading subjects' have made some contribution to the reading effort." He points out that "Assessment of the other two objectives has not been easily accomplished. No published tests are available which measure how well students read to gain information in specific courses. Furthermore, correlations between scores on standardized reading

[17] H. Alan Robinson, "Developing Lifetime Readers," *Journal of Reading*, vol. 11, no. 4 (January 1968).

tests and reading achievement in specific content areas are not high. The reading power of a student may differ markedly from one discipline to another."[18]

In evaluating the first objective, Congreve reports that three out of four teachers who teach "reading subjects" at U-High, make some contribution to the reading program. He states that the other two objectives are not as easy to measure but that some of the subject matter teachers at the University of Chicago Laboratory High School are contributing their own tests based on actual course materials. The students fill out a questionnaire related to their reading activity and the librarians ". . . contribute their insights into the students' attitudes."[19] Congreve also points out that "Day-to-day observation provides excellent evaluative data that many people overlook. These data are quite valid and provide an index to what is actually happening in a school."[20]

It is by now a cliché that evaluation is continuous, that it is most valuable as a part of the total curriculum rather than as a simple measurement taken at the beginning of a program and at its end. All aspects of the curriculum are subject to evaluation, objectives as well as procedures, materials, and tests. Without doubt, the real contributions of an all-school reading program can be evaluated only in *relation to the total school and community population.*

A chief function of the school administrator is to be sure that the status quo is being challenged and modified whenever necessary. Sometimes the members of a reading committee and the reading consultant, and even a faculty, become so close to a program (especially when they have developed it) that they cannot or do not want to see its weaknesses or its unsuitability to a changed school environment. The administrator's knowledge of the program, and his past performance in giving the program positive and openly expressed recognition will serve him in good stead as he raises questions. It is most important that the administrator follow through and react continuously until evaluation and necessary changes begin to take place, and that he earnestly and heartily praise the efforts of those involved in suggesting and planning such changes.

Criteria for a Sound Reading Program

The secondary school principal is certainly the leader of his school. Though he must delegate duties to others, he is ultimately responsible for all of the activities in the school. Obviously he needs to know what is going on and he needs to support such activities, for they are, in reality, his activities. While the reading consultant and reading committee represent the personnel delegated to improve reading instruction, the secondary school principal is responsible for its weaknesses and strengths, its successes and failures. He too is responsible to

[18] Robinson and Thomas, op. cit., pp. 41–42.
[19] Ibid., p. 42.
[20] Ibid., p. 43.

a superintendent who will expect him to be intimately involved in what goes on his school. Throughout this chapter it has been urged that the principal be knowledgeable about the reading program and that he actively and openly support it. He must also be ready to criticize, but in so doing he must be willing to involve himself in improving the program.

A program is based on criteria growing out of a philosophy. Criteria are the bases for building the program and evaluating it. This chapter concludes with a list of twelve criteria for a sound secondary school reading program which may be of use to the administrator as he views his reading program.

1. A sound reading program is planned cooperatively by the total staff or by an adequate representation of the staff.
2. It is directed toward specific goals leading to independence in reading.
3. It is balanced and is, therefore, concerned with all aspects of reading.
4. It provides for basic skill instruction with directed application to a variety of reading situations.
5. It provides for the individual reading needs of all students, on the basis of adequate diagnosis.
6. It adjusts instruction and materials to individual needs.
7. It makes special provision for meeting the reading needs through normal classroom instruction.
8. It endeavors to make students cognizant of their strengths, weaknesses, and goals through a continuous evaluation program.
9. It allows subject-matter teachers to teach the reading skills pertinent to their own subjects.
10. It makes in-service training a continuing factor in the reading program.
11. It is understood by students, school personnel, parents, and the community at large.
12. It is continuously evaluated in terms of specific goals.[21]

BIBLIOGRAPHY

Burr, Miriam, "What the Classroom Teacher Looks for in Leadership—Secondary Level," in David L. Shepherd, ed., *Roles of the Administrator and Parent in the School Reading Program,* Proceedings of Hofstra University Reading Conference, Part I (Hempstead, N.Y.: Hofstra University, 1966), pp. 38–40.

Congreve, Willard J., "The Birth and Development of a Comprehensive Reading Program," in H. Alan Robinson and Ellen Lamar Thomas, eds., *Fusing Reading Skills and Content* (Newark, Del.: International Reading Association, 1969), pp. 38–39.

Figurel, J. Allen, ed., *Forging Ahead in Reading,* Proceedings of the Twelfth An-

[21] Robinson and Rauch, op. cit., p. 78.

nual Convention (Newark, Del.: International Reading Association, 1968), pp. 243–247.

Robinson, H. Alan, "Reading in the Total School Curriculum," in J. Allen Figurel, ed., *Reading and Realism,* Proceedings of the Thirteenth Annual Convention (Newark, Del.: International Reading Association, 1969), p. 2.

Robinson, H. Alan and Sidney J. Rauch, *Guiding the Reading Program: A Reading Consultant's Handbook* (Chicago: Science Research Associates, 1965).

Sargent, Eileen E., "Integrating Reading Skills in the Content Areas," in H. Alan Robinson and Ellen Lamar Thomas, eds., *Fusing Reading Skills and Content* (Newark, Del.: International Reading Association, 1969), pp. 19–23.

Thomas, Ellen Lamar, "The Role of the Reading Consultant," in H. Alan Robinson and Ellen Lamar Thomas, eds., *Fusing Reading Skills and Content* (Newark, Del.: International Reading Association, 1969), pp. 47–48.

Viox, Ruth, *Evaluating Reading and Study Skills in the Secondary Classroom,* Reading Aid No. 205 (Newark, Del.: International Reading Association, 1968).

IV

Research-The Key to
the Future

14

Administrative Leadership
Through Research

Bjorn Karlsen

A school administrator is often faced with the difficult task of deciding what methods and materials to use in reading instruction in his school. The judgment of curriculum specialists, opinions of teachers, and other informal forms of evaluation are valuable, but because of the importance of reading instruction, the administrator must review experimental data as well.

The purpose of this chapter is to discuss two main issues. First, with what facets of reading research must the school administrator be familiar? Secondly, what are some of the problems in interpreting reading research data?

Ordinarily, research data are available from publishers of material or from others who have experimented with a given model. Since there are publishers who will publish or reprint only studies which are favorable to their material, some sort of external verification must be carried out. It is, then, up to the school administrator to "review the research" and make some preliminary judgment about the suitability of a certain approach to the teaching of reading for his particular school district. If a given method or set of materials appears sufficiently promising, a preliminary try-out with a few classes would be a reasonable next step.

The School Administrator and Educational Research

When someone gets a new idea or develops a new set of materials for reading instruction, who should be responsible for experimenting with the material? In 1966, the International Reading Association adopted a policy, which read, in part: "Distributors of reading devices or materials have an ethical obligation to submit their products to fair scientific trials before marketing, and to make data of these evaluations available to all prospective purchasers." It would appear, then, that in the view of IRA the publisher himself should submit his material to scentific experimentation. It is doubtful that more than one percent of the materials currently being sold have been submitted to "fair scientific trials" by an independent and disinterested party. Many publishers feel that when they have produced the best possible material, it is only fair that the public schools try it out.

Are we then going to submit our children to experimental instructional materials when we have little assurance from the publisher that the students will learn from it what we think they should learn?

One of the very fundamental principles of child development is that behavior is irreversible. When a child has been put through the first grade with a certain set of reading materials, he cannot go back. The child is now a year older, he is going into the second grade and, if the novel approach failed, he is in trouble. Therefore, the schools have been reluctant to try radical departures from proven instructional materials since such departures seem to constitute an undue risk.

Some time ago this writer received a letter from an inventor of a new kind of alphabet by which reading could be taught. He wanted this system endorsed, so that he could urge the public schools to experiment with his method. He considered this a fair request. He had produced this material and the schools should try it out. In replying to this person, it was pointed out that such experimentation was his responsibility, that he needed to try the method with a few youngsters in a carefully controlled situation and not put it on the market for general consumption before such a trial had been made. By return mail came a rather irate letter asking how I could possibly expect innovation in the field of education if I would not endorse his system to the public schools of the United States.

In return, he was informed that his system was inconsistent with what I think we know about how children learn and how reading can be taught and that I would therefore be cautious about proceeding with this new approach until at least a small and carefully controlled study had been made. The parents of the children participating in the study should be aware of the fact that it was an experimental program using a radically different and yet unproven system of teaching reading.

We have a responsibility to develop new and better ways of teaching children, but we have to proceed in a responsible way. Perhaps the best research approach is through cooperative ventures between publishers and school systems; they can work together to develop new and better ways to teach reading.

DESIGNING AN EXPERIMENT

Most of the evidence presented by various publishers seems to be of the "personal testimony" variety. When asked what kind of success they have had with a given set of materials, publishers often say that the material has been tried in school system X, and that "the teachers like it." Some publishers have even made collections of letters from happy teachers as evidence of the success of a given approach. Much of the so-called "research" which takes place in many school systems is no better than this "personal testimony" kind of research. A certain set of materials or a certain gadget is tried out and the teachers somehow come up with the conclusion that "it works." The fact that something works is not good enough. As a matter of fact, with a good teacher, practically everything works. Some sort of controlled experimentation must be provided that will compare a certain approach with what has been done in the past or, possibly, compare the approach to another new system. It would appear reasonable to expect that the strengths and weaknesses of a certain set of materials would be determined from the standpoint of improved content and comparative success of the children for whom it is intended.

It might be worthwhile to look at how educators arrive at the "it works" conclusion about a certain approach. Apparently what happens is that a certain system or set of materials is introduced and some type of evaluation is made, perhaps six months or a year later. The results often indicate that the youngsters have improved in the particular characteristic which the new approach or system was supposed to teach. A question remains to be answered, however. Did the youngsters improve more than if they had been left alone, or would they have shown the same improvement with practically any kind of instructional material?

Obviously, it is necessary to get an independent and impartial evaluation of new materials from a financially disinterested party, and the results of this type of study must then be communicated to the educational community.

COMMUNICATING THE RESULTS

It is the responsibility of the researcher to communicate the results to others in the field of education through the usual professional journals. Unfortunately, there has been a strong tendency for researchers to write for other researchers rather than for the research consumer. If the results of research are to be communicated to the educator, they must be communicated in terms that the educator can understand. Educational researchers have developed their own language, and have often been unwilling to report their data in a straightforward way. The consumer is often able to read only the conclusions, which are interpretive and which contain a considerable subjective element. It is an investigator's responsibility to present his data in such a form that an independent reader can make his own evaluation about the adequacy of the design of a study, the empirical results, and the interpretation of the data. The professional school administrator must have sufficient knowledge of research terms to be able to read and interpret research reports; it is part of being a professional.

Researchers are often not interested in studying specific sets of instructional materials, but are interested rather in studying the broader aspects of instruction. For example, people making comparative studies of basal readers versus programmed readers for reading instruction choose for comparison a series or a set of materials representing each of these two approaches. At the present time, this type of study is too general, because the approaches now being used are not sufficiently representative of a specific method, but are highly impure. Many basal readers, for example, use procedures similar to programmed readers and vice versa.

It also is a mistake, after researching a problem at a given grade level, to draw general conclusions about this particular problem for all grade levels. For example, in one study of the components of reading, a reseacher could not find a phonics component in reading. This finding may be rather surprising to those who have been working with younger children, but it is probably understandable when it is noted that the study was done with high school seniors.

READING OF RESEARCH

Perhaps the most discouraging aspect of research in the field of reading is the impression that few read it. For example, the research on the improvement of eye movements by mechanical means has produced amazingly consistent results. The research, including comparative studies, has demonstrated that the media of conventional classroom procedures using books produces greater improvements in eye movements than does the use of mechanical devices. Nevertheless, literally millions of dollars are being spent by American educators in the purchase of mechanical devices for mass application—not for further experimentation, which might be a legitimate use of funds.

Although no data are readily available, probably fewer than half of the eye movement cameras purchased within recent years by public schools have ever been put to practical use, either in research or in the classroom. Some of these same schools do not possess a school library. When a school district spends tens of thousands of dollars buying hardware for the study and improvement of eye movements, one would think that whoever made the purchases might have seen some evidence to indicate that this investment was worthwhile. Though it might be too much to expect this person to acquaint himself with all available research literature, at least he should have read one of the summaries of research on this particular piece of equipment.

GETTING RESEARCH GRANTS

American educators have been able to convince the federal government that they need money for research and that no industry has spent less money on research than has education. Congress has responded by appropriating large funds for educational experimentation, but the educational community has not had adequate staffs of trained researchers to make effective use of such funds. Although many school administrators have been trained at the doctoral level, such training has usually been geared to the realities of their profession as administrators, and has provided little training or practice in research skills.

To compound the problem, research support has often been made available on a year-to-year basis, making it difficult for school districts to hire competent researchers. Stable employment is necessary for effective recruitment. In addition, a one-year experimental program is unlikely to yield reliable data.

Since most school districts were reluctant to pass up the opportunity to participate in federal programs, they proceeded to apply for funds. Since funding was based on a written proposal, many schools hired proposal writers who then proceeded to propose innovative programs in preschool education, vocational education, remedial reading, cultural enrichment, special education, and in many other facets of the school program with which they were generally unfamiliar. The main qualification for these innovative "grant swingers" seemed to be their ability to determine what sort of proposals the government officials wanted and what kind of vocabulary was needed to appear knowledgeable. (A similar situation exists in the colleges and universities, but their grantsmanship is marked by much more sophisticated experimental designs.)

Too many of the so-called innovative programs proposed by the public schools represented rather sloppy research design. On the other hand, the more academic researcher shies away from the classroom, because there are so many uncontrollable variables affecting the results that when he is through he doesn't know which caused what. To the experimental purist, the classroom is too contaminated to serve as a research laboratory. But it is the problems of the classroom that the education profession is primarily interested in solving.

Is there, then, no room for pure research? If by pure research is meant a study which will reveal some hitherto undiscovered facts or a contribution to theory in some way, pure research is badly needed. There are, however, researchers who do research for the sake of research, who do a study because the problem has not been explored, justifying this by enumerating the many wonderful things that are accidental discoveries or by-products of "pure research," saying, "We might just come up with something." Such "going fishing" research is a misuse of public funds; we can not put that much faith in serendipity.

Reading Research Design and Interpretation

THE HAWTHORNE EFFECT

There are school systems which will not adopt a new approach even though their experimentation has found the new approach more effective than past methods. Such improvement is often the result of the well-known Hawthorne effect, that is, most novel endeavors generate enough interest and effort to yield favorable results not reflective of values within the new approach itself. It is, therefore, necessary to develop ways of deciding whether or not an experimental method yields a truly significant improvement over the traditional method. Most school administrators make such judgments on the basis of "common sense," but their personal biases often enter into such decisions.

There is no sound statistical approach for the determination of the degree to which the Hawthorne effect operates. The problem can be controlled through design by using a "Hawthorne group." Most experiments use the experimental–control group method, a procedure which is conducive to the Hawthorne effect. To control this, a third group can be set up which is manipulated or experimented with, but the manipulation is not related to the outcome. That is, everybody involved in the Hawthorne group somehow gets the feeling that he is involved in an experiment, which should yield some significant improvement. The extent to which the Hawthorne effect is operative can be determined by comparing the two control groups (the do-nothing group and the Hawthorne group), while the effect of the experimental variable can be determined through a comparison of the Hawthorne group and the experimental group. It should be pointed out that some studies have been reported in educational research literature which have found no Hawthorne effect.

THE PROBLEM OF EXPERIMENTAL CONTROL

The most important consideration in educational research is that of experimental control, that is, the control of variables which might conceivably affect the outcome of an experiment. The most commonly controlled factor is that of intelligence. Most studies make sure that both experimental and control groups are reasonably equivalent with respect to mental ability. Experimental control can be achieved in one of two ways. The control may be by random assignment of the children to the experimental and control groups. The alternative approach is to study the related variables and equate the groups on the important variables. The former approach is easier in a laboratory study where the pupils are taken out of the classroom one at a time.

But the realities of using a school setting for experimentation often prohibit such an approach. In a school setting, one must choose from among teachers who are interested in cooperating. This often requires the comparison of classrooms which are quite divergent in many variables even at the very outset of a study. In such situations, the variables need to be directly controlled.

The factors to be controlled are ordinarily those that according to the research literature correlate significantly with reading achievement, such as socio-economic status, sex, and age. It is important that the groups in any study do not differ significantly on any of the control variables.

There was a time when experimental subjects were selected by a process of individual matching on all control variables. This is no longer considered necessary, as long as the two groups do not differ *on the average* and in variability. If it should happen that two groups have means which are significantly different, there is a statistical technique, called the analysis of covariance, whereby the effect of this variable can be subtracted out of the experimental effect. The use of this method is generally considered a last resort, but in curriculum research it is a necessity which arises quite often.

The use of very large samples in reading research will tend to reduce the need for control of many variables, but the best research strategy appears to be that of controlling as many variables as possible and keeping the sample size relatively small. Our efforts are better spent on careful design and analysis than on incorporating large numbers of children in the experiment. The quality of a study is primarily determined by how well different variables are controlled.

In reading, one will find studies of methods of beginning reading instruction where many pupil variables have been controlled, but where the investigator came to the conclusion that the most significant variables affecting pupils' progress in reading are teacher variables. The selection of appropriate control variables is a most crucial issue. Reading studies in the future must control teacher variables such as experience, teaching ability, enthusiasm, classroom control, organization, and other hard-to-evaluate characteristics. The fact that a variable is hard to evaluate does not justify ignoring it.

INTERPRETATION OF RESEARCH DATA

There is an abundance of empirical data available in the field of reading, but many people have difficulty interpreting it. One of the most controversial books in the field, *Reading: The Great Debate,* is mainly concerned with the interpretation of the research data on phonics. Most of these data have been in the literature for years, but their meanings have been interpreted differently by different experts. The main difficulty in interpretation seems to relate to in-between data which merely indicate *trends,* rather than to data which provide more definitive and dramatic results.

One major problem with group statistics such as means and correlations is the tendency of a person to assume that all members of a group are representative members. When Terman found that gifted students tended to be of above average height, many assumed that practically all gifted students are tall. The fact was, however, that 45 percent of Terman's gifted students were below the national average in height.

An even more dramatic example of how an individual student or pupil can get lost in group statistics is illustrated by the group data on the reading abilities of all students in a school district. Assume that two students have taken three tests, covering different aspects of the reading process. On the three tests, pupil 1 scores high-low-high, while pupil 2 scores low-high-low. The group averages are average-average-average. Some investigators have even referred to this last profile as "the mean pupil." It would be more meaningful to report how many pupils have each type of pattern.

The author has developed the *Instructional Placement Report* for use with the *Stanford Diagnostic Reading Test,* which is based on the idea of determining the pattern of each pupil's set of subscores, and grouping those students who have similar strengths and weaknesses. An interesting by-product of this approach is the type of pupil accounting which is made possible. For example, instead of determining only the average vocabulary score for this group, other questions can now be answered: how many pupils in this system have inadequate vocabulary as their main problem in reading? Data of this type might not be quite as neat as a set of means, but the individual pupil does not get lost, and curricular adjustment to pupil needs will be facilitated.

Before a study of reading instruction is carried out, the people involved must have thoroughly considered the problem of interpretation, and must be willing to accept all possible outcomes. In efficacy studies of special reading programs, one certainly must be prepared for the possible result that the special program has no significant effect on pupil achievement. Or, more generally, a study should be designed so as to facilitate an accurate, objective, and educationally relevant interpretation.

RESEARCH ON GROWTH IN READING

Perhaps the most difficult kind of research study to do in reading is a study of growth. The factor which complicates this problem has to do with the measurement of growth.

A large city newspaper report of the ESEA, Title I program in that city was an annual report of the reading growth of two groups of pupils, the elementary pupils and the junior high school students. The school had released data that on a standardized reading test the elementary school pupils had made a mean gain from 2.1 to 2.9 in grade scores for the year. The junior high students average had increased from 4.8 to 6.0. The interpretation was made that the elementary school program was ineffective, since a 0.8 year gain in a year would result in those pupils' falling further and further behind. The junior high program was judged to be good, since those pupils were catching up. This interpretation was based on the false premise that reading abilities develop linearly; that is, as a straight line where a year is a year at any grade or age level.

The reading grade score is a type of norm, merely reflecting how well the average American student can perform on a reading test at a given point in his educational development. If students normally increase only two percent in reading ability from seventh to eighth grade, that increase will be represented by one year on the grade score scale. If the gain from second to third grade represents 20 percent of the total reading growth that, too, will be represented by one year. To equate these two would be a serious mistake. Why, then, is it being done?

There is no way of measuring reading growth on an absolute scale. We simply cannot determine what 20 percent of total reading growth is. But we have an enormous amount of data from objective large-scale studies as well as more subjective case-study impressions, which seem to agree as to what constitutes normal growth in reading comprehension. This growth curve appears to be S-shaped. It starts out with a period of slow development, but by the end of grade 1 it picks up momentum. The acceleration increases in grade 2. The third grade is probably the year of the greatest amount of absolute gain. This growth begins to taper off in fourth grade, and from the fifth grade on the slope is exceedingly gradual. The reading grade score, therefore, is what one might call a rubber band unit, and to compare gains along this scale is virtually impossible.

In the Title I study described above, it would seem reasonable to conclude that both programs showed significant gain, certainly gains of sufficient magnitude to warrant continuing the programs. If a decision had to be made as to which group made the greatest gain, most reading specialists would designate the elementary group. This judgment is consistent with the hypothetical growth curve in that gains in grade scores at the third grade are of the greatest magnitude, and diminish as one proceeds up the grade scale.

Information about the reading curve should help school administrators make more accurate interpretations of data regarding gains in reading; it should help explain why many remedial programs for pupils who read at second-grade level demonstrate relatively small gain in reading, and why high school remedial reading programs may appear to show much greater gains.

Conclusion

Among the many demands which will be made on the educational administrator in the immediate future is that of greater research sophistication. This would include an appreciation of the role of research in education, improved research literacy, an understanding of the problems of designing a good research study, and the ability to interpret research data. The purpose of this chapter was to cover the major issues in reading research.

Empirical research evidence is unquestionably the best single basis upon which educators can make intelligent decisions about the curriculum. But this is the case only when the research is designed properly, executed carefully, and interpreted correctly.

BIBLIOGRAPHY

Gage, N. L., ed., *Handbook of Research on Teaching* (Chicago: Rand McNally and Company, 1963).

Harris, C. W., *Encyclopedia of Educational Research,* 4th ed. (New York: Macmillan Company, 1970).

Innovation and Change in Reading Instruction, Sixty-seventh Yearbook of the National Society for the Study of Education, Part II (Chicago: University of Chicago Press, 1968). A collection of analyses of major issues relating to reading instruction.

Journal of Reading (Newark, Del.: International Reading Association). A journal containing research and descriptive articles on reading instruction at the secondary school and college level.

Reading Research Quarterly (Newark, Del.: International Reading Association). A journal devoted to research and theory on the reading process. The winter issue contains an annual review of the preceding year's research in reading.

The Reading Teacher (Newark, Del.: International Reading Association). A journal containing research and descriptive articles on reading instruction at the elementary school level.

Research in Education (Washington, D.C.: U.S. Government Printing Office, a publication of the Department of Health, Education and Welfare). A monthly journal containing abstracts of all research reports stored in ERIC—Educational Resources Information Center. The field of reading is especially well covered.

Review of Educational Research (Washington, D.C.: American Educational Research Association). A journal exclusively devoted to reviewing research on major educational topics; reading has been reviewed every three years.

Theoretical Models and Processes of Reading (Newark, Del.: International Reading Association, 1970). A collection of interpretations of reading research from the standpoint of theories regarding various aspects of the reading process.

C 4
D 5
E 6
F 7
G 8
H 9
I 0
J